Enlightenment and Change

The New History of Scotland
Series Editor: Jenny Wormald

Original titles in the New History of Scotland series were published in the 1980s and re-issued in the 1990s. This popular and enduring series is now being updated with the following published and forthcoming titles:

Kingship and Unity: Scotland 1000–1306
G. W. S. Barrow

Court, Kirk and Community: Scotland 1470–1625
(second revised and updated edition)
Jenny Wormald

Crown, Covenant and Union: Scotland 1625–1763
Alexander Murdoch

Enlightenment and Change: Scotland 1746–1832
(second revised and updated edition of *Integration and Enlightenment*)
Bruce P. Lenman

Ourselves and Others: Scotland 1832–1914
Graeme Morton

Enlightenment and Change
Scotland 1746–1832

Bruce P. Lenman

Edinburgh University Press

© Bruce P. Lenman, 2009

Revised and updated edition. First published in 1981 as
Integration, Enlightenment, and Industrialization: Scotland 1746–1832
by Edward Arnold (Publishers) Ltd
Reprinted in 1992 as *Integration and Enlightenment*
by Edinburgh University Press

Edinburgh University Press Ltd
22 George Square, Edinburgh
www.euppublishing.com

Typeset in 10.5/13pt Sabon
by Servis Filmsetting Ltd, Stockport, Cheshire, and
printed and bound in Great Britain by
CPI Antony Rowe, Chippenham and Eastbourne

A CIP record for this book is available from the British Library

ISBN 978 0 7486 2514 7 (hardback)
ISBN 978 0 7486 2515 4 (paperback)

Contents

Preface

Previous reprints of this book allowed some minor corrections of errors and a little updating of the bibliography, but no changes of substance. This second edition tries to preserve the bulk of a text for which there has been a continuing demand while updating it extensively. It also uses significant additional wordage to incorporate important issues that have risen to prominence in a generation of unprecedented vigour for Scottish history. The book is not, and within its limited compass cannot hope to be, a balanced survey of all aspects of national life. As before, the text seeks coherence and penetration by focusing primarily on the political history of Enlightenment Scotland, but tries to provide a broader picture of a lost world by setting its politics in the widest possible economic, social, religious and intellectual context. A new final chapter on the achievement and heritage of the Scottish Enlightenment has been added. The selective bibliography totally replaces an older discursive one, happily rendered obsolete by excellent recent scholarship. The author has benefited from and is grateful for friendly and shrewd advice from Professors Michael Lynch and Chris Whatley, but neither of these distinguished scholars should be held responsible for the shortcomings of this book which derive solely from the mind of the author.

Bruce P. Lenman

1

Scotland on the Eve of the Agricultural and Industrial Revolutions

The defeat of the Jacobite army commanded by Prince Charles Edward Stewart at the battle of Culloden, fought a few miles to the east of Inverness in April 1746, guaranteed long-term political stability for Scotland in the sense that after it there was no prospect whatever of a successful challenge to the reigning Hanoverian dynasty represented in 1746 by King George II. Even Prince Charles's brother Henry, 'Duke of York', appreciated the realities of the situation. In 1747 he effectively retired from dynastic politics by accepting a Cardinal's hat in the Roman Catholic Church. Repeal of the Union of 1707 with England had been a Jacobite aim. By 1750 everyone wielding significant power in Scotland was Hanoverian, by conviction or resignation. They all accepted the Act of Union and the authority of the King in Parliament in Westminster.

The Union settlement had offered guarantees for certain institutions and rights which were regarded as essential to the identity and continuing local autonomy of Scottish society. Such were the Scottish universities, the Presbyterian settlement in the Church of Scotland, the distinctive Scottish legal system and court structure, and the powers and privileges of the royal burghs of Scotland. Given the lack of any concept of legal restraint on the unbridled authority of the sovereign King in Parliament, none of these guarantees was ultimately secure but most of them were respected for a long time. The great exception was a direct result of the '45. The Act of Union guaranteed those heritable jurisdictions and offices which in the extreme form of a regality converted areas into sub-kingdoms virtually excluding the King's Writ. A consensus that these jurisdictions had contributed to Jacobitism produced the Abolition of Heritable Jurisdictions (Scotland) Act of 1747 which took effect in 1748. Already in decline, the jurisdictions which covered perhaps half of Scotland were swept away, with the exception of baron courts which were left with minimal powers. By 1750 Scotland had, just, left its medieval past behind. It remains to examine its demographic, economic, social and cultural structures on the eve of an era of rapid change.

It has been traditional to describe that change under two headings – the Industrial and Agricultural Revolutions. Both terms have inevitably attracted criticism. They are terms of art. Contemporaries like Sir Walter Scott or Robert Burns did not use them, nor did the predominantly clerical compilers of the remarkable *First Statistical Account* of Scotland. However, these people were well aware of the pace of change in their lifetimes, and often fascinated by it. Another objection is that the Scottish Industrial Revolution was just part of a wider 'British' one, especially after 1800, but the answer to that is clear enough. The great bulk of the land area of the British Isles never underwent primary industrialisation. Industrialisation was very much a regional phenomenon. In Scotland it was concentrated in the Central Lowlands and linked to the rest of Scotland by migration patterns and changes in agricultural practices amounting to an Agricultural Revolution which were partly a condition for and partly a response to industrialisation. Scottish experience of the primary industrialisation process was later, more extreme and more compressed in time than that of England. In Ireland the pattern was again different, though even there, and especially in the north-east of Ulster, developments were very similar to those in Lowland Scotland, particularly in the period when industrialisation was dominated by textiles, and especially linen. The lack of exploitable coalfields in most of Ireland and large parts of England and Scotland meant that development of the coal- and iron-based heavy industries that underwrote the post-1830 'Victorian Miracle' in the Lowlands of Scotland often simply could not occur elsewhere.

Linkages often spanned the three nations. Thus, the linen trade was to create close connections between parts of eastern Scotland, north-east Ulster and the area centred on Leeds in England. People, capital and ideas moved freely in a 'linen' subculture, just as the commercial producers of wool around the Scottish woollen manufacturing area in the south-east Borders developed close links with the Yorkshire wool-producing and manufacturing areas in England. Nevertheless, it is clear enough that the Scottish nation experienced a massive, unprecedented and irreversible change in both the rural and urban contexts between 1780 and 1830. This was not a 'Transition to Capitalism', a Marxist concept that has flourished because simple myth sells better than complex fact. Market forces and monetarisation can be found many centuries earlier than in this era, though of course all markets are socially and politically determined and those who shout loudest about economic liberty also tend to shout loudest for the coercive enforcement of their own market rules by a strong state.

DEMOGRAPHIC AND ECONOMIC FOUNDATIONS

Arguably the size and distribution of the population was the most significant single area of change in the rapidly evolving pattern of human life in Scotland between 1750 and 1832. Certainly it is only after 1755 that we can begin to speak about Scottish population statistics with any degree of confidence. It was in that year that Dr Alexander Webster, Minister of the Tolbooth Kirk in Edinburgh, produced his 'Account of the Number of People in Scotland, 1755'. A former Moderator of the General Assembly of the Church of Scotland, Webster had built up close links with parish clergymen and schoolmasters. Despite the indirect way in which he calculated his results, modern scholarship has not seriously shaken the standing of his estimate that Scotland's population came to 1,265,380 souls.

If a million and a quarter is roughly the right order of magnitude in 1755, informed guesses would suggest that this was something like a peak figure which in previous centuries would have been eventually cut back by dearth and demographic crisis of the kind that struck in the 'ill years' of the 1690s. This cycle of expansion and contraction was, however, decisively broken in 1739–41, when severe harvest deficiency was contained by extensive poor-relief measures, substantial grain imports, and above all by the existence of accumulated wealth capable of tiding Scotland over the crisis. There was a sharp regional famine in the Highlands and Islands in 1782–3, but again imports staved off total disaster. Better coastal and inland transport had already virtually unified Lowland grain markets.

Growth was so marked that the first official census in 1801 gave the Scottish population, despite significant emigration, as 1,608,000. The figure represents a retained population increase of just over a quarter in roughly fifty years, or an average increase of 0.52 per cent per annum since 1755. Thereafter the rate of population growth in inter-censal decades accelerated. In 1811 the population was 1,824,000, representing an increase of 1.27 per cent per annum in the period since 1801. In 1821 a population figure of 2,100,000 reflected 1.42 per cent per annum growth in the previous decade – the highest ever recorded. By 1831 the population of Scotland was given as 2,374,000, which implied a 1.23 per cent annual expansion since 1821. In the next decade the annual rate of increase fell to just over 1 per cent.

A higher and higher percentage of these people were crowding into the Central Lowlands, that transverse band of relatively fertile low-lying, often sandstone-based soils which lies between the older and harder rocks of the Highlands and Islands and the lower, but still relatively infertile, hills of the Southern Uplands. All the bigger Scottish towns, from Aberdeen to Dundee, and from Edinburgh to Glasgow, lay within this narrow belt which even in 1750 had a disproportionate share of the population. At that date the Highlands and Islands, covering 70 per cent of the land surface of Scotland, had a population of 652,000, or 51 per cent of the total figure. The Central Lowlands, with a little over 14 per cent of the country's area, possessed in its 464,000 people some 37 per cent of the population. With a similar area, the Southern Uplands held only 149,000 people or roughly 11 per cent of the total.

Highland population did grow overall between 1755 and 1832, but by 1832 it was clear that growth in these counties was lagging decisively behind that in the Central Lowlands. Indeed by 1831 many individual parishes in the Highlands and Islands already had declining populations, and one Highland county, Argyllshire, had a similar overall trend.

Scottish urban units were known as burghs. They came in two types: royal burghs and burghs of barony. Royal burghs were self-governing, albeit under narrow and totally self-perpetuating oligarchies whose precise composition was defined by the 'sett' or constitution of the burgh. Originally only royal burghs could conduct overseas trade or retail imported commodities. Burghs of barony, dependent on a feudal superior, had much narrower trading rights and restricted self-government. The Act of Union both confirmed the privileges of royal burghs, and authorised all Britons to trade where they wished in the Crown's dominions. It was an unstable position, and by 1743 a decisive legal case (between Kirkwall and Stromness in Orkney) had started a fifteen-year journey ending in the House of Lords and the destruction of the royal burghs' monopolies.

Though there were about seventy royal burghs and roughly 200 burghs of barony, only approximately an eighth of the population in 1750 was urban. In the next seventy years urban growth was swift. Glasgow's population of 27,451 in 1755 grew to 147,043 by 1821. Edinburgh (including Leith) started with 52,720 people in 1755 and grew fast enough still to be bigger than Glasgow in 1801, when Glasgow had 77,385 indwellers and Edinburgh 82,560. However, by 1821 Edinburgh with 138,235 inhabitants had fallen behind its great western rival. Aberdeen and Dundee, the traditional rivals for third place among the burghs, also grew swiftly. Aberdeen had 15,730 inhabitants in 1755, 27,519 in 1801 and 44,796 in 1821. Dundee grew from a figure of 12,477 in 1755 to 26,084 in 1801 to 30,575 in 1821. What was remarkable was the fact that Paisley, a smallish place of 6,799 people in 1755, had swept ahead of both Aberdeen and Dundee by 1801, when it had 31,179 of a population, and it held its lead with 47,003 in 1821.

Old county towns and secondary seaports grew at a gentler rate. Perth had 9,019 people in 1755, 14,878 in 1801 and 19,068 in 1821. Stirling had 3,951 in 1755 and 5,271 and 7,113 respectively at the two later dates. Yet it is important to remember that if in 1821 the urban fraction of the population had increased to about a third, this still left two-thirds of the national population in rural communities.

Traditional historiography saw the eighteenth-century rural scene as dominated by a gradually mounting tempo of Improvement. Improvers like John Cockburn of Ormiston (1679–1758) and John, Earl of Stair (1673–1747) were seen as starting a process which reached maturity under leaders like Lord Deskford, later Earl of Findlater (1716–70), and Sir Archibald Grant of Monymusk (1696–1778), at which stage it had reached the proportions of an Agricultural Revolution. Yet it is now clear that in the period of not very buoyant agricultural prices before 1750, self-conscious Improvement was a rich man's non-paying hobby, not a universal fever. Cockburn of Ormiston himself became insolvent and sold his estate in 1747. Empirical adaptation and gradual change, on the other hand, can be traced far back into the seventeenth century, especially on estates in Lothian near the big Edinburgh urban market.

Commercialisation and specialisation, along with social instability, came early in the south-west of Scotland, in Dumfries and Galloway, where the rapid expansion of the black cattle trade to England stimulated enclosure of land by dry-stone dykes to form large cattle parks. By the 1720s resentment by the excluded tenant-farmers had bred agrarian violence. Elsewhere premature attempts at restructuring rural society just failed. For example, from 1737 the Duke of Argyll, advised by the great lawyer Duncan Forbes of Culloden, tried to squeeze out the clan gentry or tacksmen in his country, on the ground that they held their tacks or leases too cheaply and that their sub-tenants, if turned into direct tenants of Argyll, would pay more than ever had the tacksmen. Apart from gravely undermining the military cohesion of Clan Campbell during the 1745 rebellion, the experiment did not even pay. Tenants bid high in public auction for farms, but no more cash rent was collected than under the tacksmen. The balance simply accumulated in the form of arrears. Successful change tended to be gradual and to respect commercial realities. Scottish agriculture was strongly commercial. Though farmers produced much of what they ate and wore, inter-regional trade was essential. The Highlands, for example, always produced a substantial surplus of animal products, ranging from skins to butter and cattle on the hoof. To supplement their own inadequate hardy grain crops (mostly oats and barley), Highlanders traded with the Lowlands, which in normal years produced a grain surplus. A series of market towns on the Highland margin such as Dingwall, Inverness, Kirriemuir, Dunkeld, Crieff, Dunblane and Dumbarton catered for this trade. A similar form of specialisation sustained regional trade between the Orkney and Shetland Islands. Orkney produced a grain surplus of hardy cereals such as oats or bere (a primitive barley). The lairds of the much bleaker Shetland Isles were masters of a very commercial local fishery, but it was still true, as had been said by the Reverend John Brand in 1700, that 'as Zetland could not well live without Orkney's Corns, so neither could Orkney be so well without Zetland's Money.' Surplus fish, turned into cash, were exchanged for vital foodstuffs.

In 1750, even in the relatively advanced Lowlands, many farmers still lived in fermtouns or hamlets. They held grazing in common and cultivated as individuals scattered plots in the arable area, which was divided into infield and outfield. Only the infield received any systematic manuring. Mixed farming was universal, though the balance between crops and animals varied from area to area. Much rent was paid in kind, but landlords usually converted the bulk of this to cash in the nearest urban market. Especially in arable areas from 1600 onwards there had been a steady drift towards consolidation of estates into single-tenant farms usually held on a lease of nine or more years. Improvement did not start only after 1707.

As Daniel Defoe pointed out in his *Tour Through the Whole Island of Great Britain* published in 1724–6, the huge flow of black cattle from the Highlands was ultimately geared to meeting

London's need for meat. The cattle marts or trysts at Crieff, and after 1770 at Falkirk, were simply points of organisation and departure on the road to Smithfield meat market in the metropolis. Highland rents were often settled in drovers' bills. In the Southern Uplands an increasing emphasis on sheep farming was directly connected with the raw material needs of the Scottish and northern English woollen industries. The finer branches of Scottish woollens, in decline before 1707, were destroyed by English competition after that date, but coarser woollens survived, and Scottish wool flowed into England alongside cattle on the hoof. Between 1745 and 1770 the pace of rationalisation, specialisation and change in the Scottish countryside accelerated in response to urban demand for food and raw materials, a demand often rooted in industrial growth.

Industry in Scotland in 1750 was heavily dominated by textiles. The Board of Trustees for Manufactures and Fisheries in Scotland (set up by legislation in 1727) had rightly identified linen as the most promising growth industry and the scale of expansion in this trade may be gathered from the fact that the amount of linen made for sale in Scotland rose from 2,000,000 yards valued at £103,312 in 1728 to 36,000,000 yards valued at £1,403,767 by 1815. Production doubled roughly every twenty-five years between 1750 and 1800, excluding the large quantities consumed within manufacturing households. Spinning yarn was a widely dispersed female trade. Lowland merchants even bought yarn in the more accessible Highland glens. Weaving, on the other hand, was and remained concentrated in the countries of Fife, Angus and Perthshire on the east coast and Lanarkshire and Renfrewshire on the west. The Board of Trustees tried by offering prizes and importing foreign experts to stimulate advances in technique. Its grants did help those involved in the expensive business of creating bleachfields, but linen was a winner, with or without the Board.

The growth of the linen trade was nevertheless heavily dependent on protective tariffs and export bounties. The temporary withdrawal in 1753 of a bounty on the export of coarse linens, the staple of the Tayside industry, led to a sharp depression in

Angus in 1754–5. The first signs of the grouping of looms under one roof on a scale worthy of the name of factory can be discerned in ports like Montrose, Arbroath and Dundee, where exports were always vitally important to local textile manufacturers. Growth resumed with the restoration of the bounty. London merchant houses absorbed a high proportion of Scots output, much of it for export to the colonies, so increased foreign competition and political disturbance in the American market triggered off another depression in 1772–4.

Though much rent was paid out of the price of webs of linen, the landed classes were more directly interested in mining. Coalfields occur at intervals throughout the Central Lowlands south of the Tay. Mines around 1760 were usually simple affairs worked by the landlord or a single tacksman or leasee. Apart from pits in the vicinity of the large Edinburgh and Glasgow markets, most Scots pits were on or near tidal water and were linked to saltworks where the culm or small coal was used to evaporate salt water in great iron pans. Drainage, like winding, was effected by horse power. Only half a dozen primitive steam engines seem to have been at work in Scottish mines around 1760. After that date coal prices began to move up due to increased domestic demand, with population growth and the exhaustion of Lowland peat; increased industrial demand; and significantly greater agricultural demand for lime produced in coal-fired kilns.

Chemical works such as the Prestonpans sulphuric acid works established in 1749 by Dr John Roebuck and Samuel Garbett consumed a deal of coal, but were insignificant compared with the demand from ironworks. Charcoal was for long the only acceptable smelting fuel. Several Lancashire firms even set up blast furnaces in Inverness-shire and Argyll between 1729 and 1775, to smelt imported ore with local timber. Scotland never ceased to import Swedish malleable bar iron, but in 1759 the Carron Iron Works near Falkirk opened – the first works to use local coal to smelt nearby ironstone in its furnaces. However important as a precedent, Carron had no comparable rival for twenty years.

The Scottish economy around 1750 was in some ways more poised for expansion than rapidly expanding. Even so widespread an industry as brewing showed this. Private brewing was universal but the seventeenth century had seen the emergence of a tendency towards concentration of commercial brewing within specific regional centres. Between 1700 and 1750 this trend accelerated. Edinburgh, with its large domestic market and nearby fuel supply from Lothian coalmines surrounded by barley-producing farms, was pre-eminent. However, excise returns suggest a short-term downward trend in production between 1720 and 1740. If the underlying trend was still upwards, and recovery came fast after 1740, it is still true that it was only in the 1760s that sustained expansion set in, and as late as 1765 foreign-going exports of ale and beer were, at 40,000 gallons per annum, a tiny fraction of total production valued at a mere £2,000. By the 1770s linen production, half of which was exported to England or abroad, was surging so strongly that most economic historians would regard the Scottish Industrial Revolution's first phase to be in full swing, though few would deny that its second stage was only gathering impetus by 1830.

SOCIAL AND CULTURAL STRUCTURES

The relationship between this economy and contemporary social and cultural structures can only very crudely be represented by the analogy between foundations and superstructure. In reality the relationship is infinitely more complex. Nevertheless it remains a fact that the social and political structure of Scotland in 1750 reflected broadly the realities of contemporary economic power, and that the very significant political changes which occurred at the start of the third decade of the nineteenth century were, to put it mildly, in some measure a recognition of fundamental shifts in the balance of power and influence within Scottish society, shifts ultimately determined by the pace and nature of economic changes in the period between 1750 and 1832.

Around 1750 Scotland was still overwhelmingly an agrarian country dominated politically by its landowning class. At the very top of that class stood the peers. The Union Roll, which listed Scots titles in existence in 1707, contained 154 entries. In the Westminster House of Lords there were only sixteen elected Scottish representative peers. The right to vote for them depended on being listed on the Union Roll, itself subject to debate and adjustment. Nineteen peers involved in the '15 rebellion had their names removed, as had those convicted of treason after the '45, though the latter were subsequently restored, with one exception. Between 1711 and 1782 Scots noblemen who acquired a peerage of Great Britain from the Crown after 1707 were, most inequitably, excluded from the House of Lords. One reason for this partisan ruling by the Lords was the political subservience of Scots peers who notoriously allowed the government to virtually nominate the so-called Scottish representative peers.

At the very top of the Scots peerage were a knot of magnates, most of whom managed before 1800 to achieve ducal status. Such were the Dukes of Hamilton, Queensberry and Buccleuch in the Lowlands, or the Duke of Argyll and the Duke of Atholl in the Highlands. In the north-east of Scotland the ducal house of Gordon was a power to be reckoned with in both Lowland and Highland areas. Not too far behind these mighty personages came noblemen like the Marquis of Tweeddale or the Earls of Rothes, Haddington, Hopetoun, Glasgow, Glencairn and Seaforth, all possessed of extensive estates and great influence. Below the forty or so earls came the holders of the comparatively modern title of viscount, and the holders of the lowest peerage title in Scotland – that of Lord.

The Scottish baronage comprised all tenants-in-chief of the Crown below the rank of viscount holding in free barony. The baron court was the only heritable jurisdiction not abolished by the 1748 Act, though it survived only with reduced powers. All lords were barons: not all barons were lords. The term 'laird' was vaguer, embracing barons and landlords who were not barons. If peers were few, lairds were legion in the Lowlands, while in the Highlands tacksmen, often relatives of clan chiefs, held substantial blocks of property on generous leases or tacks, sub-letting to the peasantry and acting as a laird class. Tacksmen often lent money on mortgage or wadset to their chief. Wadset was also common in the Lowlands, and since few landlords had enough surplus revenue to pay off outstanding debts, a wadset secured on land constituted virtual ownership. Ownership therefore occurred well below the level of laird.

Scotland between 1750 and 1832 was governed by a North British version of that 'open aristocracy based on property and patronage' which governed England. There are indications, as in contemporary England, that the landed elite tended to become more exclusive as time went on. In theory a successful merchant could buy an estate as the first step towards establishing a landed family, and this was a continually occurring phenomenon especially in Stirlingshire, Ayrshire and the Borders. In the county of Angus behind the city of Dundee, on the other hand, very few such families were ever established before the Victorian period. By the late eighteenth century it was notorious that the merchants of the city of Perth found it extremely difficult to buy land in Perthshire anywhere near Perth itself. Glasgow merchants in the western Atlantic trades in the late eighteenth century were an exception because of the sheer weight of wealth they could accumulate. Successful Edinburgh lawyers could afford properties in the Lothians. However, at a humbler level it is clear that many of the independent proprietors established during the great sixteenth-century boom in the feuing (that is, perpetual leasing) of ecclesiastical lands had by 1750 been bought out by bigger proprietors. A small minority escaped this fate by rising to become large landlords themselves.

Dominant and stable as they were, the aristocracy and gentry were not a caste. Primogeniture sent younger sons out into many careers, while in theory an able or lucky man could rise to any noble rank. The landed interest dominated the highest level of the legal profession. Throughout the eighteenth century some 90 per cent of entrants to the Faculty of Advocates (barristers entitled to plea before the central courts in Edinburgh) were from landed families. Any advocate rising to the top of his profession as a Senator of the College of Justice automatically joined the *noblesse de robe* with the judicial title of a Lord of Session. In control of politics, and entrenched at the top of the legal system, the landed interest could and did use its power and property to construct elaborate vertical chains of patronage and dependence tying society together under its lead.

That leadership was in no way challenged by the burghal oligarchies, themselves a small, closed and increasingly unpopular self-perpetuating caste. Each royal burgh had a 'sett' or constitution peculiar to itself but in all of them the retiring town council elected the new one, with predictable results. Even where, as in Dundee, it was normal usage that the provost serve only for two years at a time, the result was that in the late eighteenth century Alexander Riddoch, the dominant figure on the council, simply had to find a crony to act as front and provost every alternate two years. For the merchants in the smaller burghs the lairds in the landward area were often by far the biggest customers for trades ranging from wine importing to building contracting. The Adam family of architects started under William Adam as general builders in Kirkcaldy, and the proprietor progressed through contracts for country houses and resulting patronage to Master Mason in North Britain to the Board of Ordnance.

Deference and obedience were what was expected of the lower orders, the bulk of the people, divided into Highland peasants and Lowland countryfolk and townspeople. The Highland peasant was marked off by his Gaelic tongue and usually by his poverty. Because of the absence of middling classes and towns in the Highlands, the gentry and tacksmen had to act as entrepreneurs and even as bankers. By 1750 clans survived only as sentiments. The reality had been crushed and then made illegal with the abolition of heritable jurisdictions and military tenures. Highland tenants usually lived in hamlets often called townships or clachans surrounded by strips of ground suitable for arable farming beyond which lay the extensive common grazing. Legally, the joint-tenure of the clachan was precarious. Leases were rare. The law recognised no customary right.

Cattle and sheep represented the main form of exportable surplus, and were far too precious to eat, except on rare occasions.

Meal, usually oats but sometimes bere, milk, after 1750 increasingly potatoes, and fish made up the staple diet. Even so, meal had to be imported and it was reckoned that in districts like Lochaber the cost of imported meal represented half the cash surplus derived from livestock. Household possessions were seldom worth more than £5 all told, and of this a fair proportion (between £1 and £2) might be the wooden couples which held up the turf roof over the boulder-walled, earth-floored hut. Rent, when paid, was not high. Life was lived on the margin.

In Orkney townships or turnships as they were called operated a system of agriculture very like that of the Highlands but producing in a more favourable landscape surpluses of grain in the form of oatmeal or bere which a remarkable class of merchant-lairds exported to nearby areas like Shetland or sold to the many ships which put in at an Orcadian anchorage as they swung round the north of the British Isles between Orkney and Shetland. Shetland had its own class of merchant-lairds who had risen on the ruin of the class of immigrant Scottish lairds who had asserted control over Shetland in the late sixteenth and early seventeenth centuries. Keeping their tenants deliberately at the margin of survival on what were known as fishing tenures, Shetland lairds forced them by threat of eviction and by debt-bondage to concentrate on fishing for fish which had to be handed over to the laird who cured and exported them. Division of farms to secure more hands for the boats ensured that agriculture was incapable of sustaining the population for more than part of the year.

In the Lowlands too there was increasing emphasis on the absolute property in land held by landowners, a concept underlined by seventeenth-century Scottish legislation giving landlords extensive powers to reorganise and consolidate lands lying in runrig (that is, jointly farmed with arable in strips). Main tenants rented direct from a landlord. Sub-tenants or cottars rented gardens and dwellings from main tenants. Below them came the landless – domestic and field servants and beggars. Wage payments were mostly in food and access to land. They appear to have been at a subsistence level, but after 1750 part-time industrial activity was more available to help poor households supplement their incomes. With consolidation of farms accelerating after 1760, many substantial tenant-farmers controlled 100 acres or more, and could exploit the numerous urban and village markets of the Lowlands. Early in the eighteenth century their inventories already show an impressive range of domestic utensils and furnishings as well as the odd sign of luxury such as a piece or two of silver, or a set of drinking glasses.

There were plenty of craftsmen in the countryside but the biggest concentrations of skilled workers were naturally to be found in the burghs. Organised in powerful and until the end of the seventeenth century restrictive guilds, their standards of living, though below those of the ruling merchant oligarchy, were comparable with those of prosperous Lowland tenant-farmers. In the course of the eighteenth century these craftsmen lost their ability to exclude the work of outsiders from town markets, but their inventories show that they enhanced their modest prosperity. Below them the journeymen and casual labourers of the burgh were usually so close to the margin of subsistence that their notorious propensity to riot over rising food prices is perfectly understandable.

What is interesting is that the forms of social control used by the aristocracy, gentry and merchants to manage so many poor and hard-used people relied very little on constantly available physical force. There was no effective police force. The army was not usually visible. Patronage, and the public theatre of their ruling style were reinforced by the inculcation of deference and seemly obedience by kirk and school. The Kirk By Law Established – the Church of Scotland, Presbyterian in governance since 1690 – had few rivals. Roman Catholics survived only in traditional pockets in the Highlands, Islands and northeast, and may have numbered under 20,000. Episcopalians had suffered dreadfully because of their association with Jacobitism, and were in sharp decline by 1760. The landed classes tended to be attracted more by Anglican than by Scots Episcopal views and traditions. In 900 parishes and in the burghal kirks, the Church of Scotland ruled.

It was a hierarchy of courts, with the annual General Assembly in Edinburgh at its apex. In the parishes the kirk session still managed to operate a remarkable moral discipline on all but the gentry and nobility. The latter nevertheless often supported ecclesiastical discipline. After all, with the restoration of lay patronage in 1712 they nominated clergymen themselves and could influence Crown patronage. Clerical demands for augmentation of inadequate stipends were crushed in 1749–50. By 1752 that group of clergymen known as Moderates, who favoured lay patronage and were anxious to reach a dignified accommodation with the ruling political oligarchy, had emerged to preach compromise and elevated social morality.

Inevitably, schism arose from so blatant an attempt to ignore the radical implications of Presbyterianism, and to come to terms with an aristocracy which usually neither belonged to nor wholly approved of the Church of Scotland. Lay patronage was the issue which precipitated the Original Secession of 1733, led by a Stirling clergyman, Ebeneezer Erskine. Other secessions followed. Moderates preferred such people out of the Established Kirk, which they then found easier to manage. Its authority over schools, next to the pulpit the most effective means of mass communication, was never shaken.

Nor, be it said, was it very rigid. Virtually every Lowland parish had a parish school. Heritors or landowners had to bear its cost, which explains the miserable 100–200 merk[1] salary range for the teacher or dominie, who usually doubled up as session clerk and often led praise as precentor on Sunday. Subject to visitation by the local presbytery, such schools provided good cheap elementary education for all classes and both sexes, as well as preparing promising lads for university. Burgh high schools were effectively secondary schools usually stressing Latin. They

---

[1]   A merk was 13s. 4d. or two-thirds of a pound, so 100 merks was £66 13s. 4d., but this was of course in pounds Scots which survived as a unit of account for decades after 1707 and were worth a twelfth of the same value in sterling. In sterling £66 13s. 4d. becomes £5 11s. 1d.

were controlled by town councils, nearly all of whose members were elders of the burghal kirk and who also licensed the adventure or charity schools which taught elementary subjects. We simply do not know what sort of literacy rates this system produced. In the Gaelic Highlands with huge parishes and few schools, it is clear that most people were illiterate. The Lowlands probably had literacy levels higher than most of England (outside London) and higher than most Continental countries except Sweden. The Society in Scotland for Propagating Christian Knowledge tried after 1709, and more effectively after 1766, to bring literacy in English even to some Highlanders.

THE OTHER HALF – WOMEN

It had always been the intention of the Reformed Kirk, which in different forms dominated Scotland after 1560, that girls as well as boys should receive a basic education in at least reading and writing in the network of parish schools that gradually became a reality on the face of the land. Protestant concepts such as the priesthood of all believers and the personal responsibility of the individual soul to make itself in relationship to God meant it was very desirable that women, possessors of souls and rational beings as much as men, should be able to read Scripture. As a result, around 1750 many more women would have been able to read than write. In Glenartney, Perthshire, in the charity school there a generation later, none of the twenty-one girls in attendance could write, and about the same time in Monzie school, also in Perthshire, only one out of fifteen girls could write, though all could read. In both cases the fact that many of them would have been primarily Gaelic-speakers made the transition from reading English to writing it more difficult.

In the mid-seventeeth century many Scottish women had gone well beyond reading in support of the Covenanting movement against King Charles I. In the sixteenth century John Calvin had privately felt there was a case for giving women equal rights within the godly congregation, though he admitted he could not get past the misogyny of St Paul, but the Covenanting era channelled a lot of feminine activism into the prayer groups that lay behind charismatic Covenanting clergy, acting as a combination of spiritual support and think-tank for them. There was probably a decline in the intellectual accomplishment and politicisation of many upper-class women after the Restoration of 1660, and the universal reach of the parish schools was always more theory than practice even for boys. Such figures as we have suggest that attendance by girls was much thinner, for the girls were potentially more useful to their parents in the household. Nevertheless, some always did attend the parish schools, where instruction in writing, reading and basic arithmetic appear to have been available to most. Informal means of education such as cheap private schools and tutors hired by husbands for their wives after marriage helped cope with the increasing demands of both the economy and polite society after 1750. It is true that there was an increasing stress in the education of upper-class girls on 'accomplishments' such as singing, dancing and the ability to play a musical instrument, as well as a smattering of the fashionable French or Italian languages, to fit them to bid for the social mobility represented by success in the marriage market. Edinburgh in particular in the second half of the eighteenth century had many private boarding schools for girls which operated with that sort of curriculum. Inevitably, this approach fed the condescension pervading contemporary male opinion which regarded enlightened motherhood was the highest female aspiration in a world where domestic work was for servants. Lord Kames, jurist and ornament of the Scottish Enlightenment, thought that motherhood was all-important for a woman who, if prudently educated, should be fit to instruct her children and to be a 'delicious companion' to the intelligent man.

Historians tend to be over-obsessed with this genteel world, to which few women belonged. Though both ecclesiastical and secular prescriptive writers usually deplored indiscriminate association of the sexes, most women lived close to men both socially and in a world of work far from the norms and experience of the genteel. The relative poverty of the rural peasantry alone guaranteed close physical proximity. Most rural houses were essentially one room, usually no more than 20 feet by 14.

Only around 1750 did furniture such as box beds, which gave minimal privacy and a sense of division of space, begin to be common even in families with substantial tenancies, and 'luxury' items of furniture like chairs, mirrors and chests of drawers came in slowly. In the 'black houses' of the Highlands the most important internal division of the shared space was always that between people and animals, and even that, though clear enough with the cow, could not be absolute with the hens in the rafters. In urban areas such as Edinburgh's Canongate (technically a burghal regality of which Edinburgh was the superior), or in its port of Leith, a high proportion of the lower orders lived in single rooms in the attics or basements of high tenements. Servants shared beds, admittedly usually with someone of the same gender. It was a world where privacy was impossible and cleanliness difficult.

Most women had to work and usually they worked alongside men, as an essential part of a team. They dominated the large domestic service sector. On farms they did not control the horse teams that drew the ploughs, but they were critically important to sowing and harrowing and it was they who harvested with sickles and gleaned. They did heavy physical labour involving bending and carrying, as in pulling flax, carrying peats, or carrying creels of fish from fisher villages into nearby town markets. Dairy work was theirs, as was cooking and cleaning and the domestic production of everyday clothing. They cooperated with men in winnowing grain, brewing beer, and preparation by retting of flax which involved soaking it in water. Victorian fantasies about feminine fragility were unthinkable in the coal pits where women, alongside children of both genders, worked underground as part of a family unit, in which women did much of the underground haulage. Brickfields were another industrial area swarming with women and children until deep into the nineteenth century. They were central to the emerging linen industry in its preparatory and spinning aspects. Women had long been significantly entrepreneurial, as well as the main labour force, in the heavily overlapping services provided by inns, eating houses, taverns and brothels.

Despite the Kirk's distaste for 'scandalous carriage', social and sexual interaction between men and women was therefore frequent and often freely enjoyed. The Reformation and the Counter-Reformation had competed in legitimacy and puritanism by emphasising their commitment to 'Godly Discipline', but by the second half of the eighteenth century the mechanisms designed to enforce sexual discipline in Scotland were creaking rather than running smoothly. They depended heavily on a homogenous group of overlapping male worthies controlling both secular and ecclesiastical jurisdictions at local level, mainly the burghal and baron courts and kirk sessions. Under William and Mary that political homogeneity had begun to splinter fatally. Ironically just when this was happening, the need to rebut absurd Jacobite and Tory allegations that the expulsion of the main Stewart line in 1688–9 had led to national moral collapse facilitated the passage through the Scots Parliament in 1690 of draconian legislation against the emotionally charged crime of infanticide, legislation that presumed guilt rather than innocence in a capital crime on the part of the accused – usually an isolated, frightened and unmarried servant girl.

After 1750, political faction, schism in the Kirk by Law Established and enlightened disquiet with the implications of the infanticide laws saw the whole system reoriented towards a pursuit of the father of an illegitimate bairn to obtain adequate support for the child, if that were possible (sailors, for example, could be difficult to pin down). The reconciliation of the repentant couple with the Christian community remained in theory the end objective, but nothing could stop the sharp rise in illegitimacy rates from 1750 or so through to about 1855. This was clearly linked to capital-intensive industrial and agricultural change, which created unprecedented opportunities for mobility, employment and personal freedom, though the trend set in in the south-west before much of this development occurred, probably due to the enhanced value of dairymaids in a dynamic regional dairy industry and the opportunities offered there to quite young men to better themselves by widespread share-cropping arrangements. Scottish lay authority, though not ecclesiastical law, had long regarded an engagement to marry followed by sexual congress as constituting an 'irregular' marriage. By the end of the eighteenth century town authorities in particular were falling over backwards to use this very liberal concept to regularise informal cohabitation in a period of unprecedented social flux.

On the other hand, divorce became commoner between 1750 and 1800. English law made divorce (as distinct from legal separation) a rare, difficult and expensive game for the very rich, for it required a private Act of Parliament. Scots law after the Reformation allowed divorce on grounds of adultery or desertion (very often the two were combined), and a much broader social spectrum had recourse to the legal system derived from medieval canon law that ruled on matrimonial affairs to shed a partner. Litigants included many middle-class people, and not a few quite humble ones who could divorce under benefit of the poor's roll, which was the equivalent of legal aid. There was a network of thirteen commissary courts, whose business was mostly to do with debt and testamentary matters. However, the commissary court of Edinburgh had special jurisdiction over defamation, marriage and divorce. Despite predictable paranoid conservative wails that divorce was becoming as common as marriage, it was still pretty rare. Only in the last decade of the period 1760–1800 did the number of divorces granted by Edinburgh Commissary Court exceed 100, and the total for the whole period was just under 350. For the poor, physical separation or secret flight were better ways out of an intolerable relationship, especially if it were not burdened with children. Scots law was generous towards 'natural' offspring, but illegitimacy was, in a society with minimal personal documentation, hardly a great handicap to people with no serious inheritance prospects. Outside your parish you were what you could get people to believe you were. In the rural north-east, there were areas, mainly Presbyterian but including the largely Roman Catholic Enzie, where illegitimacy was so common as to be almost an acceptable norm among the propertyless. There a woman did not necessarily feel an obligation to marry someone who had made her pregnant if she did not want to do so. Increasingly, the judicial system just refused to enforce the bloody code enshrined in the infanticide laws, so that by 1809 it was possible to alter the penalty for concealment of birth followed by the disappearance or death of a child without signs of wilful assault from death to a maximum of two years' imprisonment.

THE PARADOXICAL IMPLICATIONS OF SOCIAL AND ECONOMIC CHANGE

Despite the fact that for the bulk of Scottish women the period between 1746 and 1832 probably offered them more potential freedom of choice in their lives, usually at low standards of living, than the half-centuries before or after, the theoretical foundations of respectable society were firmly patriarchal, and growing more so. Unlike English titles, most Scottish peerages could in default of heirs male be inherited by a woman in her own right. In previous ages of kingship combined with regional lordship, individual women could wield great power in the court and on the periphery. The period 1746–1832 saw centralisation of political power in an exclusively male parliamentary monarchy situated in England in London's government village of Westminster where the prime minister increasingly usurped the royal prerogative. It was not by modern standards an intrusive government, but regional power-brokers now had to be linked to the Westminster system. Politics became an exclusively male sphere.

Even traditionally female spheres like anything connected with menstruation, pregnancy and birth were being invaded by males as professionalisation of medicine saw the rise of university courses in midwifery. Though the idea of a 'man midwife' could still be something of a jest around 1750, by 1780 when the brisk and businesslike Alexander Hamilton was appointed Professor of Midwifery in the University of Edinburgh, he rapidly became the most popular obstetrician in the city. Traditional female roles in the curing arts were withering before an exclusively male medical profession, still at least partially accessible through apprenticeship but ultimately rooted in the male bastion of the universities. The Church of Scotland legally had always been continuous with the medieval one, albeit reformed, and one sign of its very real continuity was the use of medieval canon law in the commissary courts. Another was the continued use of the universities in their original medieval role as appropriate schools of divinity for the clergy of the Kirk by Law Established. Separate seminaries for clergy were an innovation of the Counter-Reformation, slowly and painfully established as a norm after the sixteenth-century Council of Trent. All three areas of professional training recognised as such in Scotland in 1750 – the Church, the Law and Medicine – were exclusively masculine. Other professions such as civil engineering, which began to emerge in this period and whose emergence was closely linked to the career of the greatest of Scottish civil engineers, Thomas Telford (1757–1834), the first President of the Institution of Civil Engineers in London, followed that example by creating exclusively male validating bodies.

Compared with England's Oxford and Cambridge, Scotland had many universities. There were three fifteenth-century foundations, St Andrews, Glasgow and King's College, Old Aberdeen, as well as two post-Reformation foundations, Edinburgh University and Marischal College in New Aberdeen. They varied enormously in size. St Andrews had about 150 students in 1730. In 1776 the smaller of the two Aberdeen universities, King's, had fifty students, while Marischal had 207. Glasgow, which was very much the university of Presbyterian Ulster as well as of western Scotland, rose from about 500 to about 1,000 students between 1700 and 1800. Edinburgh University, controlled and aggressively sponsored by the town council, was always a few hundred larger than Glasgow. The century saw a complete swing in all the universities from a system whereby regents taught the entire curriculum, to one where specialist professors taught individual subjects. Professors' incomes depended largely on class fees and the age range among their pupils was vast. The tradition of completing university studies abroad, usually in Holland, was still alive in 1750, especially in law and medicine.

Presbyterian clergymen of the Established Kirk dominated the universities, being almost invariably Principal and holding many chairs. The Chancellor of a Scottish university was usually a great noble. St Andrews even elected the Duke of Cumberland, the victor of Culloden. Intellectual boldness seldom deviated into social radicalism in Scottish academic circles. Like the Convention of Royal Burghs, the Scottish university world was normally deferential to great aristocratic politicians. Scots nobles were acutely aware of not being as rich as English ones, but north of the Anglo-Scottish border the landed interest, and its mainly bourgeois, university-educated men of business, had the power to lead a vigorous drive to modernise the Scottish economy in the usual sense of that ambiguous term. 'Modernisation theory' is at its worst a mere word game, for modern just means 'whatever is'. Those Scots after 1745 whom modern historians would call modernisers wanted, among other objectives, to make the Scottish economy more like that of the contemporary economy they most admired – England – especially for its global trade reach and its accelerating industrial growth after 1750. They also wanted Scotland to become a 'polished' as well as a 'polite' society, though their model there was likely to be France.

In 1750 nearly all Scottish men, not to mention women, were excluded from the small power- and prestige-wielding national elites. That was a European norm, from Ireland to Poland and Russia. It was true that, with appropriate patronage from someone of higher social status, the parish schools could allow a boy of relatively humble background an opportunity to gain access to a surprisingly good education, but such cases were exceptional. The lower orders were to all intents and purposes excluded from the burgh schools and in so far as the educational system allowed for a mingling of social groups it was a mingling of the middling orders and the gentry. In practice the demand for highly educated professionals was limited. What Scotland needed was not a frustrated and unemployed intelligentsia but basic growth. This was a land that in the 1750s ranked seventh in degree of urbanisation among the countries of Europe, but was fourth by 1800, and by 1850 ranked second only to

England. Strong growth in national output was essential to sustain a population that went from less than 1,300,000 in the 1750s to nearly 3 million by the 1850s. Agricultural population had continued to rise in absolute terms, of course, but it finally peaked in 1831. However, overall standards of living and wages remained below comparable English levels. There were massive pockets of deprivation, especially in the western Highlands where peasant society, as in the west of Ireland, multiplied and divided farms without increasing productivity. Unprecedented growth necessarily changed the social balance of Scotland, but it did not prevent peasants from starving in the Great Famine which followed the appearance of widespread potato blight in 1846. Scotland acquired many new immigrants, but also saw a huge and enduring wave of emigration after 1846. The rise of much larger and wealthier urban middling orders had by 1832 undermined total aristocratic domination of Scottish politics, but change that empowered Dissenting patriarchs could also paradoxically reinforce the stereotype of a separate and inferior social sphere as the only one appropriate for women.

2

The Age of Islay 1746–1761

Scotland between 1746 and 1761 was a developing society, economically, socially and culturally. Its development was, however, profoundly conditioned by the fact that it took place within a relatively unchanging framework of political power derived in its forms from two main sources. The Act of Union gave Scottish politics new parameters within which to work. The supreme prizes of the electoral system were the forty-five seats in the House of Commons and the sixteen places for representative peers in the Westminster House of Lords allocated to Scotland. In terms of population Scotland was, and remained for the best part of 200 years, grossly under-represented, but contemporaries in 1707 thought more in terms of relative wealth, and in those terms Scotland was over-represented. The actual figures were a compromise seldom argued about before the end of the eighteenth century. What was controversial was the way in which Scotland representatives were chosen.

The 'Sixteen Peers of Scotland' were nominally elected by the free vote of those Scottish peers on the Union Roll, but in practice for sixty years after the Act of Union there was no chance of a nobleman being elected against the wishes of the King's Ministers. Indeed the greatest of Scottish magnates tended to give up the idea of even standing if they could not secure official backing, as did a Duke of Atholl in a by-election of 1722, 'since I found that the Court does unanimously joyne for the Earl of Findlater'. The London government drew up a list of peers before a General Election, or nominated an individual before a by-election, and that list or person was returned. Discontent with a system which so blatantly used government influence to turn an election into something like a nomination from London came to a head as early as 1734 when a committee of malcontent peers openly protested against 'money given to many, promised to more; offers of pensions, places, civil and military preferments, acts of grace, reversals of attainders', all offered to those willing to support what was unctuously referred to as the King's list. After a brisk contest, the malcontents lost and for another thirty years peers' elections were suspiciously unanimous. Even more suspicious was the solidarity with which the bulk of peers denounced anyone who, like the Earl of Buchan in 1768, protested against the system. The fact that the thirty-six other noblemen present on that occasion publicly and solemnly denied that there was such a thing as a King's list is perhaps the most convincing possible tribute to its reality and importance.

In elections to the House of Commons the second main source of rules for the Scottish political game came into play. This was the electoral regime of the pre-Union Scottish state, for its franchises and electoral machinery were carried over into the post-Union period, modified only when modification was unavoidable. The outstanding modification was the reduction of constituencies from 159 to forty-five. Thirty constituencies were allocated to the shires and fifteen to the royal burghs. This grossly over-stated the significance of the burghs, with the inevitable result that a high proportion of the burgh seats were pulled into the aristocratic politics of the surrounding shires. Edinburgh alone had a seat to itself. All the other burgh seats represented constituencies of four or five burghs organised in what were known as districts of burghs. Much ingenuity was expended on these arrangements which only became operative, after the Septennial Act of 1716, at very lengthy intervals for the purpose of a General Election, or in a specific constituency at the time of a by-election. At these times the crucial question was who had the right to vote.

In the counties the determining legislation was an Act of 1681 of the Scots Parliament which had extended the franchise to feuars (virtual proprietors subject to fixed annual feu duty), and any others owning land to the value of £400 Scots (£33 6s. 8d. sterling) annual rent, and had also carefully preserved the old-established freeholder franchise based on the holding of land valued at 40 shillings annual rent provided the land was 'of old extent'. The last phrase was vital for it confined the right to vote at a 40 shilling valuation to holders of land recorded in an obsolete medieval taxation schedule. Legislation of 1743 insisted that this minimum holding 'of old extent' had to be proved by a legal document known as a retour of date prior to 16 September 1743. The freeholders of a county, meeting at their annual head court, had to maintain a list of qualified freeholders and this was crucial, for to vote in or represent a county a man had to be on that list. In the burghs the franchise was confined to the town council. The councils sent delegates to a meeting of representatives of burghs in a given electoral district of burghs, so to control a seat a candidate needed a majority of the four or five burghs involved to support him. Open bribery was very common in the burghs and physical violence not unheard of as a means of influencing voters. As for the counties, the manufacture of fictitious votes rapidly became after 1707 both a lucrative industry and a fine art for Scots lawyers. Before the Union there had been a reasonable procedure for appealing to the Scots Parliament or to the Court of Session against such malpractices. After 1707 no effective check existed. The legislation of 1743 tried to curb abuse in the compilation of the list of freeholders, but it too proved ineffective.

The discontented peers of 1734 made no bones about the fact that they saw the hand of a specific government manager behind the manipulation of the peers' election. That manager was Archibald Campbell, first Earl of Islay, and younger brother to the then Duke of Argyll. Between the corrupt and unrepresentative nature of the franchise and the susceptibility of the Scottish governing classes to government influence, Scotland in the mid-eighteenth century was a political manager's paradise. Only a few thousand men had the franchise and of these only a tiny fraction were capable of independent choice. No London government wanted to see a single Scottish politician establish himself as the essential channel of government favour and patronage in Scotland. That man would thereby acquire countervailing power against his English masters. On the other hand, only a Scot could hope to have the intimate knowledge of the Scottish aristocracy which was needed to distribute favours wisely and above all to work out which claimants could safely be disappointed of their hopes of government bounty. Islay undoubtedly acted as Scottish man of business to Sir Robert Walpole during the last period of that domineering politician's reign as First Minister at Westminster, but Argyll himself was in fulminating opposition to Walpole by 1740. After Walpole's fall his successors resumed a policy of balancing the two leading Scottish factions – the Squadrone, and their rivals the Argathelians (or Argyll's party), led after 1743 by Archibald Campbell who succeeded as third Duke of Argyll in that year but who will be referred to here by his better-known name, Islay.

For Islay the '45 was traumatic but immensely profitable. The Squadrone Secretary of State for Scotland, the Marquis of Tweeddale, made such a botch of the crisis that he stood out in an administration covered with well-earned odium for the bungling incompetence with which it handled the rebellion. Tweeddale actually resigned in 1746 just ahead of dismissal and with him went his office. The Secretaryship of State for Scotland was not resurrected again before 1885. Clan Campbell had not exactly covered itself with laurels during the campaign but under Major-General John Campbell of Mamore, who succeeded Islay as fourth Duke of Argyll in 1761, it did enough to underline its extreme soundness, from the point of view of Westminster. By 1747 Islay was backing, very unenthusiastically, the Heritable Jurisdictions Bill, and bargaining with Henry Pelham and his brother the Duke of Newcastle, who had assumed at Westminster the mantle of Walpole. Islay collected £21,000 compensation for his own abolished jurisdictions (three times as much as anyone else) and reached a tacit working arrangement with the Pelhams, based on his own massive territorial base and his supremacy in the minutiae of Scottish politics. It was always a delicate relationship. Islay had to be discrete. His position was always resented by Newcastle, that greatest of patronage-mongers, and yet it survived the death of Henry Pelham in 1754. Newcastle himself said in 1761 that Islay died 'the absolute Governor of one of His Majesty's Kingdoms'.

It was an exaggeration. Islay could not, for example, secure the Lord Presidency of the Court of Session for his candidate Charles Erskine. In 1748 Henry Pelham compromised by giving the Lord Presidency to Robert Dundas, and compensating Erskine with the Lord Justice Clerkship. Nevertheless, it is clear that Islay controlled most government patronage in Scotland in exchange for delivering a phalanx of MPs and Representative Peers well disposed to the administration. In 1747, for example, only ten Scots MPs were 'unsound', as compared with twenty-three six years before where John, Duke of Argyll and the Squadrone were united in opposition. Between 1747 and 1761 Islay quietly dominated the scene, often from London. In Scotland his chosen, and very able, man of business, Andrew Fletcher, Lord Milton, Lord Justice Clerk 1735–48, attended to the day-to-day running of the system. Within the framework of what contemporaries openly called Islay's vice-regalty significant developments in Scottish economic and cultural life occurred. The Scottish world of Islay was still generally conservative but change was in the air.

It was primarily a world made safe for Whig Hanoverian land-lords, and for their dependants. Islay himself had sufficient flex-ibility of mind to grasp, when he succeeded to the ancestral dukedom in 1743, that Duke John's offensive against the Campbell tacksmen, designed to squeeze them out as 'useless mouths', was not only failing to produce higher real returns from the Argyll estates, but was also unpicking the seams of Clan Campbell as a military unit, so he threw the policy into reverse. However, one major result of the '45 was the forfeiture of the estates of a large number of proven rebels. Mostly but not exclu-sively these estates were situated in the Highlands. There was a general determination after the '45 to act firmly to ensure that there was no recurrence of Jacobitism and for a time these estates became the vehicle of policies designed to 'civilise' the Highlands by turning them into models of 'the Protestant religion, good Government, Industry and Manufactures and the Principles of Duty and Loyalty to His Majesty, his Heirs and Successors'. To this end an Act was passed in 1752 annexing thirteen of the forfeited estates 'unalienably' to the Crown. From these islands of economic, political and spiritual virtue beneficent influences were supposed to spread through the Highlands. The state itself seemed determined to replace the ducal family of Argyll as the principal catalyst of social and economic change in the Gaelic-speaking regions.

In practice, developments failed to live up to these exaggerated expectations. Interest in official circles faded extremely quickly after 1752, so that the appointment of Commissioners to manage the forfeited annexed estates had to wait until 1755. Islay as Duke of Argyll was inevitably one of them, but His Grace never went so far as to attend one of their meetings. Due to legal complications several of the annexed forfeited estates only came under the control of the Commissioners as late as 1770. Like the managers of many modern nationalised industries, the Commissioners were given objectives to aim at which proved ultimately contradictory. They were to endeavour to encourage economic and social change in the direction of a more commercially oriented, modernised, reorganised Highland agriculture, but they were also warned that it was imperative to encourage loyalty to the House of Hanover among the tenantry. This latter injunction deprived them of the single most effective device for compelling tenants to modernise their social relationships and agricultural methods – a raising of real rent levels.

What the legislation of 1752 did do was give the government a permanent administrative structure for a huge chain of Highland estates previously in Jacobite hands. Both in the wording of the Act and in the behaviour of the Commissioners an ideology of improvement and assimilation to Lowland patterns was emphatically asserted. The time was not ripe for such over-simple plans. The numerous mineral surveys carried out at considerable expense by the Commissioners were unable to locate any significant commercial mining prospects. In 1760 virtually the only saleable Highland commodity was still cattle. Nevertheless, there was a very real sense that a Hanoverian, Whig ascendancy had come to stay in the Highlands and the confidence of its protagonists was well expressed in the protracted creation of the Duke of Argyll's own new residence at Inveraray on Loch Fyne. Roger Morris planned there in 1745–6 the first major neo-Gothic house in Scotland, a great crenellated square block with circular angle-towers and a clear-storeyed central hall which completes the medieval image as it rises above the roof-line like a central keep. Islay also had plans for sweeping away the old burgh of Inveraray, inconveniently close to the ducal seat, and re-creating it in a neo-classical mould further away, but it is typical of his era that only a couple of the new buildings were completed in the 1750s.

In general, the period 1746–61 saw the confirmation of the authority of a Whig landed ascendancy rather than the use of that authority to produce drastic change in the patterns of daily life among the lower orders. Another very good illustration of this point is the struggle for formal control of the funds used for poor relief in Scotland which came to a head in the years 1751–2. Established in the late sixteenth century along lines broadly similar to those of the Elizabethan poor law in England, Scots poor relief was based on the parish, seems to have been reasonably liberal in its view of those entitled to relief, and made free use of both voluntary and compulsory stenting or assessment for the raising of a poor rate when the kirk session of the parish found that its funds from other sources were inadequate to deal with the problem. Stenting involved the levying of a tax for a period which could be short or long, half to be paid by the heritors or principal landowners of the parish, and half by the other inhabitants who were inevitably almost all heritors' tenants. Mounting resentment among landlords, who could be and often were Episcopalian absentees, at the idea of a kirk session full of the virtually propertyless disposing of large sums of money resulted in a series of test cases before the Court of Session. That court was political in the sense that its members owed their seats to their known loyalties to Westminster politicians, so it is hardly surprising that its verdicts reflected the consensus in the landed political class to which Lords of Session themselves belonged. Heritors gained absolute control over poor relief funds, including very often substantial bequests in time past to kirk sessions 'for the poors behoof'. The General Assembly of the Kirk rightly protested against the gross Erastianism implicit in the change, when the Crown Rights of the Redeemer had been weighed in the balance against those of Property, and found wanting, but elders who were landlords or judges and Moderate clergy combined in future Assemblies to ensure that the issue was allowed to drop out of sight. The practical consequences, in terms of the working of the system, seem at first to have been small.

In the burghs the situation was fundamentally different. The incidence of urban destitution was greater and the failure to provide church accommodation to match the population ensured that voluntary collections were almost bound to fall short of the mark necessary to cope with the needs of the poor. Glasgow led the way in 1733 with the establishment of a Town's Hospital designed to house and employ the destitute. All the relevant bodies, the town council, the church, the Merchant's House and the Incorporated Trades were involved in its foundation and administration. Very rapidly it became clear that outdoor relief would have to be provided for those destitute persons who could not be housed in the new institution. Nevertheless similar workhouses were established in Aberdeen in 1739, Edinburgh in 1743, Paisley in 1752, Dumfries in 1753, in the parish of St Cuthbert's (part of Edinburgh plus a landward area) in 1759, and in the Canongate (physically the east end of the 'Royal Mile' of Edinburgh, but legally a separate jurisdiction) in 1762. In a sense these institutions were part of the price which the ruling oligarchies paid to ensure that the level of tension and resentment among the poorest indwellers of their burghs was kept below explosion point. Whereas the countryside never experienced peasant uprisings, the burghs were perpetually at risk of serious riot, especially when grain or meal prices rose. Despite its three workhouses, the biggest urban unit in Scotland, Edinburgh, was particularly susceptible to riot. Lord Provost James Stewart, who succeeded the most persistent of Edinburgh Lord Provosts, George Drummond, after the latter's last term in office in 1764, promptly faced serious meal riots in 1764 and 1765.

One reason for the unusually volatile nature of Edinburgh society was that the city itself was changing rapidly. Like other Scottish burghs it had witnessed the atrophy of the ancient system whereby both merchants and craftsmen jealously guarded their virtually hereditary privileges and tried to exclude any outsider from participating in them. The Merchant Company of Edinburgh gave up trying to fine 'unfree' merchants (that it, non-members of their company) after 1726. A spasmodic attempt to revive the exclusive system in 1736 had no life in it. The Merchant Company complained about hawkers, pedlars and 'English riders' in the 1750s and 1760s, but to no effect. By then very serious plans were afoot vastly to expand Edinburgh by draining the marshes and Nor Loch to the north of the Castle Rock prior to building a bridge over the resulting dry valley to the empty acres of Bearford's Parks to erect there a New Town. *Proposals for carrying on certain Public Works in the City of Edinburgh*, published in 1752, made it clear that the objective was the expansion and embellishment of Edinburgh as a capital city for Scotland capable of imparting to the Scottish economy at least some of the stimulus which it was widely realised the English economy derived from the pre-eminent vitality of London. Behind the drive to create a new Edinburgh stood the influential figure of George Drummond, Presbyterian, Whig, and indeed for many years the leading agent and sycophant of the Hanoverian regime in Edinburgh. He was Lord Provost in 1725–7, 1746–8, 1750–2, 1754–6, 1758–60 and 1762–4. In 1746 he succeeded the unfortunate Alexander Stewart, Lord Provost at the time of the seizure of the city by the Jacobite army of Prince Charles Edward. Resistance would simply have exposed the inhabitants to the dangers of storm and sack, but an angry London government prosecuted Stewart for complicity in the bloodless Jacobite occupation. Honourably acquitted in

1747 after a long trial in which Drummond did his best to destroy him, Stewart abandoned Edinburgh politics for banking in London. Drummond had replaced him in 1746 after a poll of all burgesses, which was rendered necessary by the lapse of elections in 1745, and which showed that Drummond had support outside the magic circle of the town councillors.

Even so, it must be said that the only significant new scheme completed by 1760 was the Royal Exchange (now the City Chambers), which formed a neo-classical square fronting on to the High Street of the old Edinburgh. Without support from the Bank of Scotland and the Royal Bank it would have been neither started nor finished. This was not inappropriate, for the economic confidence underlying the attitudes of men like George Drummond was largely the product of successful mercantile capitalism and of the financial institutions created to sustain the operations of mercantile capital. Those financial institutions were in fact precociously developed in Scotland, given the relatively undeveloped nature of its economy as late as 1750. The Bank of Scotland, one of the earliest of European public banks, was established in 1695. It pursued in solitary state a profitable but hyper-conservative policy of lending almost exclusively on the security of heritable real-estate until in 1727 its chartered monopoly was breached by the establishment of the Royal Bank of Scotland. In 1727 it was alleged, with some truth but more exaggeration, that the Bank of Scotland was tainted with Jacobitism. The Royal Bank was certainly furiously Whig with close connections with the arch-Whig Clan Campbell and its High Chief, Argyll. It also pursued a much more flexible lending policy than the Bank of Scotland. By 1728 it was offering a cash credit facility or overdraft to any businessmen who could produce two adequate cautioners or guarantors. It had much closer London links than its older rival. Unlike the Bank of Scotland, the Royal Bank rapidly established important connections with the rising tobacco trade of the west coast of Scotland, allowing importers significant cash credits and in exchange securing access to much of the liquidity, such as short-dated bills payable on London, which the tobacco merchants brought into

Scotland. By 1741 Glasgow was importing 8 million pounds weight of tobacco. In 1743 the figure was 10 million, and by 1745 it was 13 million.

The Bank of Scotland was obliged to follow its rival into the field of cash credits, though its first venture into branch banking was brief. The so-called 'dual system' between 1727 and 1745 was therefore stimulating but limited in scope. It left the field open for other institutions, and above all for private banks. The latter developed fast. Between 1745 and 1772 Scotland evolved a complex, advanced 'multiple system' of banks. A new public bank emerged in an unusual way with the establishment in 1746 of the British Linen Company. Here the moving spirit was Andrew Fletcher, Lord Milton, Islay's right-hand man and from 1735 to 1766 a power in Scottish life. Islay himself had been first Governor of the Royal Bank. Milton cooperated with George Drummond, through whom Milton effectively controlled Edinburgh, in negotiations with the government on behalf of that bank, but Milton, through his interest in the Board of Trustees for Manufactures and Fisheries, became convinced that the linen trade was the key industry in the country and that a new institution was needed to provide working capital for that industry. Entitled both to trade and to bank, the British Linen Company became increasingly a bank, though one with close links with the Royal. An attempt by the Royal and the Bank of Scotland in the early 1750s to crush the development of private banks outside Edinburgh fortunately failed in the vital case of Glasgow where the Ship Bank and the Arms Bank were sustained by the tobacco trade. By 1761 a third Glasgow bank, the Thistle Bank, was set up. There were fifteen or so private banks in Edinburgh, all deferential to the public banks. An Aberdeen private bank had been crushed by the two old public banks in the 1750s, but by 1761 it was clear that future private banking developments outside Edinburgh could not be stopped. Already the banking system had largely overcome the old Scottish problem of a chronic shortage of metallic coin, especially gold and silver. Business in Scotland by the 1760s was conducted mainly in banknotes or commercial bills.

Several major trades were booming after 1750. The demographic surge in both Scotland and England helped to lift their economies out of a doldrums which had lasted for thirty or forty years. Grain prices, low for nearly forty years after the Union, at last became buoyant. It is no accident that the first private banker to become Lord Provost of Edinburgh was John Coutts in 1742–4. His family were originally grain merchants in Montrose. John Coutts appears to have abandoned their hereditary Jacobitism for tepid Whiggery. His own early grain dealing clearly did him no harm socially. It was quite a good way of becoming acquainted with at least the agents of those 'People in Power' who, as the Bank of Scotland and the Royal knew to their cost, believed that 'the greater the Number of Banks so much the better for the country'. Easily available credit was most important to two other growing trades with an important bearing on rent rolls. One was linen. The export of Scottish yarns was sufficiently great for Scots weavers to complain that it raised the cost of yarn to them, but in 1748 the Board of Trustees in their annual 'State of the Linen Manufacture' noted the 'remarkable change' which had occurred in the shape of a great expansion in the export of coarse linen cloth, an expansion which it ascribed partly to the bounty on the export of coarse linens and partly to the establishment of the British Linen Company. By 1761 no less than 11,995,494 yards of linen were stamped for sale in Scotland, a quantity valued at £516,354. Black cattle flowed southwards either into expanding Scottish urban markets or, to a vastly greater extent, towards England. No two observers agreed as to the precise scale of the trade. All agreed that it grew steadily, funded mainly by cash credit from banks. When James Boswell and Dr Samuel Johnson reached the Isle of Skye in 1773, searching for an experience of a primitive patriarchal society, they found that the lairds' rents were mostly paid in bills which the tenants had acquired from drovers who moved into the Highlands armed with credit and emerged with cattle which they drove south. Falkirk Tryst was replacing Crieff as the great internal cattle market, so the Edinburgh banks were represented there after 1750 at all major cattle sales.

Dizzier still, though geographically exceptionally concentrated, was the rise of the Glasgow tobacco trade. Strictly speaking it was an Atlantic trade which involved trading in the cotton, coffee, sugar and rum of the British West Indian islands, and in cargoes of goods outwards from Scotland, as well as in the importation and re-export of the tobacco of the southern colonies of British North America. As such, it was well established, on a limited scale, in Restoration Scotland between 1660 and 1685. It was illegal under English law, but not under Scots law, and the English government was no more capable than any other early modern government of efficiently policing distant colonies. Expansion after 1707 was limited mainly by the inadequate financial resources of Glasgow merchants. However, the legal requirement under the English Old Colonial System that tobacco be first landed at a port in the mother-country before re-export to third countries placed the Clyde in a strong position as it was the handiest safe haven for ships traversing the North Atlantic from the tobacco colonies. Due to the unimproved nature of the upper reaches of the Clyde, the minority of Glasgow merchants involved in the transatlantic trade were obliged to ship their goods through Greenock or Port Glasgow. However, the trade was a capital-hungry one, and the capitalists were Glasgow men. By concentrating their trade in relatively few hands these capitalists facilitated huge bulk deals with customers such as the Farmers General of the French Customs, who usually accounted for a third or so of tobacco re-exports from the Clyde in the Golden Age of the Scottish tobacco trade between 1740 and 1775.

By the 1750s and 1760s Glasgow tobacco merchants were normally organised in groups incorporated in formal partnerships. They were dominated by a limited number of families, some of which, like the Ritchies, Bogles, Dunlops and Murdochs, could trace their connections with the tobacco trade back before 1700. On the other hand, there were, in a trade which was always unpredictable, plenty of new dynasties like the Glassfords, the Speirs and the Cunninghames. None of the latter three was even native to Glasgow. Nevertheless the tobacco merchants rapidly evolved into a closely knit kinship group. Intermarriage was common and often crucially important due to the value of dowries. Alexander Speirs was only a man of modest fortune before marriage into the Buchanan dynasty of tobacco traders accelerated him to the higher reaches of the league. These merchants were often landed before 1750 and they all bought land or indeed more land as an investment and tangible sign of success as soon as they were in a position to do so. They did not retire from business. On the contrary, when they acquired land their landed respectability enabled them to tap by way of loans the accumulated savings of the upper and middling orders of society in the west of Scotland, savings which, due to lack of alternative outlets, were more than adequate for even the needs of transatlantic trade. Manufactures were secondary in significance. Indeed they were often financed by tobacco money and geared to the need for outward cargoes for the colonies.

Commercial development in this period therefore reinforced rather than undermined the hegemony of existing local elites. Central government in the eighteenth century was largely confined to war, diplomacy and the raising of revenues. To the local elites local government was far more significant in their daily lives, and in this sphere the ascendancy of the local oligarchs was absolute. All sheriffdoms were Crown appointments after 1747, but the Sheriff-depute appointed in each Scottish county to exercise shrieval functions was invariably a leading member of the aristocracy. He was the principal executive officer of the Crown in the localities and usually appointed a Sheriff-substitute or substitutes to help him with his work. Usually these were young Edinburgh advocates. Most future Lords of Session had served as a Sheriff-substitute. After the Sheriff-depute in importance came county Commissioners of Supply responsible for raising the land tax, roads and bridges, catching and holding criminals, and keeping the parishes up to the mark in education provision. Chosen from the ranks of Justices of the Peace, the Commissioners led the way after about 1756 in the development of county meetings as means of articulating upper-class opinion on political issues. Justices of the Peace never assumed the importance they had in contemporary England. The Commission of the Peace simply reflected the composition of existing county and burghal elites, to the point where known Jacobites managed to stay entrenched on many Commissions until just after the '45. The Sheriff Court left Justices of the Peace only a minimal jurisdiction over oaths, licenses, and weights and measures, while the parish handled the problem of the poor, subject to the financial control of its landowners as heritors. A wise ruler like Islay used his powers of patronage, which included thousands of appointments from those under Commissions of the Peace to those under the Board of Customs, to reinforce local ruling groups, if they were generally amenable to the regime, rather than to challenge them.

This rock-like stability in both the social and the political structure of an increasingly prosperous land was the essential precondition for the continued flowering of Scottish intellectual and artistic life, and this was for two reasons. Firstly, prosperity generated the revenues required for the enlightened patronage of the arts and learning. Secondly, the governing classes were not tempted by fear of social upheaval into a blind opposition to any form of critical thought. This latter point is peculiarly important in view of the apparent paradox that from 1740 that intellectual phenomenon we call the Scottish Enlightenment of the eighteenth century had, ticking away underneath it, a time bomb capable of challenging some of its basic assumptions. This was David Hume's *A Treatise of Human Nature* (1738–40). Reason lay at the heart of the Scottish Enlightenment, expressed as much in the balance and neo-classical form of its visual arts as in its reasonable religion, common-sense philosophy, and belles-lettres. Hume argued that the traditional analysis of cause and effect was indefensible. Causation, the basis of logical argument in all fields of human knowledge other than logic and mathematics, was, according to Hume, only 'a lively idea related to or associated with a present impression'. Certainty was therefore unattainable, as much in moral as in physical matters. Hume himself recorded that the *Treatise* 'fell dead-born from the press', and an attempt by the author to stir interest in it by publishing an *Abstract* of its main argument was even more unsuccessful.

Nevertheless, the Scottish Age of Reason could not ignore the fact that it had spawned a systematic anti-rationalist. Hume's *Treatise* was alive enough by 1745 to lose him the succession to the chair of Moral Philosophy in the University of Edinburgh. Hume was an agnostic at best, though more probably a closet atheist, palpably unfit to occupy a chair whose duties involved instructing future clergy of the Kirk by Law Established. Tenure of the chair clearly required commitment to the validity of the Christian Revelation. His defeat was tied up with a struggle for power on the town council and William Cleghorn, the eventually successful candidate, was the candidate of the Tweeddale faction on the council. What is impressive is that the heretical Hume was seriously considered and indeed supported by several prominent Moderate clergymen such as Robert Wallace, Minister of the New North Church, Chaplain to the King, and Moderator of the General Assembly in 1743. Hume was an intellectual radical but not a social or political radical. Scion of a minor Berwickshire laird's family, he early sought a tutorship in a noble household and achieved it in 1745 with his attachment to the Marquess of Annandale, who most unfortunately turned out to be mentally deranged. Though well aware of the element of humbug in the Whig ideology of the Glorious Revolution, Hume was a firm anti-Jacobite and supporter of the established order, as his *Three Essays, Moral and Political* published in 1748 made clear. After acting as secretary to his distant kinsman General St Clair on military and diplomatic missions in Europe, Hume settled in Edinburgh in 1751, and in 1752, the year when he published his *Political Discourses*, he became Keeper of the Advocates' Library, a job which underlined his acceptability to the Edinburgh social establishment.

Hume's predecessor as Keeper had been Thomas Ruddiman, a living demonstration that the intellectual roots of the Scottish Enlightenment ran back into the fertile soil of Restoration Scotland. Ruddiman was a conservative in all things, a great Latinist even by the exalted standards of Scottish Latinity, a printer with a patriotic anti-Union spirit, and a sentimental Jacobite. By the time of his death in 1752 intellectual fashion had turned strongly against men like Ruddiman, or the much younger Jacobite poet William Hamilton of Bangor, who fought in the '45 and wrote verse which in some ways prefigured the literary triumphs of Scotsmen in the wider English-speaking world of the later eighteenth century. In culture as in politics the victory of Whiggism was inevitable. Philosophically, the foundations of that triumph had been laid by Francis Hutcheson, Professor of Moral Philosophy in the University of Glasgow from 1730 and one of the long succession of Ulster Presbyterians whose talents enhanced the quality of eighteenth- and nineteenth-century Scottish academic life. He taught and deeply influenced Adam Smith, a future holder of his own chair and author of a fabulously successful textbook in the well-established discipline of political economy, a subject which was by no means identical with the later concept of economic science. Hutcheson's moral philosophy, summed up in two posthumous works, a *Short Introduction to Moral Philosophy* (1747) and a *System of Moral Philosophy* (1755), was set in a Christian context but assumed that man is endowed with an innate moral sense capable of indicating what is right, and that on the whole the sum of moral actions would tend to the progress of the welfare and happiness of mankind. A sense of original sin was not a prominent feature of Hutcheson's thought, but a self-consciously Whig approach to society and politics was. He was an upholder of a constitution formed of checks and balances and with a close relationship between the possession of property and the exercise of power. So far from hankering after royal absolutism was he that he regarded people in general as 'too tame and tractable'. David Hume was more of an establishment Whig. Though his secular vision of politics accepted the need to limit the power of arbitrary government, it also totally rejected the sovereignty of the people. Hume feared anarchy more than tyranny. Protection of property was for him the prime purpose of government. The status quo suited him very well.

It was, however, less by its technical moral and political philosophy, which comparatively few understood, than by its contribution to general literature that the Scottish Enlightenment impinged on the consciousness of the polite world in the 1750s. Hume's contemporary reputation rested on the six volumes of his *History of England* which appeared between 1754 and 1762. Significantly, in 1760 the town council of Edinburgh established a new chair of Rhetoric to which they appointed the Reverend Hugh Blair, a leading Moderate clergyman of the city. By 1762 a royal commission had turned Blair into a Regius Professor of Rhetoric and Belles-Lettres in the University of Edinburgh. Already another Moderate clergyman, John Home, incumbent of Athelstaneford in East Lothian, had written a play, *Douglas*, successfully produced on the Edinburgh stage in 1756, and later in London, with acclaim well beyond its minimal merits. It had caused uproar in the General Assembly of the Kirk on a scale greater than that accompanying an abortive attempt in the previous year, 1755, to arraign David Hume and the judge Henry Home, Lord Kames, another prominent writer with discursive but vaguely disturbing interests, on charges of heresy. In 1757 the General Assembly passed an Act forbidding clergy to attend the theatre. It proved unenforceable. John Home resigned his charge, went to London, and became personal secretary to Lord Bute and tutor to the Prince of Wales, soon to be George III.

The 'literati' were too well connected with decision-taking members of the political class to be crushed. In Edinburgh lairds, judges, politicians, artists and writers mingled in such convivial clubs as the Select Society, which David Hume helped to establish in 1752. William Cullen, Professor of Medicine at Glasgow and later holder of chairs of Chemistry and Medicine in Edinburgh, was a fine physician, but his early career owed much to the patronage of the 'Argyll Interest'. Lord Kames had introduced him to the Earl of Islay in 1749. Islay, that canny Scots lawyer who dressed no better after he became Duke of Argyll than he had before, presided over a process whereby the leaders of Scottish intellectual life became spokesmen, overtly or tacitly, for that very conservative court or establishment Whiggism which was the prevailing ideology of Hanoverian Britain. Islay merited at least some of the respect in which even David Hume privately held him. This arch-manipulator had created a system

which gratified, at the price of continual shuffling, juggling and
adjustment, several major interests at the same time. Islay's interest lay in exploiting his grip on the Scottish constituencies to
enhance his own social and political weight in London. The
British government was interested in disposing of as large a bloc
as possible of obedient North British votes at Westminster,
preferably without having to pay the price of attending to specifically Scottish political problems, which does not mean that from
time to time the Scottish representatives at Westminster could
not unite to apply significant pressure to protect what they saw
as Scottish national interests. Nevertheless, the Scottish ruling
classes were obsessed with, rather than merely interested in,
access to government patronage. When Ramsay of Ochtertyre
described Islay as 'the most enlightened patriot Scotland has produced', he is best understood as saying that Islay secured more
jobs for boys who mattered than anyone before him.

However, Islay's fully developed political system predeceased
him, partly as a result of changes of personnel and power patterns in the highest circles of British politics and partly because
of a more deep-seated long-term change in the general political
atmosphere. The death of George II in the autumn of 1760 and
the accession of the 22-year-old George III was bound to be followed by changes, for nobody questioned the right of a new king
to appoint new ministers to conduct his business, if he so wished,
though practical considerations usually ensured that the exercise
resembled nothing so much as a shuffling of a well-worn pack of
cards. What made the accession of the new sovereign so significant to the uncrowned king of Scotland was the fact that George
III was very much under the influence of Islay's own nephew,
John Stuart, third Earl of Bute. Bute was an early example of the
Anglo-Scot. Educated at Eton and in the Netherlands at Leiden,
he did not actually live in Scotland before 1739 and he left the
country again in 1745 for good. As a man he was proud, haughty
in manner and lacking in common sense, but it mattered not, for
by 1755 he had become confidential adviser to the widowed
Princess of Wales as well as the beloved mentor of her son, the
future George III. Born in 1713, Bute was twenty-five years older

than the prince, to whom he undoubtedly became a sort of father figure. Bute was not at all wealthy but his association with the future ruler made him so obviously a coming man that by 1756 a small group of Scots MPs, led by Gilbert Elliot and by Bute's own brother James Stuart Mackenzie, had separated themselves out from the phalanx of Argathelians and were looking quite openly to Bute for leadership.

That year was also the year in which Britain became involved in the Seven Years' War. This great struggle was, from the British point of view, a world war against the power of Bourbon France which was reinforced at a later stage by the power of Spain, on whose throne sat another branch of the Bourbon family. Under the charismatic leadership of Pitt the Elder, ably supported by the political talents of that arch-manager and compulsive fusspot the Duke of Newcastle, Hanoverian Britain recovered from early reverses to scale unprecedented heights of conquest and glory. Despite the fact that the new King of Britain and his principal adviser Lord Bute were anxious to bring about an early and moderate peace settlement, the Peace of Paris of 1763, which brought hostilities to an end, left Great Britain the dominant European power in both North America and in the sub-continent of India. From an early stage in the war it became clear that a new generation of articulate Scots had emerged which looked forward to a degree of integration with and participation in the global British monarchy well beyond that taken for granted by their elderly political leaders. Not that Islay himself was at all unenthusiastic about the war. On the contrary, his rock-like support for measures needed to raise more and more troops endeared him, for the first time, to the German soldier who sat on the throne as George II. Standing in such high regard with the King even gave Islay the edge in his endless guerrilla warfare with the jealous and suspicious Duke of Newcastle, who would dearly have liked to take Scottish patronage into his own hands and to reduce Islay's satrapy to the status of one of the larger English counties like Yorkshire.

By 1760 Islay's position, with royal backing, was strong enough for him to make Newcastle swallow what to Newcastle was an unpalatable demand from the Duke of Atholl that his nephew and eventual heir John Murray, son of the Jacobite general Lord George Murray, be court candidate for Perthshire in the next General Election. In 1759 Islay had refused to give way to Bute in an extremely complex quarrel over the representation of the Ayr district of burghs at the impending election. Bute seemed poised for defeat when death handed him victory by striking down George II. Yet Bute undoubtedly represented more than the result of a toss of the dice of mortality. There had been widespread resentment in Scotland in 1757 when the Militia Act passed in that year specifically excluded Scotland on account of English distrust of the nation which had spawned the '45. One of the two most important Edinburgh social clubs in the late eighteenth century, the Poker Club, was so-named to commemorate the considerable agitation in Scotland over the need for a national militia, as much to underline the integration of Scotland into Great Britain as to defend the United Kingdom against its foes. The title of the club, which lasted from 1762 to 1784, was suggested by Adam Ferguson, one of the most interesting of the intellectuals of the great age of the Scottish Enlightenment. It referred to the need to 'poke-up' Scottish sentiment into a blaze on this issue. Ferguson was a Gael and a son of the manse from the parish of Logierait in Perthshire who had served as a chaplain in the Black Watch for ten years, seeing active service on such bloody Flanders battlefields as Fontenoy. Chagrin at the failure of the Duke of Atholl to nominate him to a parish drove him out of the clerical profession and to Edinburgh, where in the Select Society and elsewhere he rapidly became a prominent figure in the social life of the more intellectual circles in the city. An appropriate chair not being available, he was in 1759 jobbed into the chair of Natural Philosophy (that is, physics) in the University of Edinburgh. To his friends such as David Hume and Adam Smith his known ignorance of the subject when appointed was a topic for amusement. Only in 1764 did he secure the infinitely more appropriate chair of Moral Philosophy. In the Poker Club he rubbed shoulders not only with fellow authors like Adam Smith and David Hume (whom he had succeeded as Keeper of the

Advocates' Library in 1757), but also Moderate divines like 'Jupiter' Carlyle and Principal Robertson, as well as lawyers like Henry Dundas and peers such as the Earl of Haddington and the Duke of Buccleuch. They were all (apart from Hume and Smith, who joined the club in the hope of defusing the issue and confusing a cause they did not truly share) hungry for more respect from England.

Islay had seen no point in becoming excited about Scotland's exclusion from the Militia Act. He pointed out that there was nothing to stop a Scots nobleman from taking advantage of still-valid legislation of the seventeenth-century Scots Parliament to raise a fencible regiment in his own county, and this both he and the Earl of Sutherland did, as Lords Lieutenant of their respective counties. He himself was by 1760 the symbol of triumphant Scottish integration into the central government. Islay, nothing if not a realist, knew the arrival of Bute in power was bound to restrict his previous freedom of action, but his ability to accept this fact gracefully enabled him to escape total eclipse. Precisely because Bute, like George III, gloried in the name of Briton, he did not want to become immersed in the provincial complexities of Scottish politics. When it became clear that the former manager of Scotland was prepared to accept a more subordinate role, his expertise became too valuable to lose. Islay was reappointed Keeper of the Great Seal in Scotland as a sign that he was still in favour. The Ayr burghs quarrel was patched up by a compromise. Part of the problem had always been that Bute virtually owned one of the group, Rothesay, while Campbeltown and Inveraray were equally subject to his uncle, and Ayr and Irvine, the remaining members of the group, belonged to neither party. Indeed, Ayr town council became heartily sick of the antics of the rival noble lords and made them squirm at the end by being thoroughly obstructive towards the delicate process of setting up a satisfactory compromise. Nevertheless, in the 1761 General Election Islay, back in the subordinate role he had previously acted out under Walpole in the early 1740s, still had the details of Scottish politics in his hands to the point where he had the pleasure of ramming the odd unpalatable candidate down

Newcastle's throat. An example was Lord Lovat's son Simon Fraser who had compensated for his father's well-merited execution for high treason by raising a regiment to fight for the house of Hanover from western Europe to the Plains of Abraham in Canada. Newcastle still found it difficult to forgive Fraser for his own youthful participation in the '45.

When Islay unexpectedly died in 1761, Bute had no desire to don his mantle. Instead he tried to find a replacement in the shape of his own brother, James Stuart Mackenzie, who took his name from an estate he had inherited. Married to a daughter of the second Duke of Argyll, and a former British envoy at Turin, he was as unacceptable as any other ex-Argathelian to English politicians like the Duke of Newcastle or the very influential Lord Chancellor Hardwicke. Newcastle and Hardwicke denounced the Argyll interest and its heirs such as Bute and Stuart Mackenzie as a 'Highland' interest 'soft on Jacobitism', and argued that to counter this it was essential to support 'Lowland' influences and what was left of the old Squadrone Party. In reality the objection was to the placing of a ring fence round the daily workings of Scottish politics and the nomination of a specific Scottish manager to attend to what went on within it. Against this muttering in high circles must be set the plain fact that the Bute era of integration with general British affairs with a much reduced but still significant measure of autonomy in the management of Scottish politics does seem to have met the wishes of the more pushing Scots of the younger generation for whom enhanced patronage opportunities at the centre of British politics were the overriding objective. Indeed Bute's dominant position in government must have struck many of them as too good to be true, which is precisely what it turned out to be.

3

Integration and Expansion 1760–1775

Patronage by the powerful in London, the metropolitan centre of Hanoverian Britain, was the likeliest key to rapid advancement for an ambitious Scot in the decades before the tempo of industrialisation in Scotland itself became so hectic as to offer an alternative series of routes to wealth and status. Earlier in the eighteenth century, individual Scots had managed to carve brilliant London careers for themselves, though they often had difficulty, however outstanding their talents, in maintaining a stable patronage base. The mathematician James Stirling (a cadet of the Stirlings of Garden), for example, was fatally hampered by his family's Jacobitism and by his own passionate High Tory principles when it came to capitalising on the remarkable reputation he built up while yet an undergraduate at Oxford. Despite the friendship of Newton, he had to retire abroad whence he returned to become a leading light in the 1730s both at the Royal Society and in the circle of intellectuals around the fallen angel of Tory politics, Viscount Bolingbroke. However, in 1735 he returned to Scotland as manager of the Leadhill Mines. He corresponded with mathematicians of European repute, such as the Swiss Euler, but in 1754 he resigned his membership of the Royal Society. He died in 1770 at the age of seventy-eight after an outstandingly successful managerial career.

James Gibb or Gibbs, the Aberdonian architect who came from a Roman Catholic background and was trained in Rome under Carlo Fontana, the leading architect of Pope Clement XI (1700–21), was greatly helped when he returned to London in

1709 by the patronage of the Earl of Mar and later by the support of Robert Harley, first Earl of Oxford. Both men were in total political eclipse by 1716 but Gibbs was fortunate in that his career had already taken off by then and in any case he continued to have the private patronage of the still-wealthy Harley family. He died in 1754 after over a decade of retirement in London, leaving behind writings and a remarkable range of buildings from the royal parish church of St Martin-in-the-Fields to the Senate House at Cambridge and the Radcliffe Library at Oxford. His late-baroque style, influenced by the fashionable, lighter Palladian or neo-classical school of eighteenth-century England, had an enduring influence over his successors but by the early 1750s the man himself was an anachronism, a survival from the brief age of Tory ascendancy under Queen Anne. Even a solidly conformist Scots literary adventurer like the poet James Thomson could have problems connected with the rise and fall of his patrons. Thomson, an ex-divinity student who went to London to seek his fortune in 1725 and against the odds succeeded in becoming a successful poet with his series of poems known as 'The Seasons', was patronised by Whig politicians such as Lord Chancellor Talbot and George Lyttleton. Lyttleton was a member of the group of men around Frederick Louis, Prince of Wales, and when he and the prince quarrelled Thomson's grip on a political pension became insecure. It was in fact withdrawn in 1748, the year of his death.

Such vicissitudes of fortune are no doubt rather typical of most patronage systems and it is a nice question whether the accession of Bute to power marked a huge shift in the scale on which pensions, places, contracts and favours flowed towards Scotsmen, as distinct from Englishmen or Irishmen. The fact that Bute was a man of wide and cultivated interests, which he passed on to his pupil George III, at least ensured a continuity of enlightened patronage. However, the important point is not reality but contemporary perceptions of the situation. Scotsmen on the make were undoubtedly buoyed by the thought that a fellow Scot, who had used Scots agents like his brother James Stuart Mackenzie as well as the architect James Adam and the painters

Allan Ramsay and Jakey Seton to purchase Italian art, stood near the pinnacle of the political system. The early life of the architect Robert Adam is illuminating on this, and other aspects of the relationship between art and patronage in Britain in the 1750s and 1760s, the more so as he returned to London from his Grand Tour of the Continent full of hopes as to what Bute himself might do for his career.

Robert Adam was the son of William Adam, the outstanding Scottish architect of the first half of the eighteenth century. Though he was as much a building contractor as what the twenty-first century would call an architect, William Adam was intellectually distinguished as well as financially successful. His business successes enabled him to turn himself into a laird in Kinross-shire by the 1730s. His distinction as an architect was embodied in his buildings rather than in the collection of designs of public buildings and country houses entitled *Vitruvius Scotticus* which he drew and had engraved for publication. In his civic buildings or his work on country houses such as Hopetoun House near Edinburgh, House of Dun near Montrose or Duff House near Banff, the elder Adam could, as in the last case, fall foul of his customers over his steep charges as a builder. In his other role as architect he showed a robustly masculine style, neo-classical in vocabulary but with a dramatic swagger consciously borrowed from the theatrical baroque tradition as mediated through the English architect Vanbrugh. The ambitious Robert Adam had already worked with his father for some years (William died in 1748) when in 1754 he committed a substantial part of the family wealth to funding an indefinitely prolonged Grand Tour of Europe for himself. The decision combined enthusiasm with calculation. The Grand Tour was the bridge across which Robert Adam meant to cross from contracts on Highland forts for the Board of Ordnance and commissions to build or alter houses for Scottish lairds to the vastly more prestigious status of gentleman-architect to the metropolitan British ruling class.

Robert Adam went on the Grand Tour as the companion of the Honourable Charles Hope, the younger brother of the Earl

of Hopetoun. By this time it was very normal for Scottish aris-
tocrats to participate in this extraordinary and expensive finishing school much used by the scions of the English aristocracy.
Variety was characteristic of the exercise but the itinerary of
Robert Adam and Charles Hope gives a good idea of the elements which went into the Tour. From London they crossed the
Channel to Calais, and after an excursion into the southern
Netherlands they worked their way down from Paris to
Marseilles and Nice whence they took ship for Genoa. Rome was
the supreme treasure house of the artistic masterpieces on which
the noble tourist was expected to form his taste, though there
were usually plenty of Scots to be found enjoying the sights of
the larger and livelier city of Naples further south. So numerous
and well organised was the Scottish element in upper-class
tourism in Italy that in 1784 Mrs Thrale Piozzi could refer to
them as 'the national Phalanx'.

Partly, this Caledonian phalanx was composed of men resident in Italy with a Jacobite background or ancestry. James
Byres, a principal of the very Scottish trading house of Byres and
Moir, which was one of the biggest firms dealing in antiquities
and art objects in Rome, was an example of a man with a
strongly Jacobite family, but no active Jacobite record. Others
like Andrew Lumsden, guide and contactman extraordinary,
were deeply implicated with the exiled court. Lumsden had
fought in the '45 and in 1762 succeeded James Edgar as secretary to James, the Old Pretender. However, Lumsden had no
illusions by the 1760s about the viability of the cause he served.
He avoided politics and was happy to oblige committed
Hanoverians. Technically, the Abbé Peter Grant, a Gaelic-speaking native of Glenlivet, was primarily employed as Scots Agent
in Rome, a post to which he was appointed in 1737. In practice
his bishop was correct in suspecting that much of the time which
Grant should have devoted to his agency for the proscribed
Roman Catholic Church in Scotland was spent obliging well-off
tourists in a fashion more shaped by national than by religious
loyalties. Wholly apolitical were the motives which led Gavin
Hamilton, a student at Glasgow University, to settle in later life

in Rome as an archeologist, art dealer, friend of artists, painter of historical themes, and theorist of the neo-classical style which he himself practised.

Neo-classicism was a most important vehicle for the talents of Scottish architects and artists. The interpretation and glorification of the heritage of ancient Greece and Rome came naturally to sophisticated Scots reared in a country where classical culture was deeply entrenched in the national consciousness. The great traditions of Scottish Latin scholarship from George Buchanan to Thomas Ruddiman still waxed potent. Indeed they were given fresh vigour and a certain lightness of touch by a cult of Greek sculpture and letters. Alexander Boswell, Lord Auchinleck, the distinguished judge and much-tried father of the diarist James Boswell, is a good illustration of this. He built for himself at his Ayrshire seat, Auchinleck House, a gem of neo-classical taste completed in 1762. Speaking broad Scots from the bench of the Court of Session, he was also an accomplished master of both the classical tongues with a particular fondness for the studied felicities of Horace among Roman poets and for the elegant trifles of Anacreon among the Greeks. That his poker-faced brand of humour and ponderously bleak style as a father both proved more than his unstable son and heir could stomach was a personal tragedy.

Other Scots managed to express more consistently the lightness and elegance which it was fashionable to admire in the heritage of the ancients. A famous example is furnished by the brothers Robert and Andrew Foulis, printers in Glasgow where Robert was appointed printer to the university in 1743. With the aid of local professors they produced editions of the Latin and Greek classics notable for accuracy and scholarship. Men applied the adjective 'immaculate' to their Horace, but the typography and book production of their best work was as stylish as the scholarship it presented. In 1753–4 the brothers founded an Academy of Arts which gave instruction in drawing, painting, engraving and sculpture. Though this academy had financial troubles and closed after the death of Andrew Foulis in 1775, it would be wrong to conclude that enthusiasm for the artistic expression of the classical tradition was not widespread in Scotland outside Edinburgh. A generation later one can find in the small county burgh of Fife, Cupar, something not wholly dissimilar to the Foulis Press. This was the Tullis Press, whose proprietor Robert Tullis was printer to the University of St Andrews. He was a bookseller and paper-maker as well as a printer, and from about 1807 he was producing, in association with St Andrews professors, editions of the classics in the 'immaculate' tradition.

It was vitally important for the careers of many ambitious Scots in the eighteenth century that various forms of classicism constituted an international cultural vocabulary immediately accessible to, and therefore saleable to, the ruling classes of what contemporaries called the polite nations. To describe this cultural community simply as 'European' is both glib and myopic. For all the cultivation of Greek learning by the eighteenth century, ancient Rome was the rock on which its various forms of classicism ultimately stood, and the heritage of ancient Rome had been handed down to even the most secular-minded of eighteenth-century men through the influence, at once preservative and distorting, of medieval Latin Christendom. However, the states born from the matrix of Latin Christendom had by 1750 created world-systems of political power, trade and culture which stretched well beyond a Europe whose limits they by no means covered. There was still a great Islamic empire, that of Turkey, in the Balkans, while across the thousands of miles of the Atlantic stretched a cultural continuum, full of strains and stresses, but impressively resilient. Imperial Spain created universities in Mexico City and in Lima in Peru as early as 1551. When in 1767 the young Virginian planter and future president of the United States Thomas Jefferson determined to build himself a new mansion, which he named Monticello, he buckled down to an intensive study of the works of James Gibbs, and of the sixteenth-century Italian architect Andrea Palladio. Later he used as a consultant in his work on the state capitol building of Virginia in Richmond one Charles-Louis Clérisseau, a man important in the genesis of neo-classicism, who had cooperated with Robert and James Adam in their studies of classical ruins in Italy and on the Dalmatian coast in the 1750s.

It is significant that the cult of Palladio, whose restrained yet light classicism was to capture completely the eighteenth-century English country house, had been launched early in that century by a young Scottish architect, Colen Campbell, and his patron Richard Boyle, third Earl of Burlington. The relationship between the great Scottish artistic and literary careerists of this era and the cultural traditions they exploited, partially created and constantly modified was complex. Most of them were self-conscious about what they were doing. The Grand Tour was, after all, a construct based on a conception of classical civilisation that looked back to the Italian Renaissance, but which was much more the product of northern and non-Roman Catholic Europe's classical obsessions than of contemporary realities in either Rome or, even more so, Greece. Italians very sensibly took advantage of the opportunities to build up a tourist industry and to fleece gullible foreigners, not least by selling them dubious, 'repaired' or downright forged antiquities. The idea that modern Italians were the heirs of the ancient Romans, as opposed to being adjacent to their monuments, would rightly have been regarded as risible by sophisticated Scottish visitors such as Lord Fortrose. He toured Sicily with William and Catherine Hamilton, before settling for a spell in Naples. There Catherine in May 1770 organised a concert where Leopold Mozart and his son Wolfgang Amadeus played to an audience of Scots currently resident in the city. Fortrose later was created Earl of Seaforth, raised the first Seaforth Highlanders, and died in action in eastern waters on his way to India with them in 1781. Few tourists went to Greece, so the Greeks, despite their palpably sub-Ottoman culture, were soon able to sell an absurd self-image, not just as heirs of ancient Athens, but also as Founders of European Civilisation, to a European market where German intellectuals proved even more gullible than English ones.

One Scotsman who also grasped the importance of the European market was that eminent Moderate divine William Robertson. Bute had displayed real anxiety to act as Robertson's patron as soon as the latter made his name by publishing two quarto volumes of *A History of Scotland* in 1759. The period covered by the work was that of the reigns of Mary Queen of Scots and of King James VI until his accession to the throne of England in 1603. Robertson therefore shrewdly exploited one of the most dramatic periods in Scottish history and one with an unusually wide emotional appeal. His efforts were crowned with great success, for the book sold extremely well and was widely admired in England. When, therefore, a vacancy in the principalship of the University of Edinburgh occurred early in 1762, Robertson rapidly emerged as an overwhelming candidate backed by the Moderate party in the Kirk and by the dominant political interest of the day, managed in Scotland for Bute by the faithful Lord Milton. Indeed it would be wrong to suggest that there was any very sharp distinction between the lay and the ecclesiastical interests. The principal wheeler-dealer in the city politics of university patronage in Edinburgh, and contactman with Milton, was John Jardine, the Moderate minister of the Tron Kirk, who ran Robertson's campaign with an expertise first developed when as a young man he managed the burgh of Lochmaben for Charles Erskine of Tinwald. Robertson, as the author of an enormously successful book, deserved to become Principal Robertson, to which prize was soon added the sinecure of Historiographer Royal for Scotland with a salary of £200 a year. Yet the astute divine ignored Bute's strong advice that he provide a modern introduction to the whole of Scottish history.

Robertson wanted a topic with wider appeal. He considered writing a History of England but veered away from the idea because his friend David Hume was beginning to dominate that field. Instead Robertson turned to a sweeping European theme and repeated in 1769 his previous brilliant success when he published in three volumes quarto a *History of the Reign of Charles V, with a view of the Progress of Society from the Subversion of the Roman Empire to the Commencement of the Sixteenth Century.* Robertson's third great work, possibly his greatest single achievement, was the *History of the Discovery and Settlement of America*, which he published in London in two volumes in 1777. Starting as a by-product of his interest in Charles V, this history became a great survey of Spanish American history which had no rival in the English-speaking world until the rise to fame of the blind American historian William Hickling Prescott, whose histories of the conquest of Mexico and of Peru were published sixty to seventy years later. By any standards Robertson is an extremely important figure in the history of historical writing. It has been argued that he and Hume, and he far more than Hume, represent the first emergence of recognisably modern historical scholarship, combining the use of narrative form, buttressed by careful citation of authorities, with a capacity for penetrating thematic analysis of major issues. In this connection Robertson's remarkable survey of European civilisation prior to the age of Charles V is justly famous. He then sought out and mastered a great mass of material on Latin America and summed it all up in an analytical survey of Spanish colonial policy from the sixteenth century to the Bourbon reforms of his own day. His history of America was rightly deemed far too pro-metropolitan Spanish by the restless indigenous clerical and lay white elites of Spain's American viceralties and kingdoms, but in the eighteenth century only the Englishman Edward Gibbon, with his immortal *Decline And Fall Of The Roman Empire*, can be said to have combined erudition and analysis in a fashion comparable to Robertson, albeit with an even better prose style, and he was deeply influenced, as he admitted in his *Autobiography*, by 'the philosophic Hume' as well as by 'the vigorous sense' of Robertson.

Robertson's works were translated into all major western European languages. He was known literally from Philadelphia to St Petersburg, where the Empress Catherine the Great, as her Scottish physician Dr Rogerson told Robertson, read and admired the *History of the Reign of Charles V*. Such fame no doubt fuelled the self-satisfaction and amiable, if tedious, pomposity which characterised the Reverend Principal in his latter days, but fame alone was not the prize. Starving in a garret for the sake of Art or Truth was not a lifestyle admired by the Scottish intellectuals of this period. They all tried to make money.

By his own standards Robertson made a great deal. The 'copy money' he was paid for the manuscript of *Charles V* was no less than £4,000, for its day an unheard-of sum. Yet Robertson managed to have his cake as well as eat it. Latterly he eschewed the parochialism of Scottish themes, but when he went to London to find a publisher for *Charles V*, he settled so advantageously with William Strachan who had changed his name to Strahan after moving from Edinburgh to London. Strahan became King's Printer and an MP. It was a period when the distinction between printer and publisher hardly existed in its modern form. Strahan published Gibbon's *Decline and Fall*, as well as the works of the literary pontiff or mastiff of the age, Dr Samuel Johnson. He also printed and published a clutch of famous Scottish names including David Hume, Robertson himself, and in 1776 Adam Smith's *Wealth of Nations*. The Scots literati tended to operate on two different but not contradictory levels. Their material they deliberately tried to make as universal as possible, but in the manoeuvres which presented them with the crucial opportunities to seize Fame and Fortune they took it for granted they would be supported by a phalanx of fellow-Scots.

The fact that ambitious Scots thought in this way was only too obvious to non-Scottish contemporaries and is one explanation of the strong currents of anti-Scottish feeling which were to be found in England and more especially in London during the political apogee of Lord Bute. They would never have received the encouragement they did in high places but for the bitter hostility with which Bute's administration was regarded by men such as William Pitt the Elder and his ally Richard Grenville-Temple, first Earl Temple, whom Bute had ousted from power. It was a client of Temple, John Wilkes, who raised Scotophobia to unparalleled heights in the columns of the paper which he started in 1762 and entitled derisively the *North Briton*. Exploiting anti-ministerial passions with verve, impudence and total lack of scruple, Wilkes managed eventually to become the hero of a protracted struggle between the House of Commons and the electorate of Middlesex, whose repeated endorsements of Wilkes as their MP, in the face of equally stubborn refusal by the House to admit him, rendered the life of His Majesty's Government hideous in the years 1768–70. Yet Wilkes was never a straightforward character. He had been educated at Leiden where Scotsmen, of whom there were many at that distinguished Dutch university, were his favoured companions. 'The Middlesex Patriot' himself denied that his animus against Scotsmen could be separated from the political circumstances which raised Bute to power. This particular assertion was uttered in the circle of the arch-Tory Dr Johnson, with whom Wilkes, 'that blasphemer of his God and a libeller of his King', was eventually very friendly. There is no reason to doubt the truth of the statement. Scotophobia in London had a long history going back to at least the arrival of needy Scots gentlemen in the train of James VI and I in 1603, but its virulence in the 1760s was inextricably bound up with the almost hysterical hatred of Bute in opposition circles. In practice Bute was not an effective politician. His nerve was broken by a crescendo of abusive and violent opposition to the point where he resigned office in April 1763. Even then, he was repeatedly and quite unfairly denounced as the secret influence behind the throne.

It was only too true that Scottish MPs and peers, as compared with their English counterparts, showed a marked proclivity to support His Majesty's Government, provided the administration of the day had the wit and ability to meet their, relatively modest, demands. Furthermore, the reign of George III did see another stage in the progressive integration of Scotsmen into the life of the British governing classes, and not just as purveyors of improving literature and fine buildings or pictures. In the diplomatic service, which was still in the eighteenth century very much subject to the royal discretion in appointments, one Scot in perhaps every twenty diplomatic posts under William and Mary eventually turned into a proportion of one in seven under George III. In between, Walpole had virtually cleared Scots out of the service, but the crucial point is that they crept back in the later 1740s and were being appointed in very substantial numbers from the outbreak of the Seven Years War in 1756. This was a field reserved for the nobility and gentry, but here as elsewhere the Scots were clearly deeply entrenched before Bute and unshaken by the fall of the man denounced, absurdly, as the 'Northern Machiavel'. In 1789 Sir Robert Murray Keith had just completed twenty years as envoy to Vienna, while Sir William Hamilton had been twenty-five years in the Naples embassy. Hugh Elliot, another Scot, was British ambassador at Copenhagen in 1789, one of a series of ambassadorial positions he had held for the best part of fifteen years. At Constantinople Sir Robert Ainslie had represented the British Crown for nearly as long. Nor was there any slacking-off of the rate of appointment of Scots to diplomatic positions.

They were more honorific than profitable. Sir Robert Murray Keith wrote from Vienna in 1774 complaining that the need constantly to dip into his own pocket was bringing him to the verge of beggary. One Scots peer, the third Earl of Marchmont, refused a diplomatic post on the ground that he was not prepared to impoverish his family abroad and then come back 'to walk about soliciting a Scots pension'. The case of Sir William Hamilton, who spent some thirty-seven years in all as British representative at the court of the Bourbons of Sicily, is exceptional but instructive. His father Lord Archibald was the seventh son of the third Duke of Hamilton. No genius, he nevertheless achieved a lordship of the Admiralty and a governorship of Jamaica. His wife was far more powerful as Mistress of the Robes in the royal household and reputed mistress of Frederick, Prince of Wales. Certainly her son, the future Sir William, was brought up as virtual foster brother to the future George III. Sir William underlines the potential for close integration between the Scottish, Irish and English court elites. His formidable mother was Irish, being third daughter to the sixth Earl of Abercorn. William's influence clearly benefited from the transition to George III and Bute after 1760 but he had no difficulty in securing the Naples embassy from Bute's successor, George Grenville, in 1764, mainly in order to safeguard the health of his beloved but tubercular first wife by moving to a warm climate. Much mocked for tolerating the liaison of his second wife Emma, whom he had acquired cheaply as a cast-off from his nephew, with Admiral

Horatio Nelson, Hamilton was in fact an amateur of the arts and sciences and a cosmopolitan European gentleman cultivating with some success the 'art of getting through life'. In Scotland Bute never faced any serious challenge to his ascendancy. He was lucky in the fact that for one reason or another the heads of nearly all the great magnate houses were ineffective. The Dukes of Gordon, Buccleuch and Hamilton just happened to be minors. The Duke of Argyll, the former Major General John Campbell of Mamore who had played such a staunch and honourable role on the Hanoverian side during the '45, was old and by the standards of his house not very bright. The Duke of Montrose was blind and the Marquess of Tweeddale a cripple. Other Scots peers and MPs, partly because of a basic lack of interest in the details of English politics and partly because of the workings of patronage, tended to be obsequiously loyal to Bute. It was therefore natural for Bute to assume that he could dispose of the satrapy of Scotland at will. Indeed he owed it to his political friends to make arrangements to protect them after his own retiral from power. To this end he made his brother James Stuart Mackenzie Lord Privy Seal in Scotland in 1763 and informed Baron Mure in April of that year that 'Scotch affairs will go on under the care of my brother, as they did under my late uncle'. It was a tribute to the memory of the subtly intelligent Islay. Unfortunately Mackenzie was not nearly so strongly placed as Islay in his heyday, and he was destroyed by the ferocious factionalism of the English Whig nobility.

The ministry which took the reins from the faltering hands of the Scottish favourite rapidly came to be dominated by George Grenville, younger brother of Lord Temple. Grenville, like all his family, was pathologically pleased with himself. He was also 'a crashing bore with a mind like a cash-register'. Obsessively anxious to be the sole channel of royal favour, Grenville was soon at loggerheads with Mackenzie. While reducing the army and navy with a zeal which commended him to tax-weary back-benchers, Grenville busied himself with a series of measures which laid the foundations of a serious Anglo-American political crisis. He was paranoid about the role of Mackenzie who was in effect chief whip for the Scottish MPs and who dealt with every other aspect of Scottish affairs, even going as far as to prepare the way for a reform bill to stop 'that abominable practice' of splitting votes to manipulate Scottish elections. Grenville sharply resented Mackenzie's control over Scots patronage and supported disgruntled unsuccessful candidates, of whom there were many, since Mackenzie tried to make appointments to posts on merit. Personally unambitious and conscientious to a fault, Mackenzie was implicitly trusted by George III. By May 1765 Grenville was able to blackmail the King by refusing to serve in office unless Mackenzie was deprived both of his political function and of the privy seal (worth £3,000 per annum). The semi-autonomous manager for Scottish business, anxious to spare his sovereign more trouble, bowed out, banished by an able but power-obsessed obsessive whom the King detested and finally dismissed in July 1765, but only with support from his uncle the Duke of Cumberland and the cooperation of the group known as the Rockingham Whigs. Cumberland, whose distaste for Scots waxed rather than waned in the years after his victory at Culloden, died late in 1765, but his association with the new regime was a guarantee that integration was the watchword of policy, in so far as there was any, towards Scotland, while their lust to monopolise royal patronage made all other English Whig faction leaders averse to the reinstatement of an informal 'minister for Scotland' like Mackenzie.

During the next fifteen or so years no ministry needed, or had time to formulate, a Scottish policy. Crises came not singly but in battalions as one group after another exploited the appalling gaps between theory and practice in the British constitution, if indeed it can be held that there was such a thing, as distinct from a rather misleading mythology and a set of working arrangements. Whooping in the van of the assault came 'that Devil Wilkes'. Between 1763 and 1774 John Wilkes stimulated and used London radicalism for his own personal ends. More serious were the confrontations which developed between Westminster and the American colonies, and between Westminster and the Irish Parliament in Dublin. By comparison with other peripheral provinces of the British Crown, Scotland was quiet. It was therefore usually ignored.

The simple truth was that nearly all Scots who mattered were content, and this for a mixture of reasons within and without Scotland. Domestically the 1760s and early 1770s were an era of considerable prosperity in Scotland, and that prosperity was closely tied to the structure of the British global monarchy, as may most conveniently be demonstrated by an examination of the way in which the 'tobacco lords' of Glasgow rose to the peak of their greatness in the first half of the 1770s. Great they certainly were, for in the 1760s and '70s tobacco accounted for just under 50 per cent in value of all Scottish imports from outwith Britain and all but 2 per cent of that tobacco was imported through the ports of Greenock and Port Glasgow, which were controlled financially by the rich merchants in Glasgow further up the Clyde. The cornerstone of this commercial empire was the legislation which compelled American planters to export their tobacco to a British port before it could be transferred to the European markets which were always more important than the domestic British one. However, the rise of Glasgow to eminence as one of the metropolitan centres of the Chesapeake tobacco trade was a competitive business. As the importance of Glasgow in the trade rose, so did that of other British ports decline.

Originally the south-western parts of Britain, plus London, had been heavily dominant in importing tobacco. Not only Bristol but scores of quite small harbours in counties like Cornwall and Devon ranked as significant tobacco ports. Then came a shift to the north-west, during which the tobacco trade of London and Bristol tended to stagnate, while that of smaller southern harbours dropped away to nothing. Liverpool and Whitehaven south of the Anglo-Scottish border followed the example of Glasgow and surpassed Bristol. London never lost its individual preponderance, which was based on the domestic market, but, London apart, the significance of British tobacco ports declined from north to south. Glasgow was Scotland as far as tobacco was concerned and in the three years from 1768 to 1770 the Scottish trade reached its greatest relative importance.

In 1769, with 51.8 per cent of total British imports, the Scots tobacco trade for the first and last time exceeded that of England.

Apart from a shorter, safer Atlantic voyage from the waters of Chesapeake Bay which washes the shores of both Virginia and Maryland, Glasgow enjoyed other comparative advantages. It benefited from the changing nature of the ultimate market. As long as the bulk of the tobacco crop of the British colonies was reshipped for sale in Amsterdam, it hardly mattered where it was landed in Britain, but when French and German buyers began to buy directly in the British market, they preferred to deal with a limited number of large ports. Much of the prosperity of Glasgow in the 1760s and '70s hinged on bulk purchases by the Farmers General of the French state tobacco monopoly. Glasgow also enjoyed the advantages of unusually well-developed banking and commercial facilities, but above all it throve on low operating costs. On the Clyde, ships and labour were cheaper than elsewhere, as were refitting charges, and more profitable outward cargoes to America could be obtained. However, it was the way in which Glasgow merchants combined low shipping costs with a network of factors and stores in the colonies which seems to have been decisive.

Though their financial resources allowed the Glasgow firms to buy or hire the bigger ships which were more economical on the Atlantic run, it seems that the crucial point in the whole operation was turn-round time in the Chesapeake. A quick turn-round saved vital running costs and other charges. All the big Glasgow tobacco firms operated a store system, particularly in the inland areas beyond the falls on the rivers flowing into Chesapeake Bay where tobacco cultivation was expanding in the hands of less wealthy planters. These men could exchange their staple crop for cash, or more usually for a combination of goods and money. The factor in charge of the store tried to accumulate tobacco in time to ensure a quick turn-about for his firm's ships when they arrived. Bulk sales at the other end ensured a rapid turnover which, allied to profit on goods exported, gave the Glasgow merchants a vital margin over rivals. The price for steady expansion rooted in competitive offers of credit was mounting American indebtedness. John Glassford, a leading Glasgow 'tobacco lord', estimated that in the early 1760s he and his fellows were owed some £500,000 by planters. In 1778 the estimated planter debt to Glasgow was £1,306,000.

It was no recipe for popularity with the debtors, one of whom compared 'A North Briton' to a species of obnoxious plant, quick to root and multiply, hard to eradicate, and poisonous to the ground it afflicted. The tobacco ships nevertheless carried an important outward cargo of men and ideas which deeply affected the developing societies of colonial America. Scotland, like the American colonies, was essentially a cultural province of Hanoverian England. An acute sense of inferiority pervaded the conscious cultural life of both Scots and Americans, breeding inevitably a love-hate relationship with the metropolitan power. Robert Wodrow, that conservative Presbyterian divine, complained bitterly that 'all the villainous, profane, and obscene books and plays, as printed in London, are got down by Allan Ramsay, and lent out, for an easy price, to young boys, servant women of the better sort, and gentlemen'. One hears here an extreme form of that suspicion of London which can be found in the quintessentially English novels of Jane Austen at the very end of the eighteenth century, in which evil is so often something which comes down from London into the pastoral world of a provincial middle-class family. Very eminent Scots intellectuals of the eighteenth century could be extraordinarily apologetic about their own provincial setting, at least in letters to London correspondents. David Hume said to such a one in 1756 that in exchange for valued metropolitan information he could offer only 'provincial stories which are in no way interesting'. Adam Smith in 1759 obsequiously remarked that such was the tedium of life benorth the Tweed that no Scots correspondent could hope to offer entertaining matter to a sophisticated southerner. All this is of a kind with the excitement with which the young American Benjamin Franklin read an issue of the London *Spectator* and resolved to mould his own prose style on its metropolitan rhythms.

However, Scots society was closer to that of the south of England in most ways than was provincial American society.

Scotland had a far more elaborate and old-established educational system, for example. Its social structure, so decisively dominated by aristocracy and gentry, was similar to that of contemporary England, whereas the social structure of the American colonies was significantly different. Scotland could therefore mediate metropolitan culture to America and that in various ways. Scottish teachers found their way to America in some numbers. James Blair, an alumnus of Marischal College Aberdeen and of Edinburgh University, had in 1693 been largely instrumental in the foundation of what was later to be the College of William and Mary in Virginia. William Smith, another man with an Aberdeen background, became the first provost of the new College of Philadelphia in 1755, and played an important role in the transformation of American colleges from schools for clergymen into institutions more like universities. By far the greatest of these figures was the Reverend John Witherspoon of the Laigh Kirk in Paisley, who was persuaded in 1766 to go out to be sixth president of the College of New Jersey which subsequently grew to be Princeton University. Trained in the philosophical and rhetorical traditions of the University of Edinburgh in the middle of the eighteenth century, Witherspoon undoubtedly gave a sharp impetus to a process of culture-transfer which was already active. Scottish 'rhetoric and belles-lettres' was a subject designed to facilitate precisely that acquisition of sophisticated, upper-class tastes and values which was the ambition of so many Americans. Equally, Scottish philosophy of the common-sense school provided a body of generally acceptable intellectual positions compatible with orthodox Christianity and particularly important as cement in the theological life of American Presbyterianism.

Yet the fact remains that the American colonies were, to those Scotsmen wielding power and influence who were not tobacco merchants, a subordinate facet of contemporary life. Nor were they at all a focus of disaffection, as New England certainly was from the very first days of its effective settlement to certain elements within English society. A small but significant segment of Scottish society was being forced to emigrate to America in the decades before 1776, yet once in America these people were remarkable for their loyalty to the British connection rather than the reverse. The key group in this movement were Highland tacksmen, those Gaelic-speaking gentlemen to whom the landlord chief was wont to lease large areas at low rents in exchange for political and military service. The dukes of Argyll were among the earliest Highland magnates to adopt a policy of squeezing tacksmen out on the grounds that they were useless mouths. That view was an over-simplified one and many tacksmen survived for a long time in parts of the Highlands. Nevertheless, after 1763 tacksmen left the Highlands in substantial numbers, selling up their stock and property and taking with them large numbers of their sub-tenants and other dependants. The experience of soldiers in Highland regiments who had served in North America during the Seven Years War between 1756 and 1763 helped to give direction to what became a steady flow of emigrants. Six vessels carrying 1,200 persons from the Highlands and Islands sailed in 1770. In 1771, 500 people from Islay and 370 from Skye took ship for North Carolina. A year later, 200 people from Sutherland sailed for the same place. In 1773 Dr Samuel Johnson and his friend James Boswell were touring the Highlands during a summer full of the bustle and talk of emigration. Neither man approved of it. On Skye Boswell deplored the forcing out of tacksmen on the grounds that men of substance could withstand bad years better than a poor rack-rented tenantry, while on Coll Dr Johnson remarked, crushingly, that 'the Lairds, instead of improving their country, diminished their people'. Contemporaries believed that 20,000 people in all emigrated. Modern estimates are of the order of 10,000 or more, but the impressive aspect of the emigration was that it was led by men who had refused to accept a reduction in social status at home and who saw in America an opportunity to re-create a hierarchical society with themselves in an enhanced rather than a reduced position within it.

Jacobite exiles and sympathisers had emigrated to America after 1746. James Burd was one who went to Pennsylvania, and Hugh Mercer, who settled in Virginia, another. The great heroine of the aftermath of Culloden, Flora MacDonald, no Jacobite despite her key role in preserving the fugitive Prince Charles, emigrated to North Carolina in 1774. She moved just in time. By 1775 a worried British government facing a mounting crisis in the American colonies had banned further emigration. Flora's husband, Allan MacDonald of Kingsburgh, was a tacksman from Trotternish in the north-east of Skye. No great business-man, he was forced into emigration by a combination of bad years and a grasping landlord chief, Sir Alexander MacDonald of Sleat, whose harsh rent demands compared shamefully with the rebates which helped to preserve the tenants of other Skye chiefs such as Macleod of Macleod and Macleod of Raasay. Nevertheless, when under pressure from rebel activists to join them in 1776, MacDonald of Kingsburgh never hesitated. Like most of the Highland gentlemen newly settled in North Carolina, he became a Loyalist and turned out to fight for King George III against the Patriot or Whig rebels.

This Highland Loyalism shows how the British Hanoverian state system could offer to ambitious Scots opportunities for enrichment and advancement which, however often they proved illusory in the case of specific individuals, were real enough to head off any serious discontent. That state structure was complex and unstable, spanning as it did the North Sea, the Irish Sea and the Atlantic. It stretched literally from the Elbe to the Mississippi, with an important extension after 1757 on the Ganges. However, there is no doubt that it was the opportuni-ties, political, economic and social, offered by its core state, the United Kingdom of Great Britain, which primarily determined the attitudes of the important Scottish elites during the 1760s and 1770s. The tobacco trade, for example, was in absolute terms important in the Scottish economy, but its impact was highly regionalised. Trades operating primarily within a British framework had a far wider impact on Scottish fortunes.

A good example is the accelerated expansion in the cattle trade after 1750. In the immediate aftermath of the '45 the breakdown of traditional authority in the Highlands led to more rather than less cattle thieving and in 1747 Graham of Gartmore estimated the direct and indirect loss to farmers and landowners in the Highlands, through stealing and blackmail, at no less than £37,000 sterling per annum. Slowly but surely small military garrisons and regular patrols of key routes and passes reduced the level of theft while the state gradually extended effective control over such strategic thieves' kitchens as the Moor of Rannoch, though it had to wait for the death of the indomitable and much-forfeited Alexander Robertson 'Elector of Struan' to do so. It was recorded in an official report that 'It was a saying of the late Strouan's [sic] that be the roads never so bad, his friends would see him and he wanted no visits from his enemys'. By 1755 a military road was being built to link Rannoch with the outside world. The progress of agriculture in those parts of the Lowlands adjacent to the Highlands, especially in connection with the new cultivation of turnips and artificial grasses, imparted an even more important stimulus to the cattle trade than the pacification of the Highlands. It is important to recognise that these new crops could be introduced without a root-and-branch reconstruction of traditional agricultural practices. This was just as well, for when Andrew Wight, a progressive tenant farmer from East Lothian, was charged by the Commissioners of the Forfeited Estates with the task of surveying the progress of new agricultural methods in Scotland it was said when he departed on his tour in July 1773 that 'the bulk of our farmers are creeping in the beaten path of miserable husbandry, without knowing better or even wishing to know better'.

Counties like Berwickshire, East Lothian and Ayrshire were gratifyingly 'progressive' by Wight's standards. That is to say they had abolished the distinction between an intensively cultivated infield and a less worked and less cared for outfield. They were expanding their arable acreage and were levelling and straightening the ridges which were typical of the old agricultural methods. New crops, breeds and tools were being adopted. Elsewhere in the Lowlands it was a different story. Lanarkshire in the 1770s was so conservative as to distress Wight. He took it for granted that improved methods had to be imposed from above on a mean-spirited tenantry. 'It is in vain', he lamented, 'to expect improvement from them, unless some publicspirited gentlemen would take the lead'. Longer leases and new methods might then become the order of the day. Perthshire in 1772 was remarkable for the variety of its agricultural methods. Large parts were totally traditional, but around the city of Perth and on the estates of enlightened landlords like Sir William Stirling and Lord Kames great changes had occurred. Sir William was an enterprising laird who, shortly after the '45, brought English experts and tools to Drummond Castle, which became a centre of experimentation in fallowing methods and the sowing of artificial grasses.

Lord Kames was a much more complex character whose life and career tell us much about eighteenth-century Scotland. The son of an impoverished Berwickshire laird of Jacobite and Episcopalian stock, but who had the wit to join the Hanoverian forces in the '15, Henry Home, Lord Kames was born at Kames in Berwickshire, a mere three miles from the English border. Educated at home and in Edinburgh, he made such a slow start to his legal career that he at one time thought of volunteering for the famous Giant Grenadier Regiment of very tall soldiers maintained by Frederick William I, King of Prussia. However, he remained in Edinburgh, pushing his name into prominence as much by his varied writings as by his hard work in the courts. He compiled a collection of precedental decisions by the Court of Session. He wrote on what we would call the philosophy of law. The fullest development of his legal thought is to be found in his *Principles of Equity* (1760) which shows his view of law as being rooted in human nature, defined as much by its emotions and drives as by its rational faculties. His writings on religion were not much favoured by the Kirk, but they were in fact conservative compared with those of his friend David Hume, refusing flatly to accept Hume's attempt to reduce belief to the status of a particularly lively sense-impression. Home's elevation to the bench owed much to the patronage of the ducal house of Argyll and was achieved in 1752 despite a last-minute hitch when the Duke of Newcastle was told of the Jacobite background of the Home family and had to have the Hanoverian volunteer of the '15 paraded before him to calm his fluttering nerves.

As a Lord of Session, Lord Kames went on writing to the end of a very long life on topics ranging from law to history to education. With his *Elements of Criticism* published in 1762 he became a best-selling author within the English-speaking world, rather to the surprise of David Hume who had loyally interested his own London publisher Andrew Millar in handling the London issue of the book but who suspected that it was 'too abstruse and crabbed ever to take with the Public'. It was certainly complex, yet it was rooted in principles which proved eminently acceptable. To Kames, human nature, rightly understood, was the basis of aesthetic theory, and human knowledge to him was a product of the senses, both external and internal. The latter was defined as the inbuilt capacity to apprehend abstract qualities like virtue and beauty. Kames contended that 'we are framed by nature to relish order and connection'. Nevertheless, operating as he did within a psychological and empirical framework, Kames was bound to regard the aesthetic response as more emotional than intellectual. It was eminently susceptible of analysis and categorisation which Kames supplied with all the enthusiasm, humanist learning and social awareness of the contemporary Scots legal intellectual.

For all its ultimate naïvety and lack of real philosophic depth, the *Elements* sold well in the British Isles, where half a dozen editions appeared in the author's life. It became a standard philosophic text in North American colleges until the middle of the nineteenth century. In France its reception was blighted by the wrath of Voltaire, an admirer of the historical works of Hume and Robertson, but no friend of Kames, who was rash enough to criticise one of his poems in the *Elements*. The German translation first appeared in 1766, being re-issued in 1772, 1785, 1790 and 1791. While the great contemporary German writers on aesthetics like Johann Friedrich Herder and Gotthold Ephraim Lessing necessarily changed and transcended the message of Kames, they knew their *Elements* and held it in high esteem. Kame's *Essays on the Principles of Morality and Natural*

Religion helped to establish another major Scots export to America – the Scottish Common Sense school of philosophy which was to be given its classic formulation by his friend Thomas Reid.

Intellectual and professional success on this scale inevitably gave Kames access to power and to the supreme contemporary embodiment of power – land. He was a member of the Board of Trustees for Manufactures and Fisheries in Scotland, as well as a Commissioner for the Forfeited Annexed Estates, and a gentleman farmer. His literary and other extra-legal activities, allied to a decided eccentricity of manner, led latterly to a measure of criticism of his performance of his judicial duties. In 1766 his wife became heiress to the estate of Blair Drummond on the upper reaches of the Forth near Stirling, where her husband arguably made his most permanent mark on the Scottish heritage by beginning a very long-term project to clear the vast mosses or bogs which lay 6 to 12 feet above good alluvial land for 12 miles or so up the Forth valley between Stirling and the Menteith Hills. The mosses were cut up and floated down new-cut channels into the Forth by Highland peasants induced to settle by favourable terms offered by Kames. Financially rewarding in the shape of new rents, the enterprise was later said, on dubious grounds, to have had a very bad effect on the salmon population and oyster beds of the Forth. Yet eventually it altered the strategic geography of Scotland by creating a broad corridor of good dry land where in previous centuries had lain only a narrow passable track totally dominated by the soaring fastness of Stirling Castle Rock.

Andrew Wight found that agricultural methods were not necessarily more affected by innovation in counties close to Lothian. Fife, just across the Firth of Forth, disappointed him by the conservatism of its farming. There was excellent reason for this state of affairs. Available drainage techniques were quite incapable of dealing with the mosses, moors and myriad small lochs of central Fife at an economic cost. In any case, such operations could hardly be justified except as the prelude to a substantial increase in arable farming, but the buoyant demand in the agricultural markets of Fife was that of English drovers for black cattle, which could be produced within the context of existing agricultural patterns. Forfarshire or Angus, on the northern shore of the Tay, was a much more progressive county, from Wight's point of view, than Fife. Partly this was because it was larger. Dundee, the largest urban unit, was cut off from the rest of the county by the Sidlaw Hills immediately behind it. In the vicinity of Dundee potato husbandry was notably advanced, while the export-oriented production of grain on the light soils of the southern slopes of the Sidlaws continued to flourish. Beyond the Sidlaws the county of Angus embraced both a great Lowland area in the shape of the Vale of Strathmore and a large Highland area linked to Strathmore by five great glens running like the thumb and fingers from a palm into the massif of the southern Grampians. Lowland Angus was famous for its oats and cattle. One of the earliest improving lairds in Angus had been the Honourable James Stuart Mackenzie, Lord Privy Seal, who had brought experts from England to instruct his tenantry, but Wight reported that zeal for improvement 'has now laid hold of almost every person who hath a bit of ground to cultivate'. From its own Highland area, and from further afield, Lowland Angus received cattle for fattening on its pastures before they were sold to English drovers.

It is true that in the county of Kincardine north of Angus Wight was depressed by the fact 'that agriculture in this county makes little figure, except among a few patriotic gentlemen' such as Barclay of Ury, while in Aberdeenshire improvement as he understood it was confined to the vicinity of the city of Aberdeen and to the home farms of the landowners, but agriculture was only one facet of a general current of expansion. Textile production grew and diversified, albeit at a price. The long-established woollen industry was of purely regional importance by the 1760s. Stirling, with 160 woollen looms at work in 1771, was a centre for the production of cheap woollens such as serges, plaids and carpetings. In Aberdeen in the same year no fewer than twenty-two business houses were engaged in exporting woollen stockings hand-knitted by the country folk of Aberdeenshire and

Kincardine, though the development of a more mechanised industry in the Borders using stocking frames posed a challenge to the Aberdeen firms. Linen continued to be the outstanding growth sector of Scottish textiles. Its main centres were the counties of Forfar (or Angus), Fife, Perth, Lanark and Renfrew. Increasingly, all but the last two of these produced more and more coarse linen, much of it for export. Lanark and Renfrew in 1768 produced together 23 per cent in volume and 40 per cent in value of Scottish linen production by specialising in fine goods such as lawns and cambrics, which replaced imports in the British market after legislation of 1748 had prohibited the importation of French lawns and cambrics. However, change and instability were the price of progress.

Change was most significant in the increasing use of cotton wool in the western Lowlands, where a new cotton industry, based on the Clyde's extensive trade with the West Indies, was growing out of the linen industry. Cotton wool imports rose from 105,831 lb in 1755 to 157,127 lb in 1767, to a peak (not surpassed until after 1785) in 1770 of 466,589 lb. Some pure cotton cloth was being made but the bulk was used in hybrids with linen warps and cotton wefts. Naturally, the credit facilities required by so buoyant a textile trade had expanded well beyond those originally supplied by the older chartered banks like the Bank of Scotland and the Royal Bank, with their conservative lending policies and suspicion of branch banking. The British Linen Company, sponsored by Lord Milton, the Argathelian branch manager for Scottish politics, and chartered in 1746, had originally intended to enter the mercantile side of the linen trade, which indeed it did, but by 1747 it had taken the first steps towards the banking business which engrossed more and more of its efforts. It began to issue notes to weavers and manufacturers. Unlike normal banknotes, these were effectively receipts for goods and originally the lowest denomination was for £5, but very quickly notes for £1 and indeed 10 shillings were issued and became acceptable as currency all over the country. Despite hostility from the older banks, the British Linen Company persisted in what it found to be a very profitable line, though up to the

1770s it still specialised in cash credits to linen manufacturers, linen merchants, or to the relatively heavily capitalised bleachers, who not only bleached but also carried out other finishing operations which often required substantial machinery. Smaller local banks sprang up in various towns. On 1 August 1763, for example, thirty-six persons signed a contract of co-partnery to trade as The Dundee Banking Company in a town where previously there had only been a few shopkeepers willing to give cash for bills on London or to sell bills on London to those wishing to make remittances to elsewhere. The nominal capital of the new bank was £12,600. No fewer than six new banks were founded in Perth in 1763. In 1766 they fused into the Perth United Company.

Such vigorous growth was bound to involve dangers and tensions. The role of state expenditure in the economy, for example, varied much, but in wartime it could be huge. The Seven Years War, especially when policy was dominated by the Elder Pitt, was a notable case of fiscal incontinence. Government demand for food, goods and loans distorted the market. It was believed (though statistics were lacking) that Scottish deficits on cross-border trade soared. Certainly premiums on payments on bills of credit drawn on London soared and that, along with the existence of opportunities for quick returns on investment in London, led to a run on specie in Scotland, for export to London. It required close cooperation between the Bank of Scotland and the Royal Bank to clamp down on specie withdrawal and on the expansion of credit by local banks to contain the crisis. Legislation of 1765 endorsed by the Bank of England institutionalised restrictions on banknote issue. Credit extension is always hazardous if done with more panache than judgement. Large-scale manufacture oriented towards external markets is always susceptible to occasional slumps in demand.

The next financial crisis showed that the safeguards could too easily be relaxed. The third chartered bank, the British Linen Company, adopted a more expansionist approach to note issue. In 1769 the cautious Earl of Elgin was driven off the Bank of Scotland board by private banker interests just as Douglas Heron and Company, better known as the Ayr Bank, was established with the admitted aim of increasing the supply of finance for industry and agriculture. Its chairman was the wealthy Duke of Queensberry, noted agricultural improver and chairman of the newly established Forth and Clyde Navigation Company which was trying to link the firths of Forth and Clyde by canal. With a nominal capital of £150,000, of which £96,000 was subscribed, and the backing of many wealthy landlords in the western Lowlands of Scotland, the bank embarked on an aggressive lending policy which stretched its own resources to the limit, leading it into devious paths such as excessive note issue and above all by raising credit by chains of bills on London. The bank's misfortune was that it commenced business towards the end of a long period of rising economic activity and had barely time to over-commit itself before the peak of the economic boom was past in 1771. By 1772 all the indices of production turned down. It is true that there was virtually no fall off in the linen trade, for the period 1769–72 inclusive saw over 13 million yards stamped annually in Scotland, but the total for 1773 fell sharply to 10,750,000, which suggests that very large stocks proved unsaleable in 1772.

General contraction proved fatal to the Ayr Bank, which failed on 25 June 1772. By August 1775, no fewer than 114 out of 226 partners in the Ayr Bank were insolvent, so the repayment of creditors inevitably involved the sale of estates. It was esti-mated that no less than £750,000 of landed property changed hands as a result. Many private banks closed for ever between 1772 and 1775. The two senior chartered banks resumed their hegemony, cooperating with cautious London banks of Scots origin like Coutts and Co. and Drummond's. Above all, the two big banks moved back into close alliance with the stable members of the aristocracy and the network of influence wielded by the increasingly dominant political boss, Henry Dundas. The crisis was contained.

Scotland also saw serious food riots in 1772–3, which was hardly surprising. A survey of Britain between 1735 and 1800 revealed that roughly two-thirds of all popular disturbances seem to have been triggered off by absolute shortage or high prices of food. Since the end of the '45 Scotland had enjoyed an exceptional run of average or better than average harvests, with occasional bumper years such as 1759–60 when fine harvests brought good, cheap living to working people whose diet was dominated by a few staple items. Demand for these items was, however, notably inelastic so when, as in 1772, basic food prices soared at a time when real earnings were in decline, the resulting tension could become explosive. From 1764 the weather had become more unpredictable and in 1772–3 the poor harvest in the European grain zone was so general that foreign supplies were not available to alleviate internal shortages. Rioting broke out in Dumfries in 1771. It spread to Tayside in 1772–3, mainly as a form of direct action against shipment of grain out of the region to more lucrative internal markets. The riots assumed the form of an urban-rural confrontation with mobs from the burghs of Tayside like Perth, Newburgh, Cupar and Dundee trying to seize grain stored in the warehouses or barns of corn merchants or farmers. They were resisted by not only the gentry of the region, but also by the bulk of the country folk in the affected areas.

Episodes like the Ayr Bank failure or these grain riots neither threatened the ascendancy nor sapped the morale of the Scottish ruling elites as a whole. There was no reason why they should. The Ayr Bank collapse only struck hard at the pockets of a particular regional group. It bore none of the moral stigma that surrounded similar occurrences in the Victorian era, when the middle-class cult of respectability reigned supreme. The gambling instinct was built into the lifestyle of the aristocracy, which gave its own tone to the rest of eighteenth-century society. Some men had played for high stakes and lost. Others would win. Whereas in England the market for estates may well have gradually narrowed as oligarchic tendencies grew stronger among the eighteenth-century aristocracy, in Scotland this was not so. Bankruptcies such as that of the Ayr Bank or of the York Buildings Company, which bought huge tracts of confiscated Scottish Jacobite estates after the '15 and finally lurched into admitted bankruptcy in the early 1770s, simply made available to rising mercantile interests, like the tobacco lords of Glasgow, many attractive estates. The tobacco lords, by and large, were able to restrict their purchases of land to counties adjacent to Glasgow. Around Perth it was a different story. The stability of the local aristocracy was such that merchants anxious to purchase estates had to go far afield. It was unusual in the county of Angus or Forfarshire for a merchant to become a substantial landowner outwith the immediate neighbourhood of Dundee. Nevertheless, it was possible, however difficult, for rising men of business to buy estates in Scotland, and that fact could but cement their loyalty to the political and social order.

Though judges waxed eloquent against 'the licentious practice of mobbing', it was not, in the form of a traditional grain riot, a threat to the established social order. Rather was it an attempt to assert a traditional moral economy which did not allow men to exploit market mechanisms to the full in pursuit of profit when such behaviour was hazarding their neighbours' lives. It did not set rich against poor, so much as town against country, and Westminster had the wit to liberalise the protective Corn Laws so as to ease tensions by facilitating the import of foreign corn in times of internal dearth or high prices. Confidence among the possessing classes in Scotland was profound and reflected in their very high propensity to invest with a view to future profit. That was one reason why they enthusiastically supported new banks with a liberal lending policy which, in a country chronically short of specie, inevitably meant a credit structure based on various forms of paper. Scotland's endemic balance of payments problem, when outside funds were withdrawn, could create crises as in 1762–3. The older banks had then insisted on a deflationary policy, but many in Scotland in the 1760s and '70s seem to have been ready to gamble on growth despite unmistakeable evidence that they lived in an economy given to spasms of expansion and deflation.

This aggressive optimism was not confined to the neighbourhoods of Glasgow or Edinburgh. It was diffused over the face of the kingdom. Work on the Forth and Clyde Canal linking the two most important Scottish regions began in 1768, but by 1773 the great engineer James Watt was surveying for the line of the Caledonian Canal which was to run through the very heart of the Highlands to join Inverness with Fort William by continuous water communication. In 1770 Watt spent several weeks in Strathmore, the great Lowland valley between the Sidlaw Hills north of Dundee and the Highland boundary fault, surveying for a canal linking Perth with Forfar. The idea was sponsored by a leading Coupar Angus linen merchant, George Young, and by the sixth Earl of Findlater, a nobleman notable for his zeal for improvement. The plan proved abortive, yet its very existence is a measure of the vigorous ambition of Perth which had opened its new bridge across the Tay in 1771, and which was expanding in area and in its manufacturing sector, especially linen. Nor was Perth alone among provincial burghs in its zest for improvement. Between 1758 and 1764 Aberdeen nourished in the venerable cradle of Old Aberdeen, a still distinct but unmistakeably suburban community clustered around St Machar's Cathedral north of the main city, the Gordon's Mill Farming Club. There progressive landed gentlemen such as Sir Archibald Grant of Monymusk, or Mr Silver, a successful Jamaica tea-planter who had purchased estates when he returned home, discussed recent advances in agriculture along with professional people including members of staff from the two Aberdeen universities, Marischal College and King's College in Old Aberdeen. There was also an active Aberdeen Literary and Philosophical Society in which Dr Thomas Reid, the father of the Scots 'Common Sense' school of philosophy, was prominent before his translation to Glasgow. Another member of this society, Dr David Skene, a local physician, was a natural scientist of international repute, an esteemed correspondent of the great Swedish botanist Linnaeus, and a man whose interest in applied geology led him to visit coalmines both in Fife and in northern England.

Recovery from the severe but temporary cyclical depression of 1772–3 was inevitable in a buoyant society confident of its potential for growth and well integrated into the prevailing social and political systems. However, the British world was an Atlantic phenomenon and in the mainland colonies in British

North America a grave crisis had been building up, certainly since the end of the Great War for the Empire in 1763. In 1776 that crisis came to a head in a bitter civil war, primarily within the Atlantic-divided English culture, but involving many other groups and leading to the break-up of the Hanoverian Atlantic monarchy. Scotland's elites had invested heavily since 1746 in an overarching British identity designed to match the Atlantic and indeed the global potential of the Hanoverian monarchy. During his brief political ascendancy, Lord Bute's enlightened patronage of Scots politicians such as Gilbert Elliot or James Oswald, the artist Allan Ramsay the Younger, architects like Robert Adam and writers like Hugh Blair and William Robertson, had shown Scots the full potential of access to such a wealth of opportunities. American Englishmen, who composed the majority of the white settler communities there and whose political culture was totally dominant, never really became British. Their priorities followed their own perceived interests and those interests lay elsewhere than in further integration into a monarchy whose grip over them was already minimal. In short, no sooner had Scots successfully adjusted to one particular British entity than it started disintegrating before their eyes.

4

Scotland and the American Revolution 1775–1784

The second half of the eighteenth century saw a crisis of cohesion in the British Atlantic community. Spaniards and Frenchmen had been expecting it for years and even the Italian who had become the first-ever professor of economics had forecast it in the 1760s. The British Empire was the first of the great European Atlantic empires to crumble from within, but it had always been the most ramshackle of them, having neither the religious uniformity nor the institutional framework of the Spanish imperial system. Nor did it possess any capacity to generate alternatives once the attempt of the Stewart monarchy to move the institutional structure of its dominions in the direction of the Spanish imperial model had collapsed in the Glorious Revolution of 1688. In England itself, Tory exaltation of authority survived 1688. It became a potent element in that very complicated structure of views, prejudices. and practices which was the working creed of the eighteenth-century British ruling class and which can only at the cost of some misunderstanding be described by the adjective 'Whig', to which some residual radicalism adhered. Real concern for liberty, however defined, was always to be found in eighteenth-century Britain, but concern for order and for the security of property were equally strong.

In 1763, after the overwhelming victory over France and Spain in the Seven Years War, Scots did very well when governorships of the new British territories in North America and the Caribbean were handed out. Scots troops had fought with distinction against the Bourbon powers in America, but they had also been drawn

into the clashes between white settlers and the Cherokee Indians
that had broken out on the Virginia frontier in 1758 and culminated in formal war between South Carolina and the Cherokee in
1759–60. Two Highland regiments were sent to stiffen colonial
military capacity in 1760. They broke the Cherokee offensive, but
by the time a Cherokee chief, Attakullakulla, and a Scot, Colonel
James Grant, sat down to smoke a pipe of peace in 1761 it was
clear that Grant, like other middle-ranking Scots officers such as
Archibald Montgomery, had developed great sympathy for the
Indians. Both men would have been educated in the ancient
Roman and Greek vocabulary of 'savage' and 'civilised' peoples,
but they were not fools and they had rightly concluded that in
terms of murderous greed, obliterative cruelty to opponents and
irresponsible warmongering, the savages in America were the
white colonists and not their predestined Indian victims. An imperial imperative to protect native peoples from these offensively
self-righteous aggressors was widely recognised, not just by Scots
soldiers, but also eventually by the Scots Indian traders out of
Charleston, who were busy fathering a significant element among
the Cherokee and Creek Indian chiefs.

Yet white Americans were bent on the seizure of Indian land,
regarding it as a God-given right. Particularly in the Carolinas,
there was to be mounting resentment among the settlers at the
close relationship between a network of Scots holding key positions in government and trade and the Indian peoples. Governor
James Glen, who governed South Carolina from 1743 to 1756,
is a good example of what irritated expansionist colonists. He
wanted alliances with Indian tribes to strengthen the British
position against the French. A logical consequence of this was
that the strength of allies such as the Chickasaws must be kept
up. With his fellow-Scot the great Indian trader James Adair he
concerted a plan to win over the important Choctaws to the
British alliance, and though it did not succeed, it did split that
Indian nation between two factions, one still inclining to France
and one to Britain. In the 1760s, when John Stuart, son of a
Jacobite-inclined bailie of Inverness, and a former Charleston
Indian trader, became Superintendent of the Southern Indian

Department created after the Seven Years War, anti-Scottish feeling reached alarming heights especially in South Carolina. There it was whipped up by one of the two rival Charleston newspaper proprietors, partly on the grounds that Stuart gave intelligence of Indian affairs exclusively to the other editor, a fellow-Scot. Stuart, like the Irishman Sir William Johnson in the Northern Department, was far from opposed to the spread of settlement, but he wanted it to be modest and in areas contiguous to existing settlement. He died an exiled, forfeited Loyalist in Pensacola, in a designated Loyalist refuge area in 1779. One of his sons, John Joseph, fought with the British army in the southern campaigns of the Revolution, went into exile after it and rose to be a knighted lieutenant-general as well as a Neapolitan count on the strength of defeating a Napoleonic army at Maida in Calabria in 1806.

It was a chronic problem for the sprawling, incoherent British monarchy that peripheral parts of the English-speaking world had a habit of turning Revolution Principles into populist rights, much more readily than the sophisticated and worldly-wise men who presided over the political organs of the core state, the United Kingdom. At the time of the debates over the parliamentary union with England in early eighteenth-century Scotland the most articulate opposition to the incorporating union proposed had come from the Scots Whig Andrew Fletcher of Saltoun. His friend the Irish Protestant Whig William Molyneux had as early as 1698 in his *Case of Ireland being bound by Acts of Parliament in England* protested passionately against the way in which the English Parliament, with no legal let alone moral justification, was taking over the absolute sovereignty claimed by the later Stewart monarchs. Scots acting as George III's praetorian guard in politics and war after 1760 had by definition accepted incorporation and naturally hoped a more cohesive monarchy could deal with the problems of holding a fairer fiscal and political balance between the different peoples of a now multi-cultural imperial kingship, where the periphery was lightly taxed, the core burdened with huge war debt, and native peoples threatened by settlers everywhere.

The American colonies, which stretched from Canada to the
southern Caribbean, were particularly sensitive to the ideological contradictions at the heart of the British imperial system. The
New England colonies in particular had a long history of barely
nominal allegiance to the Crown. Virtually autonomous, usually
disobedient, and ideologically deviant, they had felt the justified
wrath of James VII and II who had revoked their charters and
pulled them into a unified Dominion of New England under a
royal governor. Balanced perhaps by a southern dominion, New
England, like Scotland, was meant by James to be one of the
component parts of his British Atlantic world organised rather
like the Spanish empire into a series of technically equal kingdoms held together by royal authority reinforced by bureaucracy
and naval and military power. In practice, this vision crumbled
in 1688–9. The individual colonies reasserted their identity as the
Dominion of New England sank. Though the Crown's role was
not officially altered, in a sense the first assault on the only principles capable of holding an untidy complex of dominions
together came from the Whig grandees whose aristocratic quasi-
republican politics reduced the first two Georges to sit on the
British thrones not exactly to ciphers, but certainly to political
prisoners of the aristocratic factions alone capable of generating
a working majority in the Westminster Parliament. George III
was, not unreasonably, determined to curb the arrogant pre-
sumption this system had bred in some Whig dynasts, but ironically he could only do this by operating vigorously as the King
in his Westminster Parliament. Technically, that Parliament was
not inherently sovereign without him, for it was merely an aspect
of his sovereignty, but was taken for granted by Westminster
politicians that they were the ultimate imperial authority.

The vague possibility that the overseas plantations might
revolt was alluded to by such late seventeenth- and early
eighteenth-century English political economists as Sir Josiah
Child, Charles Davenant, William Wood and John Trenchard,
but none of these specifically admits a right to rebel on the part
of colonists. The first influential statement of that right can be
found in the teaching of Francis Hutcheson. Holder of a Glasgow

chair from 1730 to his death in 1746, Hutcheson published only a short summary of his teaching materials in his lifetime, and that appeared due to the initiative of the printer Robert Foulis, one of his former students. However, a complete *System of Moral Philosophy* was published from his manuscripts nine years after his death. It contains a lengthy argument to the effect that if:

> oppressive laws are made with respect to the colonies or provinces; and any colony is so increased in numbers and strength that they are sufficient by themselves, for all the good ends of a political union; they are not bound to continue in their subjection, when it is grown so much more burdensome than was expected. Their consent to be subject to a safe and gentle plan of power or laws, imposes no subjection to the dangerous and oppressive ones.

Like other professors in the Scottish universities of his time, Hutcheson regarded moral philosophy as including a discussion of natural law, the nature of civil society and the concepts of contract and rights. However, it must be stressed that his application of radical Whig doctrines to imperial matters was in no way typical of Scottish opinion in his own time, let alone a generation later. Hutcheson was an Ulsterman. He never lost contact with radical Whig Protestant circles in the Dublin where he originally made his name. By the time the American crisis came to a head in the 1770s, it had been clear for decades that neither in theory nor in practice were Scottish politicians likely to endorse demands for a reconstruction of a British central government within which they had worked so hard and successfully at maximising their leverage.

Because of their success in so doing, Scotland had become one of the least troublesome of British provinces. This was not just because of repeated purges of recalcitrant members of her ruling classes after the Jacobite rebellions of 1715, 1719 and 1745. Equally important was the process whereby the Jacobite families were reintegrated into civil society. It was a process that in retrospect rather distresses romantic believers in the sanctity of lost causes and the need to die for them, but which was, sensibly, regarded as in no way dishonourable at the time. Ex-Jacobite local power-wielders had to make it clear that, whatever their theoretical principles towards a lost cause, they would cooperate with the Hanoverian settlement. In exchange, they could resume the pursuit of their central social duty – the defence and enhancement of their own and their family's standing. They could then resume cooperation with the bulk of the Scottish elites in pursuit of those political, military or naval careers which required the systematic cultivation of metropolitan society in the south of England. Representation in the House of Lords gave some Scots peers vital political leverage, provided they were generally reliable from the point of view of the administration of the day. The second Duke of Argyll became Commander-in-Chief of the British Army in 1742 after helping to drive Walpole from power and he was succeeded by another Scots peer and field marshal (the rank was created in 1736), the second Earl of Stair, another staunch ally of the new administration. The Royal Navy was less popular as a career for Scots noblemen. Lord Duffus was prominent in it under Queen Anne, but he proved a Jacobite in 1715 and subsequently fled into the Russian service, with a significant number of sea officers of the same persuasion, thereby making British governments hyper-sensitive to reports of Russian ships off the Scottish coast. By the time the seventh Lord Colville of Culross achieved the rank of a rear admiral in 1762 the Jacobite scare was dying and it was quite dead when another Scots peer, the sixth Earl of Northesk, became Admiral of the White in 1778 at the height of the American war. As we have seen, in politics and diplomacy the Scottish nobility and gentry did very well for themselves in a British context after 1750.

Apart from anything else, the monetary rewards for success in London-centred careers were vastly in excess of anything which could be picked up in Scotland. Ordinary Lords of Session, among the most prestigious of resident Scots, had their annual salaries raised from £500 to £700 in 1759 and again to £1,000 in 1766. At the same times the salary of the Lord President of the court went up from £1,000 to £1,300 and then to £2,000. In London a Lordship of the Treasury such as a Scot like Gilbert Elliot of Minto obtained was worth £2,500 per year. Even a

Lordship of Police, of which there were nine and they all pure sinecures held with other jobs, ranged from £400 to £1,200 per annum. A mere handful of spectacularly successful Edinburgh advocates may have contrived to earn over £1,000 a year at the Scottish bar in the eighteenth century, though most earned far less. Other professional careers were paid pittances by English standards. The Principal of Glasgow University was paid £150 in 1753, a year when the Professor of Divinity at Edinburgh had emoluments of £160 as well as his free house. The 900 or so livings in the Church of Scotland ranged from about £140 annual value down to £30 in 1751, with the great bulk being at the lower end of the scale. A not very bright but astutely obsequious minor politician in Westminster could easily pick up much more than a resident Scot at the top of his profession.

Not much wonder that capable adult members of the landed magnate class in eighteenth-century Scotland were nearly all absentees. They looked after their Scottish interests through resident agents, of whom it has become fashionable to argue that a large proportion were Edinburgh lawyers and to whom it is equally fashionable to ascribe a fair measure of autonomous initiative. Neither view seems wholly tenable. Scotland was and is more than Edinburgh, though the brilliance of certain aspects of life in the Scottish capital between 1750 and 1832 always tempts intellectual historians to think otherwise. Agents of various kinds were required all over Scotland for the purpose of political or property management and they were drawn from several social groups including merchants and lairds as well as practising lawyers. Nor had these agents any very significant capacity for innovative initiative. They were normally, in all but the most routine of dealings, subject to the will of their ultimate masters. Only when those masters were themselves susceptible to an ideology of change could their agents hope to give shape to major policies, and such a time had hardly come by the 1770s. At a political level only Andrew Fletcher, Lord Milton (1692–1766), the Argyll man of business in Scotland, appears to have been able to have a significant, if very limited, ability to influence major policies. The last thing most Scots peers and MPs at Westminster wanted to do was to present political as distinct from patronage requests from their constituents. They were primarily out for their own interests, eager for jobs and advancement. Raising Scottish issues embarrassing to government was no highway to success. Only Edmund Burke, an Irishman and a Whig of the Rockingham group, gave more or less open expression to the view that an MP's first duty was to his Westminster faction and not to, in his case, his Bristol constituents, crowning it with the statement that if his constituency dared reject him, he would think the more of himself. Such public arrogance was ill-judged, but probably reflected many of his discreeter Westminster colleagues' thoughts.

Few parts of the English-speaking world were less likely to offer sympathy to totally irreconcilable Patriot demagogues like Sam Adams of Boston or Patrick Henry of Virginia than Scotland. That is not to say that Scotsmen were not interested in America. The reverse was the case. In the period when the American crisis was at its most acute – from the early 1760s to the Peace of Paris in 1783 – a total of fifty or so newspapers and periodicals circulated in Scotland at one time or another. Their proprietors had to cater for a very strong interest in American news. Indeed, the proprietor of the *Caledonian Mercury*, when about to turn his thrice-weekly paper into a daily, appealed to the appetite for transatlantic information by saying he would 'omit no American information that he can procure and depend upon as authentic'. In most other Scottish periodicals the American section was often the largest one. When *Ruddiman's Weekly Mercury* received information of the disastrous British defeat at Saratoga in 1777, it turned over the entire contents of one issue to American affairs. It was very common for American intelligence to take precedence of major domestic news items. In 1775 the *Caledonian Mercury* delayed printing its report on the General Assembly of the Kirk By Law Established in order to publish accounts of the outbreak of the first serious fighting between British regulars and American rebels. Nor was significant Scottish opinion hawk-like during the train of crises which led to the musket-shots at Concord and Lexington in 1775. The

Glasgow merchants were vocally in favour of conciliation with America during the crisis sparked off by the passing of the Stamp Act by the British legislature in 1765. A petition and deputation from Glasgow helped secure the repeal of that legislation in 1766, and in 1775 Glasgow merchants again cooperated with London interests in pressing for conciliatory measures, to secure trade. The Glaswegians specifically denounced 'the unnecessary and oppressive acts passed last session'.

When, however, it became clear that recurring episodes of appeasement had failed to defuse the underlying problem, and that there was no sign of any constructive suggestions from the other side for sustaining a meaningful Atlantic political community as distinct from a mere sham in which the King had no authority whatever in a large proportion of his dominions, Scottish opinion was overwhelmingly behind the efforts of His Majesty's Government to bring the disloyal to heel. Active sympathy for the rebellious Patriot element in the American colonies there could hardly be in Scotland on any scale, for the Scots were emphatically on the Westminster side of the great ideological fissure which disrupted the British world of the eighteenth century. It was essentially a divide between those who were convinced that the liberties secured by the Glorious Revolution were fundamentally threatened by the growth of executive tyranny and corruption, and those who simply did not share this, often paranoid, obsession. The latter could be divided into two groups: the so-called 'vulgar Whigs', who were happy to parrot slogans used by the regime to justify itself, and the very much more sophisticated thinkers like David Hume, who were totally committed to the political statusquo without accepting much of its crude and contradictory public self-justification. Such categorisation is itself excessively crude. What existed among that section of the British peoples resident in Great Britain when they thought, if they thought, about their system of government was a spectrum of opinion, not a polarisation.

What was lacking on that spectrum was any significant segment of opinion dedicated to clarifying the avowed 'Revolution Principles' on which government rested, and restructuring the machinery of state to ensure that it was capable of holding together different and far-flung identities. Earlier in the century, with an unpopular one-party Whig ascendancy and episodes like the South Sea Bubble when the government, almost certainly including the royal family, could be seen as trying to swindle the general public out of its money, total disillusionment had been not uncommon. With the accession of the palpably well-meaning George III in 1760 and the end of discrimination against what was left of the Tories, general satisfaction with a 'mild and regular government' was much commoner. Yet the King himself was one of the few who ever publicly stressed his sense of glorying in the new supra-national identity of being a 'Briton'. It tended to be Scots like Sir John Sinclair of Ulbster, Caithness laird and member of the Highland Society as well as first President of the Board of Agriculture in 1793, who worried about the need to preserve national or perhaps, if he were to be more politically correct, 'local' identities such as Scottish, Welsh, Irish and English, as a necessary source of vitality to the United Kingdom.

In David Hume the Scots even produced a man who stressed the danger to the existing system of over-enthusiastic support. In the first volume of his *History of England* he deprecated excessive emphasis on the pedigree of English liberties:

> Above all, a civilized nation, like the English, who have happily established the most perfect and most accurate system of liberty, that ever was found compatible with government, ought to be cautious of appealing to the practice of their ancestors, or regarding the maxims of uncultivated ages as certain rules for their present conduct.

Hume was anxious to see his fellow subjects 'cherish their present constitution' rather than be snared into the dangers of adjusting it because it did not live up to the full promise of its supposed historical antecedents. What little chance there was of long-term harmony between still predominantly English elites on opposite sides of the Atlantic involved at the minimum a willingness to support a reconstruction of the make-up and claims of the Westminster Parliament. A few metropolitan English politicians like George Grenville, author of the much-resented Stamp

Act, came to see that American MPs would be an unavoidable first step, but this was the last thing that men like Sam Adams and Patrick Henry wanted. Hume was unusually sophisticated in the sophistry he used to justify his refusal to contemplate serious political reconstruction, but not atypical of the very self-satisfied Scottish elites of his day in his immobilism. His response to the American crisis was unusual but logically consistent with the conservatism of the views he shared with so many others.

His 'sceptical Whiggism' led him to declare before his death in 1776 that he was 'American in my principles', which in terms of daily politics he was certainly not. What he meant was that he would prefer to be rid of an insoluble problem which might also act as a catalyst of political change in Britain. He wished to see the American colonies 'revolted totally and finally'. The colonies, 'no longer in their Infancy', could not be crushed. 'Let us therefore', he wrote, 'lay aside all Anger; shake hands, and part Friends'. The proposal was wildly unrealistic. The colonists, and especially their leaders, were rabid imperialists who demanded the unconditional abandonment by the King of his Indian subjects, as he saw them, allies as they saw themselves. Aggression against Canada was an integral part of the American Patriot programme (clearly to be followed later by aggression against other territories such as Spanish Florida). Negotiating the terms of exit would in any case have verged on the impossible because the 'American Way' in negotiation was already in place in the sense that the self-righteousness of the militant colonists precluded serious negotiation. They wanted to retain all the privileges of membership of the monarchy as they left it. Only at a very general level was Hume's basic gambit, of conserving the existing order at the core by sacrificing exposed positions on the periphery, to be of practical significance.

Most contemporary Scottish intellectuals, when the crunch came, were for repressing rebellion by force. Lord Kames was sympathetic to American problems and corresponded with Benjamin Franklin about some form of federal union with American representatives in the British Parliament, but by 1774 he was denouncing colonial claims that they could not be taxed if not politically represented. Principal Robertson was vaguely benign about American aspirations but clear by 1775 that independence was unacceptable and that dependence was to be maintained if necessary by force. These were mild positions compared with, say, the views of the painter Allan Ramsay. From 1775 Ramsay had favoured the public with his opinions under the pseudonym 'Britannicus'. In 1778 he published *A Plan of Re-Union between Great Britain and her Colonies*, and his last pamphlet on the American question was called *On The Right of Conquest*. Despite a systematic use of various *noms de plume*, Ramsay's authorship was well known and his views at one stage denounced by a London critic as 'Scotch mists'. They were perhaps unrealistic by 1778 but there was nothing soft or wet in their nature. He preached a systematic devastation of property and if necessary life in the revolting colonies in order to bring them back to appropriate subjection to the Crown. Though the drastic nature of Ramsay's proposals shook some contemporaries, his general position was understandable. In his book on the *State of the Arts in England*, whose English version appeared in 1755, the Frenchman Jean Rouquet had remarked on the need for political patronage there for any artist who wished for advancement. It was hardly a penetrating insight: the same was even truer of France. In the United Kingdom Ramsay was Principal Painter to the King.

Both at home and abroad articulate Scots opinion was overwhelmingly behind the British war effort. For example, at the start of the war cities like Edinburgh and Dundee and smaller burghs like Arbroath produced loyal addresses calling for the firmest measures against the rebels. The Scottish press was enthusiastically in favour of recruiting, particularly after the rebels allied with the popish despotism of France in 1778. General conservatism seems to have been an important constituent in this consensus, for the American cause was often identified with that of levelling republicanism, factious opposition to His Majesty's Government in Westminster, or even with individual British radicals from Lord Chatham to John Wilkes. More justifiable was a general revulsion from the savagery with which the American Whig or Patriot rebels habitually dealt with the substantial pro-British Loyalist element in their society. Anxious to uphold British ascendancy, and exclusive trading rights under the Acts of Navigation, Scottish opinion adjusted itself only slowly and reluctantly to the possibility of defeat. Nor was this reluctance solely the reflection of vulgar jingoism. The philosopher Adam Ferguson shared it in full measure.

He had been liberal in his attitude as the American crisis came to a head and had early doubts as to whether the war could be won. These were shared by Secretary at War Lord Barrington, who was in office at the start of the war. His view was that British military activity was unlikely to be effective much outside Canada, Nova Scotia and the Floridas, and that naval blockade was the only recourse for dealing with the middle colonies. Ferguson, however, had no doubts at all about the rightness of the British case, to the point where his public defence of it helped secure for him the secretaryship of the peace commission led by the Earl of Carlisle that was sent to America by the premier Lord North in 1778 to negotiate with the rebels. It offered to give up Westminster's right of taxation, withdraw all objectionable legislation, and recognise the American Congress as well as consider American MPs in Westminster, in exchange for continued regulation of trade, reinstatement and compensation of Loyalists, and withdrawal of the Declaration of Independence. By 1778 there was no way such terms would be accepted. Ferguson returned from this unsuccessful mission a hard-liner, arguing in 1779 that Britain must not lose the will to fight on, for half the population of the colonies was loyal (a gross exaggeration) and vigorous action would isolate a rebel leadership full of 'the most abandoned Villains in the World'.

Another flower of Scottish Enlightenment culture, the soldier Patrick Ferguson, a man of extraordinary physical and mental courage, also regarded the offer made by the Carlisle Commission as clearing his conscience of any remaining qualms about fighting the rebels. Inventor of an early breech-loading rifle, and a leader of Loyalist militia, he died at the battle of King's Mountain in South Carolina in 1780, the only non-American in a force surrounded and slaughtered, in many individual instances after surrender. He, for raw courage, ranks as one of the great heroes of the War of American Independence, and he was sure he died in a good cause. Lieutenant Colonel John Maitland, the Scottish commander who in 1779, in a reverse version of the earlier battle of Bunker's Hill, inflicted a crushing defeat on a massive Franco-American assault on Savannah, Georgia, in 1779, was a great soldier of the King. He died later that year. The Abercromby brothers, mildly radical Whig lairds from Clackmannanshire, demonstrate the complexity of the issues at stake. Sir Ralph, who went on to win the first British victories against Revolutionary France in Egypt in 1801, declined to serve in America, though he did not enter formed opposition to George III. His brother Sir Robert, with exactly the same political princi- ples to the point of later succeeding him in 1798 as MP in the same interest in Clackmannanshire, had no hesitation in accept- ing commands in the American war where he saw another brother, James, killed at the battle of Brooklyn. Robert went on to a distinguished military career (and a large salary) in India, where he ended up Commander-in-Chief. What was lacking in America was any realistic alternative strategy after it became clear that most colonies were beyond control, though not beyond pres- sure from a surprisingly effective naval blockade. The King would have been better off without twelve of his American provinces and there were means of getting them out of the monarchy with a healthy respect for it and checks on their potentially overween- ing power, but the Scots soldiers who fought so loyally for the Crown were serving a pusillanimous government latterly inca- pable of creating a realistic strategy or chain of command in the field. Their sacrifice was in vain.

The Scottish community with the most intimate connections with the American colonies, the city of Glasgow, showed res- olute optimism about the colonial crisis until 1777–8. Most major tobacco merchants in early 1775 believed, as John Herries the Scottish agent for the Farmers General of the French customs reported to his employers, that differences between mother country and colonies would soon be settled and tobacco prices would then return to former levels. In Glasgow uniquely high tobacco stocks were on hand in 1775–6, mainly due to vicissitudes of harvests and prices, and credit eased rather than froze after the outbreak of war, so the giant firms run by the Glassfords, Cunninghames and Speirs weathered the initial shock of war easily. The greatest bankruptcy of the period, that of Buchanan, Hastie and Company, with allied firms like Bogle, Jamieson and Company, and James Jamieson and Company, seems to be explicable in terms of long-standing financial and management problems rather than in terms of comparatively moderate American losses. Of course, there were very substantial losses for many Glaswegians, as defaulting debtors were prominent in the rebel leadership. William Woodford, who commanded the rebel forces which burned Norfolk, Virginia, and with it the property of several Glasgow merchants, was quite open about the fact that he owed Scots merchants more than he was worth or ever intended to pay. He and his kind reinforced pro-government sentiment, in so far as it needed reinforcing, in Glasgow.

What is clear is that the Glaswegians consistently underestimated the gravity of the war. At the start they had no conception of the capacity of the colonists to resist firm action by regular troops. They did not understand the sheer scale of the logistical problems involved in supplying a large army on the other side of the North Atlantic. In 1775 French intervention was hardly recognised as a possibility. Only after defeat at Saratoga and the French declaration of war did Glasgow appreciate the grim nature of its situation. Then indeed credit tightened, the Glasgow Regiment was raised, and merchants began to seek the classic compensation for depressed trade due to war, by investing in privateering. However, it must be said that the Glasgow merchants throughout assumed a degree of resolution, firmness and common sense which on the part of the British government proved sorely wanting. George III by 'abolishing party' had opened the gates to 'an orgy of faction'. Aristocratic factions meant to subvert his authority. The politicised nature of the British high command proved catastrophic in the all-important early stages of the war. Lord Amherst, the best-known British general, refused to serve, as did Lord Cavendish. Admiral Keppel, a member of the Rockingham faction, refused to serve until the war became a war with France. Admiral Lord Howe and his brother General Sir William, the supreme commanders at the start of the war, insisted on very generous powers to negotiate a settlement. These powers they abused to the point of insubordination, and until relieved they pulled their military punches when they needed to be driven home. The upshot was a demonstration of the futility of half-measures which failed to conciliate the disaffected, and gave them time to rally, while eroding the morale both of the government forces and of the Loyalist element.

The Scottish aristocracy and gentry did not join in the near or downright treasonable politics of the wilder elements among the English Whig elites. On the contrary, the war provided them with a splendid opportunity to show their talents as military entrepreneurs, for the government had great difficulty securing troops. Only in August 1775 was an increase in the establishment from 33,000 to 55,000 men authorised. Attempts at virtual conscription of the 'idle and able-bodied' proved ineffectual save in the rather specialised instance of reprieved criminals who in 1776 made up three whole regiments of the British forces in America. Yet as late as 1781, 34,000 troops were available to British commanders in America. Some were German mercenaries. The Hanoverian state-system was partly German so there was no rational argument against the use of Hessians and other German-speaking professional soldiers by what was, ultimately, a north German dynasty. However, the great bulk of at least nominally voluntary recruiting drew on two other traditional reservoirs of military manpower – Ireland and Scotland.

Proposals for raising troops for the British service in the Highlands had been advanced as early as 1738 by Duncan Forbes of Culloden, the great Whig lawyer and laird. After the '45, suggestions from the Duke of Argyll that regiments be raised among the disaffected clans were considered and rejected. Government policy, as Lord Findlater reminded the Duke of

Newcastle in July 1748, was to root out the military spirit in the Highlands, not to sustain it by extensive recruiting, and Westminster tended to draw no fine distinctions between loyal and disloyal Highlanders. With the outbreak of the Seven Years War in 1756, Newcastle did tentatively suggest the raising of regular regiments in the Highlands, only to see George II veto the scheme. Defeats in that year, allied to a serious manpower crisis in the British army, produced a reassessment of the situation. Late in 1756 the Duke of Cumberland recommended the raising of Highland regiments and the idea was enthusiastically adopted by the Elder Pitt, who persuaded King George and his ministers to swallow it. The avowed objective was to transport potential Jacobites to foreign battlefields where they could be slaughtered fighting the French, rather than leave them to plot subversion at home. The first regiment, the 77th or Montgomery's Highlanders, was commanded by Colonel Archibald Montgomery, a son of the Earl of Eglinton, but it was deliberately recruited in areas with a Jacobite past, while the second Highland regiment embodied in 1757 was the 78th or Fraser's Highlanders, raised by its future commander, Simon Fraser, son of the executed Jacobite Lord Lovat. Young Simon was busy working his passage back into Hanoverian favour.

The success of this particular experiment in the 1750s naturally led to offers to raise units from Highland landowners in the 1770s. Though there was a significant outlay involved in raising a corps of any size, there were government grants which covered most of the costs, such as clothing and bounty money to encourage recruits, while any loss made by an aspiring colonel was obviously more than compensated for by political and patronage gains. Such gestures of loyal enthusiasm were nicely calculated to assist a gentleman's career in arms or politics or both. At the same time, the commissions in his regiment gave the colonel a formidable instrument of patronage among the local gentry. Six new Highland regiments were raised for the war in America in 1777–8. They fought alongside older Highland regiments with their usual courage and dash. They certainly did not find their duties contrary to the spirit of the bulk of their fellow-countrymen in the colonies. On the contrary, Scottish emigrants tended to be staunchly loyal to the British cause. Even former Jacobites exiled for their convictions were far more likely to turn up under the banner of King George than in the rebel ranks. The Highlanders of North Carolina formed a small Loyalist army in which Flora Macdonald's husband held a brigadier's commission before the battle of Moor's Creek in 1776, when they were caught and shattered by a superior force of rebel Whigs. In the southern colonies Scottish emigrants were divided in their response to the heightening of military activity which followed the large-scale British invasion of the region in 1780 under Lord Cornwallis. Scots could be found both in the ranks of Loyalist units and (especially in the case of those who had emigrated soon after the '45) in those of the Whig or Patriot forces. They displayed nothing like the radical solidarity of the Scotch-Irish, those embattled settlers from Presbyterian Ulster, who when the die was cast formed perhaps the toughest ethnic phalanx in the rebel line of battle.

Even Anglican Ireland distrusted the British government, which it saw, not without reason, as only too ready to neglect, subordinate and betray the Protestant interest in Ireland. By the end of the American war Irish politicians were using the lever provided by the rise of the Irish Volunteers, initially a home defence force for a country stripped of troops and vulnerable to American privateers and French attack, to prize Westminster's fingers away from key levers of power within the Irish political system. Despite their own overwhelming Protestantism, the response of the Scots to the American crisis most closely resembled that of the Roman Catholic Irish. Both communities had a long history of armed resistance to English power. Both by 1776 were anxious to win the favour of Westminster by a display of enthusiastic loyalty to the British cause. To the Catholic Irish the objective was help in breaking the discriminatory system operated against them by their fellow Irishmen. The Scottish objective, to be attained by a similar cultivation of English goodwill, was political and material advancement. Not much wonder that 'a free exportation to Scotchmen and Tories' became a common

toast in Patriot circles in America. It is even less surprising that
the minutes of the New York Saint Andrew's Society, established
in 1756 to provide relief for Scotsmen in distress in New York
State and modelled on a similar society already in existence in
Philadelphia, are discreetly missing for the years 1775 to 1784.
No doubt if extant they would reveal just how Loyalist was the
tone of an organisation whose seat was New York City, itself
occupied by British forces for most of the war.

Exceptions in the shape of prominent home-domiciled
Scotsmen consistently sympathetic to the American cause tend
merely to prove the rule that most Scots of consequence were not
so disposed. There was an obscure group of impoverished Scots
Whig peers who opposed the war. The one outstanding Scots
parliamentarian who systematically opposed the government's
American policy was George Dempster, MP for the Perth Burghs
between 1761 and 1790. Apart from Dempster, who by 1778
was convinced that American independence should be granted,
Scots MPs and peers merited the taunt hurled at them by, among
others, the relentless Wilkes that no body in Parliament was
a more reliable supporter of the royal government and its
American policy. Significantly, Dempster, an outstandingly independent man, was a vocal critic of the arbitrary and unrepresentative nature of the contemporary Scots parliamentary franchise
and a champion of demands for its radical reform. In this, too,
he was atypical of the leading Scotsmen of his day. The great
English county of Yorkshire showed more critical and independent spirits active in politics in the latter part of the American
crisis than Scotland. The Reverend Christopher Wyvill was the
moving spirit in the Yorkshire Association which was widely
supported by men of substance and which agitated for a reduction in government influence in Parliament, an increase in the
number of independent county members, and triennial elections.
Admittedly only half a dozen other English counties had associations pledged to the full Yorkshire programme, but in Scotland
a man like Professor Adam Ferguson could regard the activities
of the Yorkshire reformers with real alarm.

In 1780 Christopher Wyvill addressed a circular appeal to the

Scots. Ferguson hoped for early military successes to silence such subversion on the home front. Ferguson did accept that the Anglican rulers of Ireland would have to be appeased in the short run, though he hoped to draw their fangs, in the long run, by an incorporating union. Here he was by no means typical even of conservative Scots contemporaries. James, second Lord Fife, held an Irish peerage though a devoted Banffshire laird, because Irish peerages were easier to obtain than the British one he eventually secured and were compatible with his membership of the House of Commons at Westminster. He visited Ireland in 1782 after Henry Grattan had led its Parliament to legislative independence, and enthused about Ireland's 'great situation'. He even thought about investing in Irish land. As long as there was a common and not notional sovereign and social stability, freedom from any dependence on Westminster for Ireland worried him not at all. Of course, in enjoying the accessible and gay world of the Irish upper classes with their unique version of rococo style, he singularly failed to grasp the depth and intransigence of Ireland's clash of religious cultures.

Even in Scotland it was only religion that could create emotions strong enough to mobilise a vocal opposition to government policy during the American crisis. That party in the Church of Scotland known as the Evangelicals showed signs of sympathy with the American rebels, partly no doubt by way of reaction to the pro-government line of their Moderate rivals, but partly because of genuine sympathy with a cause itself deeply influenced by radical American Presbyterianism. The best-known example of this sympathy was the Reverend John Erskine who published a pamphlet entitled *Shall I go to war with my American Brethren* in 1769 and again in 1776. Both in the General Assembly of the Kirk and at the level of local synods, there was considerable tension over the American issue during the war years. The government's system of management proved adequate to head off the Evangelicals' challenge, but that challenge was itself part of a rising current of opposition to a stranglehold from which the Kirk had benefited only to a limited degree. Islay had early on built up a structure of control in the General Assembly, based on the extensive ecclesiastical patronage of the Crown, and employing after 1736 the Reverend Patrick Cumming of the Old Kirk of Edinburgh as his principal manager. Islay set a firm example of using Crown patronage with no respect for or consultation with parishioners. Other lay patrons, previously often conciliatory towards the views of congregations, tended to follow suit. Cumming and others of his kidney argued that by being conciliatory to Islay, a man of little religion and less respect for the cloth, they could secure practical concessions. In fact an attempt by the General Assembly in 1749–51 to secure augmentation of ministerial stipends, many of which had become with time miserably inadequate, elicited no support whatever from the civil power, and provoked a quite remarkable display of belligerent meanmindedness from the landed gentry of virtually every Scottish county.

By 1761 Cumming's leadership of the church was at an end and his successor in that capacity, Principal William Robertson of Edinburgh University, was a more independent figure though a militant champion of patronage. He and his supporters believed that by cooperating with the state on equal terms and by interpenetrating the influential levels of contemporary secular society it was possible for the Church of Scotland to resist 'a slavish corrupting dependance' on the political boss of the moment in Scotland. However, even Robertson's talents, eminence and commitment to conciliatory and reasonable policies could not stop the process whereby Moderatism was placed on the defensive after 1776. His own resignation from leadership in the Assembly in 1780 was not unconnected with the American crisis, though the linkage was such that he could regard the gesture as an expression of his belief in religious toleration. Government attempts to cope with its need for troops by encouraging recruiting among British Roman Catholics had led logically to a mild proposal to relieve Roman Catholics of a few of their many legal disabilities. Dissenters and Evangelicals of the established churches at once reacted with a fit of suspicious no-popery agitation expressed in Protestant Associations which found a charismatic leader in a young Scots MP, Lord George Gordon, a brother of the Duke of Gordon and the bore, despair and scourge of the House of Commons.

Lord North had already tried to buy him out of politics with
the lucrative Vice-Admiralty of Scotland, so when he became a
key figure in a frightening mass agitation North's offers went up.
Lord George was mentally unstable, but he was impervious to
bribery as well as a sympathiser with 'the worthy patriots of our
injured colonies'. The culmination of his career came in a
week in early July 1780 when, after the House of Commons
had refused to take seriously the petition of the Protestant
Association, London was dominated by a reckless, drunken and
radical mob acknowledging the somewhat nominal leadership of
'the mad Scotchman', Lord George. Eventually the rioters were
crushed and dispersed by regular troops, militia and middle-class
volunteer units, directed to act by an unlikely combination of
George III and John Wilkes. The latter, always a calculating
egotist, was not prepared by 1780 to see popular agitation divide
the ruling class, of which he was a member, and threaten the
social order.

Lord George, a deeply religious man who later converted to
Judaism, had become a symbol of the half-articulate resentments
of the lower orders. The London riots were paralleled by less
extensive disturbances in Glasgow and Edinburgh. The thinly
veiled secularism of the ruling cliques at Westminster was bound
to be a source of weakness to governments chosen on an arbitrary and unrepresentative basis which was justified at least to
some extent by official propaganda on the grounds that the
regime operated a 'Protestant Constitution'. However, with Lord
George in hiding and later firmly in Newgate jail, it was possible
to defuse the crisis simply by withdrawing the relief bill.
Principal Robertson, like his hero the Emperor Charles V, chose
to retire from the public stage before his time, ostensibly to
devote more effort to historical studies. Privately, he deplored the
revival of religious bigotry. At a deeper level he, who had like
many self-conscious liberals lost interest in conciliating those
who differed from him, may have sensed the tide was turning
against his own Moderate ascendancy.

The London government expected Scottish Presbyterians to
be more responsive to radical American principles than most

Britons, but its fears were misplaced. The ruling groups in Scotland were behind the war which, throughout Britain, was a popular war until after the defeat of Cornwallis at Yorktown in 1781, when it became increasingly clear that it could not be won. Heavy Scottish losses were incurred from start to finish, and not purely by rebel action. The pattern of Atlantic summer gales in the 1770s and 1780s was exceptionally severe. Cyclones frequently came roaring directly across the 3,000 miles of sea from America to Scotland rather than moving as usual into the latitudes of Iceland and Norway. The convoy which set out from the Clyde late in April 1776 carrying the Highland Brigade to reinforce General Howe in his Manhattan campaign was so battered and scattered by the fury of the elements that it eventually lost seven ships and 800 men, nearly as many as the British had lost at the bloody engagement at Bunker's Hill. Their superiors could not stomach such losses with equanimity. British forces were grossly inadequate and losses virtually irreplaceable.

Perhaps there would have been more of an anti-war outcry if the Scottish economy had seen its steady recovery from the depression of 1772–3 seriously interrupted by the war, but this did not happen before 1780. Capital was abundantly available in 1775 and 1776, at rates as low as 3 per cent. A series of good harvests kept grain prices low and breweries and distilleries busy. The construction industry was eventually affected by diversion of funds into government loans, but not before 1779–80. After 1780 there was a deficit on the visible balance of trade. War with two big naval powers such as France and Spain was bound to affect overseas trade. Re-exports of colonial produce naturally declined, but internal British markets seem actually to have expanded. Scottish ironworks profited from war demand, as did Scottish producers of leatherware such as boots and saddles. Only at the very end of the war can it be shown to have been holding back expansion in the growing Scots linen and cotton manufactures. The disastrous harvest of 1782 was a more alarming crisis than any purely commercial downturn in the wartime Scottish economy. So grave was the situation that the landlords and the government had to combine to avert the threat of famine.

The Royal Navy shipped grain and peas to the worst-affected parts of the Highlands and Islands. Peace in 1783 came timely to the shaken economy of North Britain.

The rising figure in Scottish politics, such as they were, at this time was undoubtedly Henry Dundas of Arniston, a half-brother of Robert, second Lord Arniston, President of the Court of Session. Henry Dundas sat as MP for Midlothian and became Lord Advocate in 1775. At the start of the war he was trying to expand his electoral influence in Scotland, to increase his bargaining power at Westminster. To curry favour in London he made such exaggerated objections to the odd groups of religious Seceders who passed motions in favour of conciliating the American colonies that George III found him egregious and described him in 1778 as a pest. Dundas duly toned down his style and did what Lord North told him to do, albeit grudgingly since North did not heap favours on him. Dundas resented not being made Keeper of the Scottish Signet for life and by 1780 was beginning to realise, with many others, that the American war was lost. Nevertheless, in a snap election called in 1780 to try to strengthen North's ministry, Dundas did his electoral duty. Out of forty-five MPs from Scotland, forty-one reliable supporters of government were returned, and of these Dundas personally controlled twelve. The Scots votes were increasingly important to the government after a despairing North resigned in 1782, and Westminster descended into extreme instability. Rockingham, the leading opposition peer, formed a ministry. Dundas served him as he had North. When Rockingham suddenly died and the much-distrusted Lord Shelburne took over, Lord Advocate Dundas sat tight, reaping rich rewards as Shelburne drifted towards the political rocks. With the life Keepership of the Signet under his belt, Dundas, leading his file of wonderfully reliable Scots MPs towards the voting lobbies, survived and prospered in the midst of political hurricanes. He was full of ideas for coalitions to replace the sinking Shelburne, but the eventual Fox–North coalition he could not live with.

Charles Fox simply could not abide the Scotch 'Sycophant-Fiscal' to George III and replaced him as Lord Advocate in 1783 with Henry Erskine. Dundas had no option except to align himself with the King's 'only resource', William Pitt the Younger, who along with his cousin and political ally Lord Temple was manoeuvring to use support from the monarch and House of Lords to strike down faction bosses trying to rule from a narrow base only in the House of Commons. From 1781 or so, Dundas had made a speciality of the complex problems of the East India Company, the very issue on which Fox and North fell because it was feared that they were trying by proposed regulatory legislation to lay hands on enormous Indian patronage. There was undoubtedly a steady swing of opinion towards the 24-year-old Pitt after George III named him First Lord of the Treasury and Chancellor of the Exchequer in December 1783. The opposition politicians, ever since Rockingham achieved office, had made it clear that they were interested primarily in power, rather than reform. The voice of Edmund Burke, principal apologist for Rockingham and Fox, rose to a shrill 'scream of passion' at the mere suggestion of parliamentary reform. Opinion at large in the political nation deplored the bullying of George III, especially by Charles Fox who was an unattractive alternative to his royal enemy. Pitt actually managed to win over the existing House of Commons, after a desperate early struggle, and in a General Election in 1784 a sustained surge of support in the electorate, aided but not created by Crown and East India Company influence, saw him through to a famous victory.

Dundas was a rock of dependability, producing the usual phalanx of pro-government MPs from Scotland. Even at the height of George III's troubles only seven Scots MPs had voted in 1780 for John Dunning's famous, but quite untrue, motion that 'the influence of the Crown has increased, is increasing, and ought to be diminished'. It was carried by 233 to 215. Twenty-three Scots MPs opposed the motion while fifteen others were absent. By 1784 any competent premier could have counted on general support from Scots MPs, but out of the forty-five Scottish seats Dundas had some sort of closer grip over twenty-two of them. Nor was his political power anywhere near its zenith. Islay was come again, but the new manager was more powerful, for he was to be the second most important British politician after Pitt. That the Scots had not on the whole joined the Foxite attempt to eradicate George III's residual power ensured they were disproportionately favoured by the new Pittite system. It was a phenomenon that did not recur until the late twentieth century when the fact that rising Scots political intellectuals, unlike their English contemporaries, had overwhelmingly stood by the Labour Party in its era of troubles after 1979, secured them disproportionate influence with the New Labour ascendancy after 1997.

By 1784 two empires had emerged from the old Atlantic monarchy of George III. One, an aggressive imperial republic, had to rape a continent before it went global. Its expansionist policies offered opportunities to Scots, among other immigrants, though its virulently anti-British stance, predictably encouraged rather than softened by Shelburne's policy of appeasement, spelled death for older Scots-American networks. Glasgow's tobacco trade and the much-resented Scots factors on the Chesapeake vanished. The mixed-blood or mestizo Indian chiefs among the Creek Indians in particular had often regarded Scottish links as a lifeline against drowning in a sea of settlers. This was carried to the point where Creek chiefs were active members of Clan Chattan, visiting Speyside. The firm of Panton, Leslie and Company, Indian traders from north-east Scotland, was a major element of Creek independence and status. A Spanish government rightly fearful of barefaced aggression from the Americans they had helped win their war of independence licensed, quite uniquely, this firm, whose directors included heretics as well as north east Roman Catholics, to continue to supply goods to Indians in the American territory of the Catholic Kings of Spain after 1783. The great Creek chief Alexander McGillivray was a director, and he fought a long, cunning but hopeless rearguard action against American malevolence. McGillivray was as much a product of the Enlightenment as George Washington. His father Lachlan was an ardent Loyalist who retired to Scotland. Ultimately, the McGillivrays were champions of honourable but lost causes, victims of Westminster betrayal and American power. The other empire that emerged was simply what was left to the British Crown, plus an expanding continental base in India. In that seaborne empire a combination of Henry Dundas and Scotland's growing economic and commercial vitality ensured that Scots were to play an important role in creating the next sort of British entity and identity.

5

The First Phase of the Dundas Ascendancy 1784–1793

The American war had proved to the hilt the loyalty of the Scottish political nation to the political and social system centred on London. A few radicals had protested, predictably, against ministerial policy, but they had awakened gratifyingly little response in the masses of the Scottish people. The upper classes of North Britain had behaved impeccably from the point of view of Westminster. There were one or two exceptions to this last statement, but they were such that they could be dismissed as cranks or eccentrics. James Boswell, who succeeded his father as Laird of Auchinleck in 1782, had always rejected the violently pro-coercion views of his hero and mentor, the English literary lion Dr Johnson. By February 1780 Boswell had reached the opinion that the Americans were in the right to insist on independence. However, he was in other respects conservative to the point of absurdity and his American views could easily be dismissed as a product of that inner frenzy which, despite his amiable social qualities, was driving him into a destructive downward spiral compounded of manic depression, alcoholism and venereal disease.

In much the same way, David Steuart Erskine, eleventh Earl of Buchan, could be dismissed as an unbalanced, whimsical fellow whose support for the American rebels was marred by the same search for notoriety which had been prominent in the support Boswell had offered to the cause of Corsican independence and its embodiment General Pascal Paoli in the late 1760s. The earl saw some of his best ideas, such as a plan for a parochial survey of Scotland, executed by others. Buchan also had the great misfortune in advanced old age to earn the dislike of Sir Walter Scott and of his son-in-law and biographer John Gibson Lockhart. The acid comments of that formidable pair have until recently wrecked Buchan's reputation. Buchan was in fact a man of ability and public spirit whose ideas were often far in advance of his time. Educated at St Andrews, Glasgow and Edinburgh universities, he was the moving spirit behind the foundation of the Society of Antiquaries of Scotland, a body for which he helped obtain a royal charter. His vision for that society was remarkable for, from its foundation in 1780 to his own disillusioned resignation from its ranks in 1790, he tried to make it not only the custodian of an important national museum but also a general clearing house for a revitalised school of Scottish history. Buchan studied source material for Scottish medieval history in Paris and Rome. No great *Monasticon Scotiae* ever emerged, but Buchan did write several works of Scottish history.

His national projects had a higher completion rate than those of Boswell, who failed to make any progress with a Scots dictionary meant to rival Johnson's English one, not to mention a life of James IV of Scotland and a history of the '45. One of Buchan's abortive projects was a life of Andrew Fletcher of Saltoun. Buchan, essentially a radical Whig, admired the principles expounded by that patriot laird. He believed that American politicians like Benjamin Franklin or the future President of the United States Thomas Jefferson represented the living embodiment of that tradition of thought. There is certainly no reason to doubt that the Americans' approach to politics grew out of the same radical Whig principles that Fletcher embraced. Buchan admired George Washington, corresponded with him at length, and toyed with the idea of emigrating to America after the war. He was already too old for this to be practical. Instead he settled down in Dryburgh Abbey where he indulged in his literary enthusiasms. He did much to build up the cult of James Thomson, author of poems such as *The Seasons*, and *The Castle of Indolence*. Activities of this kind, along with the advocacy of such patently absurd and wrong headed causes as female education and emancipation, enabled the sensible men of his time to write him off as an elderly buffoon long before his death in 1829.

A decision to return the Forfeited Annexed Estates to the descendants of the Jacobites from whom they had been confiscated after the '45 was one consequence of the American war. It was put into effect by what was known as 'The Disannexing Act' of 1784 which cited the exemplary loyalty of the ex-Jacobite families in the recent war. The writing had been on the wall for the Commissioners of the Forfeited Estates since about 1774. Henry Dundas had begun to agitate seriously for the return of the estates in 1775 and when he himself was appointed a Commissioner in 1783 it was clear that state control of these properties was about to be abandoned. The heirs were not always pleased to find that they inherited not only the property but also any accumulated debts connected with it. However, the return of the estates was more significant as a piece of political symbolism than as a transfer of property. It set the final seal on the total reconciliation between the Scottish aristocracy and a British government which as late as 1746 had harboured doubts as to whether there was such an animal as a reliable Scotsman. The gentlemen of Scotland, with rare exceptions, had proved on the battlefield in the American war and in the lobbies in Westminster they could be relied upon to support the King's government and forward its business.

The Younger Pitt always talked of himself as a national British leader, but he also ruled as man of business to the possessing classes. Pitt had a reputation as something of a reformer and the wit to see that few things tarnish a political reputation so badly as an over hasty jettisoning in office of genuinely held convictions of the need for moderate reforms. Not without skill, he contrived both to express limited support for a few reforming causes such as the reform of parliamentary representation, and to preside over their progressive decay when it became clear that there was no consensus for passing them. Concessions to reforming agitation which threatened to dismantle the existing social and political hierarchies were never part of the new régime's programme. In Scotland such agitation was hardly prominent.

However, the discrediting of a divided and feuding political elite through its inability to run effectively an American war or even invent a winnable one had helped to provoke a movement for reform in that most indefensible and corrupt part of the Scottish political power structure – burghal government.

The agitation was launched by a rich Edinburgh merchant and burgess, Thomas McGrugar, who in late 1782 and early 1783 published so-called 'Letters of Zeno' in the Edinburgh newspaper the *Caledonian Mercury*. The self-perpetuating cliques which formed the town councils of Scotland were wildly unrepresentative even of the wealthier classes in their communities, so the fact that only the town council had the vote in parliamentary elections was particularly offensive. Nor was 1782–3 a good time for the doctrine of 'virtual representation' whereby Westminster habitually tried to persuade those who were not represented there that in some mystic way they really were. McGrugar was no popular demagogue. He resented the fact that only twenty-five men chose Edinburgh's MP, but he argued only for the granting of the franchise to the propertied middle class, not to the swinish and uneducated dregs or bulk of the urban population. His writings had by 1783 stimulated the creation of a central committee dedicated to Scottish burghal reform. It demanded changes both in the parliamentary franchise and in the notoriously corrupt and inefficient internal government of the burghs. By March 1784 the movement could assemble delegates from half the sixty-six royal burghs in a convention in Edinburgh.

At local level the agitation was carried on mainly by merchants consumed by a social, moral and financial contempt for what they saw as a disreputable and incompetent gaggle of *rentiers* who monopolised municipal government. The Edinburgh committee which tried to coordinate and lead the movement was, like so many Edinburgh committees, dominated by lawyers. Prominent were younger members of the Society of Advocates such as Archibald Fletcher and Henry Erskine, the brother of the Earl of Buchan and a man who shared most of Buchan's radical enthusiasms though not his eccentricity. John Clerk of Eldin was another lawyer active on the committee which in Lord

Gardenstone even boasted a Lord of Session. Despite the respectability of those involved, it rapidly became clear that the legislature would entertain no proposals for parliamentary reform. By 1785 the Scottish burgh reformers had accepted this and abandoned hope for all but internal burgh reform.

Their proposals were for the enfranchisement of all burgesses and an end to self-selected councils. Instead it was proposed that on the same day all over Scotland there should be an annual election of councillors. The voters were also to select seven auditors of accounts to oversee the traditionally crooked ways of the council with burgh revenues and the 'common good' or burgh assets. Test cases in 1784 and 1787 underlined the urgent need for reform, for they confirmed that there was no legal sanction against absentee councillors and no survival of the power wielded by the old pre-union exchequer of Scotland which entitled it to audit burgh accounts. The British state simply washed its hands of the matter and every single Scots MP, including some self-styled reformers, refused to introduce the reform proposals to the House of Commons. Only the advocacy of the London-Irish playwright and Foxite Whig MP Richard Sheridan gave them a hearing there, but Henry Dundas was too busy exploiting old abuses to support new reforms. He opposed and crushed the proposals.

Dundas did not particularly want to change anything. His political power was based on existing social structures. In 1784 his influence was still centred on the Lothians where he was hand in glove with Henry, third Duke of Buccleuch, a nobleman with no taste for high office but with the closest of ties with governing circles in London. Buccleuch's mother, Lady Caroline Campbell Scott, was a daughter of the second Duke of Argyll and widow of the heir to the dukedom of Buccleuch. Her second marriage was to 'that splendid shuttlecock' Charles Townshend who was a notably kind stepfather to the Buccleuch children, but died in 1767 after making a major contribution in office to the coming of the American Revolution. His stepson Henry lived until 1812, managing the ducal estates and Scottish elections in the Dundas interest. Withal he was a man of culture tutored by Adam Smith in France between 1764 and 1766. Smith was subsequently a frequent visitor at Dalkeith Palace, the principal Buccleuch residence, as was Sir Walter Scott. In 1783, when the Royal Society of Edinburgh was established to further the study of physical science and by implication to do down Buchan's Society of Antiquaries with its faint radical tinge, Buccleuch became its first president.

The world of the regional magnates was one which Dundas knew and understood. He was not one of their number, though his membership of the family of the Dundases of Arniston gave him the necessary standing for familiar access to and intercourse with the greatest in the land. Henry Dundas was the son of a Lord President of the Court of Session and Anne, daughter of Sir William Gordon of Invergordon. In 1760, as he grew to manhood, his older half-brother, Robert, became Lord President. The Arniston family was undoubtedly at the very pinnacle of the *noblesse de robe* of Scotland. The fact did not guarantee any solidarity with them on the part of other members of that order. The other branches of the Dundas family were remarkable for their sustained hostility towards what they saw as the upstart house of Arniston. Until his death in September 1781 Sir Lawrence Dundas of an elder branch of the family controlled and represented the city of Edinburgh in a spirit of virulent hostility to Henry Dundas. The latter moved in on Edinburgh over the grave of his kinsman and in the closest possible alliance with the Duke of Buccleuch. Even so, there were plenty of relatives left to oppose the rising Arniston ascendancy. Until he became a peer in 1794, Sir Thomas Dundas, head of the Dundas of Dundas family, repulsed all attempts, fair and foul, by Henry Dundas to unseat him as representative of Stirlingshire. Some small consolation was available to Henry in 1790 when he did unseat another hostile relative, Colonel Thomas Dundas of Fingask, in the remote Orkney constituency.

Hardly surprisingly, Dundas expanded his empire of electoral influence not through collateral branches of his own family, most of whom loathed him, but by tactical alliances with local magnates. His 'conquest' of the north-east, that shoulder of Scotland whose regional capital is Aberdeen, was a classic illustration of his technique, and of its subtlety. The foundation of Dundas's campaign was an alliance with Alexander, fourth Duke of Gordon, the head of a once-mighty family long in decline. His Grace was afflicted with such staggering debts that he could hardly show his face in the metropolis during a London season. All this was hard on a man who had tried to purge any trace of Jacobite connections in his family by recruiting a fencible regiment (the first of four he raised altogether) in 1759 when he was aged only seventeen. The congenial obscurity of Gordon Castle was even less attractive to his eccentric and tempestuous wife, Jane Maxwell. Late in 1783 the Duke of Gordon embraced Henry Dundas as his political guide, philosopher and friend, mentioning only an English peerage as an appropriately modest object of his ambition. Financial embarrassment among Scots peers was, incidentally, always a great help to Dundas. About the same time that the Duke of Gordon moved into the Dundas orbit, Lord Napier, another impoverished North Briton burdened with debts incurred to purchase a company commander's commission in the era of the American war, wrote to Dundas successfully soliciting an increased pension from the state in exchange for stolid support for the official line in such matters as Scots peerage elections.

Yet the Dundas–Gordon axis rapidly proved inadequate in the face of the rival electoral interest of the Earl of Fife, to which was allied men of local substance like Lord Findlater and Sir James Grant. Dundas had no real reason to quarrel with the Earl of Fife, a man interested in improved farming methods but otherwise fanatically conservative and a sincere admirer of William Pitt. By September 1787 Dundas was engaged in ramming a compromise with Lord Fife down the reluctant ducal throat. His Grace eventually swallowed hard. The enlarged alliance by 1790 swept the north-east as far indeed as Inverness, where Dundas successfully negotiated with Sir James Grant and the Frasers of Lovat for the return of a suitably 'reliable' candidate, Norman Macleod. Dundas was ever a man who respected strength. Faced with opposition from an MP whom he thought he could safely isolate and crush, he was ruthless. His normal technique was to seek to deprive that MP of even the most minimal and routine patronage without which it was difficult for the unfortunate man to retain any standing in his own constituency. Faced with a vested territorial interest backed by hard cash, Dundas usually tested its strength and if the opposition failed to crumple under his assault, he tried to come to terms with it. For example, it was a pact with the Earl of Eglinton, finalised about 1789, which gave Dundas control of Ayrshire.

It was a measure of the lack of common sense of the diarist James Boswell that he tried, with of course absolutely no success, to insert himself as a candidate for Ayrshire in defiance of these arrangements. It was typical of the generosity Dundas could show to a fallen opponent who did not threaten his power that in 1791 he gave Boswell's brother David a job in the Navy Office worth £100 a year that Boswell had been seeking for his sibling for years. Fully to secure the Dundas grip on a complex county political scene could be the work of many years. Thus, in the county of Fife Dundas discovered by the educative experience of losing elections that he needed the support of both the Wemyss family and that of the Earl of Fife. The Wemyss interest he had bought by 1788 with British and West Indian appointments. Lord Fife, as has been demonstrated, was the subject of elaborate negotiations covering his interest in the north-east as well as in Fife before he could be safely gathered into the Dundas camp. Those who played along with Dundas seldom violated their basic conservative instincts and all derived benefits from access to central political power. The Duke of Gordon achieved a hereditary seat in the Lords in 1784 when he was made Baron Gordon of Huntly and Earl of Norwich in the United Kingdom peerage. He was able once more to hold court in his London house in St James's Square during 'the Season', or rather his wife did, marrying off three of her five daughters to dukes and one to a marquis (the fifth had to settle for a mere baronet, but he was a millionaire banker).

Viewed from the top downwards, the Dundas ascendancy could look like little more than a laager around William Pitt into

which the ruling class in Scotland progressively moved, partly
out of conviction and partly because cajoled by Dundas, who
happened to be Pitt's personal friend and drinking companion as
well as an important minister and the acknowledged manager of
Scotland. The only change most of these people wanted was
change in the economy in order to make them richer. Yet the
Dundas era was more than just a period of political and social
immobilism. The regime of the Younger Pitt, of which Dundas
was so devoted a servant, was a distinct political system. The
British peoples were and are defined by their political systems,
since their state has no other basis than the monarchy, which
achieved unprecedented public popularity as a symbol in the
latter years of George III, just when it was sliding into irrelevance
as an effective part of government due to the mental illness of the
King. British political systems claim bogus antiquity (often by the
misuse of old names like 'Tory') but are in fact sharply discon-
tinuous. The Pitt system was to stagger on, latterly in damaged
form, until 1832. It was necessarily rooted in change as well as
stability, because it had, minimally, to fashion a more efficient
and acceptable state after the political instability and debacles,
briefly interrupted by Lord North's peacetime premiership,
of the period 1760–83. At the General Election of 1790
dynamism was not the keynote of the political process in
Scotland, for only nine counties and seven burghs were contested. Imprecise though any figure was bound to be, it was reckoned that thirty-four out of forty-five MPs were of the Dundas
interest. Yet Dundas owed this measure of success to some extent
to the fact that he represented the internal and external expansion of the British state.

India is a good example of the way in which Dundas creatively
exploited opportunities he often helped create. Indian patronage
was to be very important indeed in binding together his domestic political empire. Despite the failure of the proposals put
forward by Fox and North, it was clear that the British state
would have to assume a much larger measure of responsibility for
the territorial empire established in the Indian sub-continent by
the Honourable East India Company, so in August 1784 Pitt's

India Bill was passed into law. It established a joint regime of Company and Crown for British India. The Directors of the Company retained control of commerce and patronage but a new Board of Control consisting of six unpaid privy councillors was entitled 'to superintend, direct and control all acts, operations and concerns which in anywise relate to the civil or military government or the revenues of the British territorial possessions in the East Indies'. Dundas was one of the leading members of the Board from 1784 to 1801 and in 1793 the salaried office of President of the Board of Control was created for him. He might just as well have been called Secretary of State for India, since he presided over a full department complete with secretaries and clerks. One of the early biographers of Dundas (C. Matheson) depicted his hero as both a patriotic Scot and a good British imperialist. More recent research supports a nuanced version of this interpretation. The two areas of interest were never separate. Dundas always spoke with a strong Scots accent. He came back to Edinburgh every summer to enjoy his estate and mend political fences. He even managed to roll back some of the military and fiscal controls erected to hold down Scotland in the Jacobite era, so that Scots for the first time could replace Englishmen as Commander-in-Chief North Britain or as Barons of the Exchequer in Scotland. India was undoubtedly something of an intellectual passion to him, though he never went there. He worked regularly at the offices of the Board, read every scrap of information he could obtain on India from a wide range of sources, and dominated his colleagues to the point where membership of the Board in his day was poor training for independent office in India. George Canning, a member between 1799 and 1801, agreed that Dundas was active and diligent but added that he was also 'selfish and Scotch' and that his policy was 'pillage and patronage: pillage by conquest and patronage at home'.

It is important to be clear about the parameters of the possible in 'Dundas's India'. The great age of unbridled profiteering in Bengal by Company servants was over before 1784. It hinged on the right of those servants to participate privately in internal trade and in the so-called 'country trade' from India to South-East Asia.

The Bengal over which the Company exercised effective control after Clive's victory at Plassey in 1757 was described by a Scot (A. Dow) who had served there as one of 'the richest, most populous and best cultivated kingdoms of the world'. It was also until about 1760 a country where desirable goods were relatively cheap as well as abundant. Exemption from taxation, political pressure and brute force enabled Company men to become extremely rich remarkably fast. When the unscrupulous John Johnstone retired back to Scotland in the 1760s he was worth £300,000 and could buy three estates and establish a parliamentary interest. 'Nabobs' like Johnstone were a fact of life in Scotland in the 1780s. One of them, Alexander Brodie, was so powerful in the north-east that Dundas had to come to terms, which included Brodie's unanimous election for the Elgin District of Burghs in 1790. Another nabob, George Paterson, who returned and married a daughter of Lord Grey of Foulis, bought the main seat of the earls of Strathmore at Longforgan outside Dundee in 1777, giving it back its old name of Castle Huntly which it had borne when first built by a Grey from 1452.

There was never in aggregate enough nabob money to make any significant impact on the Scottish economy, and much of it was spent very conservatively. Reforming governors, and a sense of moral outrage in Britain, epitomised by the eventually unsuccessful trial of the great Governor General Warren Hastings in the years 1787–95, eventually put an end to the worst excesses in India. Sir John Macpherson, a Scot who arrived in India in 1767 as a ship's purser and contrived to end up Governor General for a year and a bit (1785–6) when Warren Hastings returned to England, was one of the last of the old-style Company men. His nickname, 'Johnny McShuffle', was a sign of the contempt younger thrusters with political backing held him in. Had they been able to read his most private correspondence in phonetic Gaelic, they would have been shocked to discover how deep was his contempt for them. His policies as Governor General were in fact a model of the restraint and retrenchment the Company needed to avoid bankruptcy. The future lay elsewhere and Dundas did much to shape it, but Dundas always knew, and made sure that demanding friends such as the Duchess of Buccleuch knew, that he had to use his influence in India with moderation, for fear of provoking a backlash.

He still had enormous influence. Appointment to a good position in the 'covenanted' or established and exclusively British branch of the Company service was by nomination of a Director. The Directors were elected by the Court of Proprietors of the Company and could in theory be dismissed, but in practice were life-tenants of positions which were expensive to gain and gave them a vested interest in enjoying favour with Dundas who in any case set about building his own reliable power-base in the Directorate. The rate of commercial profit in Britain in 1700 seems to have normally ranged from 6 to 12 per cent. In 1776 Adam Smith thought 8 to 10 per cent a good profit. In Bengal in 1767 normal profit in internal trade reputedly ranged from 20 to 30 per cent and access to this world for a Scot was usually by nomination. Inevitably many Scots had bought East India stock for the sake of influence in the Court of Proprietors and what Adam Smith grimly described as a share 'if not in the plunder, yet in the appointment of the plunderers'. Dundas represented after 1784 a cleaned-up, to some extent centralised, and almost respectable version of what could be saved from the old rackets.

He did help to export his countrymen in large numbers to India, though he was pilloried by English cartoonists like Gillray for this propensity. Dundas knew full well that there were limits beyond which he must not go for fear of giving some unscrupulous demagogue like Wilkes the chance to whip up a violently anti-Scottish agitation. In 1787 Dundas warned the new Governor of Madras, Sir Archibald Campbell, that:

> It is said with a Scotchman at the head of the Board of Control and a Scotchman at the Government of Madras, all India will soon be in their hands, and that the County of Argyle will be depopulated by the emigration of Campbells to be provided for by you at Madras.

Nevertheless, Dundas undoubtedly in his Indian appointments favoured his fellow Scotsmen and looked after his relatives. In 1821 Sir Walter Scott referred to the Board of Control as 'the corn chest for Scotland'. Part of the explanation for this was simply the enormous expansion of British India in the Dundas era, which created many opportunities for civil and military appointments and for the lucky survivors (the death rate was always high) opportunities for spectacular careers. Colonel Colin Mackenzie, for example, the son of a Stornoway merchant, rose to be first Surveyor-General of India in 1815. He owed his initial appointment to the Madras Engineers in 1782 to the patronage of the Seaforth family, the once-Jacobite Mackenzie chieftains. The Earl of Seaforth actually died at sea on his way to India with a regiment in 1781, while his heir died in India in 1783 of wounds received in battle with Maratha pirates. Colin Mackenzie went on to campaign against Tipu Sultan, ruler of the south Indian state of Mysore, in the army of Arthur Wellesley, the future Duke of Wellington. Surveys of conquered territory in India interspersed with service in the Dutch East Indies against a Dutch regime allied to Revolutionary France were the background to his final elevation in 1815 to a post he held until he died at Calcutta in 1821. Mackenzie was an immensely professional surveyor and a man with a deep scholarly interest in Indian culture, but patronage and successful war lay at the base of his career.

Expansion on the scale that happened in India was hardly envisaged by anybody in 1784. The debacle in America had coincided with a debacle in British India. British territory was organised in three presidencies: Bombay, Madras and Calcutta. Only the last-named had anything like a territorial empire. Madras controlled an area known as the Northern Circars from which, as Dundas was only too aware, it drew depressingly little revenue. An attempt by the Bombay presidency to seize an enlarged territorial base on the Malabar or western coast of India led to humiliating defeat at the hands of Tipu of Mysore and the Treaty of Mangalore of 1784, whereby Bombay surrendered rather than gained territory. The Company debt stood at £8,000,000. Pitt's India Bill specifically renounced war and annexation. Yet expansion came, partly at any rate because Dundas was open to arguments ultimately rooted in the conviction of the Bombay presidency officials (most of whom were also private traders on a large scale) that force must be used to secure control of products necessary for the booming China trade. Here rather than in India was where the Company made its money, by importing ever-increasing amounts of China tea into Britain where a mass market was being created by Pitt's policy of drastically cutting the duty on tea to discourage smuggling. In the absence of any profitable large-scale European export to China, tea was paid for by the despatch of Indian goods to China by private traders. The west coast of India produced pepper and other spices, sandalwood and, above all, the raw cotton on whose export was built the original greatness of Bombay. Two Mysore wars, the first of which ended in 1792 with defeat for Tipu and the loss of half his territory, and the second in 1799 with his complete overthrow and death, were not unconnected with British determination to control the sources of exports to China.

Pressure on Dundas for a more forward policy for the sake of the China trade ultimately derived from an interest in penetrating Far Eastern markets which had waxed strong long before the American war. One leading figure in this school of thought was Alexander Dalrymple, navigator, explorer, publicist and hydrographer. He came from a distinguished Scots family. Among his elder brothers were the judge and writer Lord Hailes; another commanded a regiment in the conquest of French Canada; one was a captain in the Royal Navy and a friend of the Pacific explorer Captain Cook; and yet another was a lord provost of Edinburgh. Alexander, who died in 1808, rose to be hydrographer first to the East India Company and then the Royal Navy. His professional standards gave Britain a world lead in a field in which she had previously lagged. His career was based on cartographic professionalism and latterly had to be passed in London, international metropolis of the British nations. Interestingly, Dundas himself had in 1804 declined to give a naval command to the Irishman Francis Beaufort. Dundas's nephew Lord Melville was as First Lord of the Admiralty in 1829 to appoint Beaufort, Dalrymple's greatest successor and author of the Beaufort scale of wind resistance, Hydrographer to the Navy.

The day of the rascally adventurer was drawing to a close. Some survived well into the Dundas era in India. Murdoch Brown, who left Scotland for Lisbon in 1750, is a good example. He somehow appeared on the Malabar or western coast of India as a consul for Maria Theresa, Empress of Austria, and later changed from Austrian nationality to French. At one stage he was Danish. After the tide of British conquest swept over Malabar he emerged from the wreckage as British Police Commissioner in Mahe. Always he looked after his pocket, whether as Scot, Dane, Austrian, Frenchman or North Briton. His like could not come again. Nor, blessedly, could the career of a predator like Lauchlin Macleane, a Maclean of Coll born in Ulster, who in twenty years between 1757 and 1777 campaigned as an army doctor in Canada, speculated dishonestly in captured West Indian land, intrigued in India, and operated as a totally corrupt and ruthless MP and stock-speculator in London. He was parliamentary agent for the Nawab of Arcot, a prince necessarily devious in dealing with the absolute villains of the Company's council of the Madras presidency. They held his huge debts, but both Macleane and the Nawab knew they dared not foreclose on unsecured pieces of paper.

The second great wave of conquest which occurred in India during the Dundas era owed little to self-seeking sharks like Lauchlin Macleane. It was basically premeditated aggression by the Marquis Wellesley, Governor General 1798–1805, which Wellesley justified largely in terms of anticipating French plots in India, in which he does not seem truly to have believed. Fortunately for him, Dundas was more inclined to take such threats seriously. Scots were prominent in the ultimate formation of a truly continental power through victory in the Mysore and Maratha wars. They served as devoted soldiers like Sir David Baird, or deeply conscientious administrators like Mountstuart Elphinstone, or that grandson of the manse Sir John Malcolm, not as self-seeking opportunists like Murdoch Brown. Scotsmen were in fact very significant in that general overhauling and professionalisation of British government which was perhaps the greatest single achievement of the Pitt–Dundas axis, and the price they and the ruling groups they served had to pay to restore the moral authority of the state after the American catastrophe. It is no accident that Scottish intellectuals and the products of Dissenting academies in England played a disproportionately important role in restructuring the prevailing concepts of the appropriate role of the state in society. The Scots combined a precocious educational establishment with a strong tradition of socially relevant analytical thought. Scottish thinkers like Lord Kames or Adam Smith regarded civilisation as synonymous with a highly organised political society whose workings were susceptible to the processes of reason. Edward Gibbon's *Autobiography* may have given an unfair picture of port and prejudice as the prevailing attributes of eighteenth-century Oxford, but certainly the two ancient English universities simply did not produce articulate thinkers on major issues of public policy to match the much-distrusted Dissenters and North Britons who clustered around Lord Shelburne, George III's first post-war premier, and later around the Younger Pitt, who appropriated without much acknowledgement many aspects of Shelburne's style and policy.

Scottish contributions to discussions on the theory of economic policy predated the Union of 1707. John Law of Lauriston, Controller General of Finances in France in 1720, came from an Edinburgh banking family and published his first tract on political economy, his *Money and Trade Considered*, in 1705 as a contribution to the debate on the revitalisation of the Scottish economy. The tradition of the faintly Jacobite Law can be seen as reaching its peak in the work of the erstwhile active Jacobite Sir James Steuart (1713–80), who expiated his sins of commission during the '45 with a very lengthy exile in France, Germany and Holland. Returning to Scotland in 1763, he showed total loyalty to the Hanoverian dynasty and published early in 1767, with encouragement from friends such as the philosophic Hume, the two imposing octavo volumes of his *An Inquiry into the Principles of Political Oeconomy*. It is a pioneering work by a man with a very real grasp of the mechanism of the market, but who also accepted the need for constant readiness on the part of the state to intervene to protect major interests. Sir James deals exclusively with economic rather than political problems. His interest is directed towards prosperity, not power, but he stressed that:

> In treating every question of political oeconomy, I constantly suppose a statesman at the head of government, systematically conducting every part of it, so as to prevent the vicissitudes of manners and innovations, by their natural and immediate effects or consequences, from hurting any interest within the commonwealth.

Seventeen years of exile on the Continent of Europe had undoubtedly attuned Steuart's mind more to Continental than to British realities. Nevertheless, after his full pardon was underlined by his presentation at court in 1772, he tentatively embarked on the role of adviser to government. On behalf of the East India Company, he investigated the currency problems of Bengal, publishing his results in an essay entitled *Principles of Money Applied to the State of the Coin in Bengal*. In 1776 Adam Smith's *An Inquiry Into The Nature And Causes Of The Wealth Of Nations* struck a mortal blow at Steuart's reputation by quite deliberately making no reference whatsoever to his work, despite its wide distribution and its at times very high quality. Smith's book was, as an intellectual artefact, vastly superior to anything Steuart wrote, for it possessed an elegance and rigour of construction allied to a persuasive lucidity of style which had never been seen before in this field of English letters, and which was seldom to be seen again.

Adam Smith was accorded quite extraordinary status by the leading politicians of his day after 1776. When it was reported in 1787 that 'Dr Smith was much with the ministry', one of the friends of the resentful and superannuated Shelburne (now Marquis of Lansdowne) remarked that he was 'vexed that Pitt should have done so right a thing as to consult Smith'. At a famous dinner party in the house of Henry Dundas at Wimbledon, William Pitt gave Adam Smith the ultimate accolade by bidding him be seated first because 'We are all your scholars'. It was partly a tribute to sheer intellectual brilliance. It was also, of course, a testimonial to the effect that Adam Smith was telling the political leaders at Westminster roughly what they wanted to hear anyway. Smith's message was acceptable as Steuart's had not been.

Because Adam Smith stands at the origins of a line of economic thinkers which can conveniently be described as the English School of Classical Economists (many of the most prominent of whom were Scottish), it was his fate to become a cult-figure for middle-class, liberal industrialists and bankers of the nineteenth and twentieth centuries. They read and misread him in the light of their own circumstances. He knew only his own. Of mechanised industrial production, be it said, he knew virtually nothing. Linen production or nail making were both to him essentially handcraft industries. The great engine of economic growth to Smith is therefore not mechanisation, nor more surprisingly that rapid population growth which so obsessed another eighteenth-century writer, the Reverend Thomas Malthus, but the rational division and organisation of labour. Though *The Wealth Of Nations* is a doric temple hewn out of the granite of self-interest, two qualifications, both of which sharply reduce the distance between it and other contemporary intellectual structures, are essential. First, like all contemporary thinkers in Scotland of any consequence, Smith utterly rejected the idea associated with the writings of Bernard de Mandeville (?1670–1733) that naked self-seeking and the social good were ultimately compatible. Francis Hutcheson had argued strongly that it was natural for men to be concerned about other members of society. Enlightened self-interest was Smith's theme. Secondly, *The Wealth Of Nations* was only part of the grand design for a general survey of man in society which began with the publication of *The Theory of Moral Sentiments* in 1759, and whose uncompleted sections have left traces in the shape of students' notes, such as those made in Glasgow at his lectures in 1763 and finally published in 1896 as *Lectures on Justice, Police, Revenue and Arms.*

Smith was pre-industrial, to some extent pre-commercial, and totally pre-democratic in his assumptions. Not for him the vague

cosmopolitanism sometimes ascribed to him. His central criterion of policy was national advantage and, as one would expect
from a keen North British admirer of the Union of 1707, he
defined the national unit as the area over which the Westminster
legislature could effectively assert its authority. He did not damn
himself in the eyes of those who mattered by an unseemly zeal
for American independence. He rejected the proposals put
forward by the English clergyman Dean Josiah Tucker for voluntary separation by Britain from the 'ungrateful, ungovernable,
and rebellious' Americans. Indeed in 1777 Smith was urging on
Wedderburn, Lord North's Solicitor-General, a type of Anglo-
American union based on the precedent of 1707. Eventually it is
clear that like Hume he had no practical advice to offer and took
refuge in an appropriate cloud of 'philosophical' detachment.
On the other hand, he regarded the loss of the colonies as no economic disaster, and rightly saw that their autonomous status
reinforced his arguments for a vast simplification of existing
trade regulations to give more scope for market forces and
regional specialisation. Britain, because of the advanced nature
of her economy, still had a great future as a market and supplier
of goods to the United States after 1783.

Adam Smith was clear that defence was more important than
opulence. He distrusted merchants, being convinced that they
seldom met even for conviviality without conspiring against the
public. He hated chartered monopoly. Free trade in the Victorian
sense of no discriminatory duties at all, he never thought feasi-
ble. Like many contemporaries he hoped for the abolition or
lowering of unnecessary or unprofitable restraints on trade. The
rambling structure of British protectionism, much of it pure
hand-to-mouth expedients introduced to raise vital cash during
war, presented an easy target, fossilised and inefficient. By chris-
tening his Aunt Sally the 'Mercantile System', Smith may well
have bestowed on it more brains than it ever possessed, but he
remained firm in his view that by creating distortions leading to
misallocation of scarce resources it had lowered economic
achievement below that attainable by 'the obvious and simple
system of natural liberty'. He never regarded his favourite system

as an absolute. There were occasional justifiable exceptions of which he thought the restrictive Navigation Acts were a good example, being essential to the naval supremacy of Britain. His Majesty's Government could clasp the bachelor Scots professor from Kirkcaldy to its bosom with no fear at all that he would turn into an academic asp. He not only did not want the political ascendancy which made him a Commissioner of Customs in Edinburgh in 1778 to fall, but was also convinced that it would not. Removal of distortions would in his view lead to more, not less, emphasis on and investment in what he regarded as the only really permanent form of wealth – improved land. His contacts with French thinkers known as the Physiocrats no doubt reinforced his emphasis on the transience of commercial as distinct from landed wealth. Nevertheless, in practical British terms he was right, in his lifetime. By 1787 he was Lord Rector of Glasgow University, where he had started his career. He died in 1790, when Pitt and Dundas, those rationalising men of business to what was still basically The Landed Interest, were riding a high wave of electoral success.

It was not only in fiscal reform that Scots intellectuals played a prominent role. They were to the fore in most areas where state power was being consolidated, rationalised or rendered more morally defensible. Patrick Colquhoun, for example, a former Glasgow merchant who became a London magistrate, was a leading figure in the debate on law and order in the 1790s. He championed the development of the penitentiary partly as an answer to a crisis in the prisons due to the loss of transportation facilities to America. He strongly urged the creation of a salaried police force for the metropolis, where London docks alone sustained a huge and minutely sub-divided community of thieves. The tone of his writings was so authoritarian that it is easy to understand the dislike of the Tory backbenchers for such eager Scotch busybodies earnestly occupied in the great task of undermining the liberties of free-born Englishmen. It was just as well that the British police tradition with its emphasis on disarmed, decentralised forces was for long deeply influenced by the revulsion raised by some of Colquhoun's proposals.

Even more striking was the role of Scottish intellectuals in the single most dramatic gesture of moral validation undertaken by the pre-1832 British social and political system – the campaign against negro slavery. Despite occasional individual protests down the centuries, it is quite clear that the main cultural currents of Christian civilisation were not inherently incompatible with the concept of chattel slavery until a surprisingly late stage in history. It was therefore of immense significance when the great French thinker Montesquieu, in book XV, chapter V of *L'Esprit des Lois* published in 1748, attacked the principle of slavery. Francis Hutcheson stood at the head of the increasingly articulate Scottish intellectual opposition to slavery in the eighteenth century. To him the structure of morality was based on the twin principles of utility and benevolence, and neither was compatible with the classical arguments for slavery. Adam Smith, his successor as Professor of Moral Philosophy at Glasgow, adopted a broadly similar stance underlining the inexpediency of slavery with the passage in *The Wealth of Nations* in which he said, 'The experience of all ages and nations demonstrates that the work done by slaves, though it appears to cost only their maintenance, is in the end dearest of all'. It would have been better if it had been true.

David Hume, though sympathetic to anti-slavery, hazarded in a famous footnote to his essay 'Of National Character' published in 1754 the conjecture that negroes were naturally inferior in capacity to whites. Henry Home, Lord Kames developed this in his *Sketches in the History of Man* (1774) into the theory that negroes were totally inferior and indeed close to the apes. Another Lord of Session, James Burnett, Lord Monboddo, was totally opposed to such views, buttressing his own pleas for the abolition of slavery with a passionate statement of the unity of all races of man and indeed of all primates. Far more important than the bickerings of these learned gentlemen was the testimony of Scots whose opposition to slavery was rooted in their strong Evangelical Christianity. The Reverend James Ramsay, an Episcopalian born in Fraserburgh in 1733, spent eighteen years as a clergyman in the West Indies before returning to England where he became Vicar of Teston in Kent by the patronage of the great naval administrator Sir Charles Middleton, later Lord Barham. Educated at King's College Aberdeen, where he made a lifelong friend of his teacher the philosopher Thomas Reid, Ramsay leapt to fame late with the publication in 1784 of *An Essay on the Treatment and Conversion of African Slaves in the British Sugar Colonies*. Before he died in 1789, Ramsay had provided leading figures in the emancipation struggle, such as William Wilberforce and Thomas Clarkson, with invaluable material full of his own passionate rejection of both the slave trade and slavery.

There is no doubt that by the last decades of the eighteenth century the Scottish thinker who was most successfully publicising anti-slavery sentiment on an international basis was Dr James Beattie, born in Laurencekirk in Kincardineshire in 1735 and appointed Professor of Moral Philosophy and Logic in Marischal College Aberdeen in 1760. Beattie was one of those literary North Britons who attained eminence by providing the English-speaking world with exactly what it wanted. He was a voluminous, influential and vapid poet, but the foundation of his enormous contemporary reputation was the publication in 1769 of the bombastically entitled *Essay on the Nature and Immutability of Truth, in Opposition to Sophistry and Scepticism*. The book was supposed to demolish the 'infidel fallacies' of Hume and Voltaire and was widely read in France and America, where Beattie was made a member of the American Philosophical Society. Beattie lacked the ability, sophistication and subtlety of Thomas Reid. So far from demolishing Hume, parts of his self-satisfied book simply failed to understand him. Yet Beattie's advocacy of anti-slavery, especially in the lectures which he published so successfully in 1790 as *Elements of Moral Science*, was of great significance. The twin strands of Enlightenment thought and Evangelical fervour gave him unique access to the mind of his age. Not for nothing did Sir Joshua Reynolds depict Beattie smugly banishing demonic influences with a languid wave of his *Essay on Truth*. The revulsion from any proposed changes which followed the outbreak of the

French Revolutionary wars delayed the abolition of the British slave trade until 1807, and the abolition of slavery itself in the British Empire until 1834, but there is a sense in which the vital intellectual battles had all been won by the 1780s and '90s, in large measure thanks to the labours and talents of men like Beattie and Ramsay.

What rendered the integration of the educated classes of Scotland into the British state system so complete in the late eighteenth century was the way in which the intellectual and spiritual influence of a limited number of outstanding Scottish publicists was supplemented by solid career opportunities for many more North Britons. To the bachelor Adam Smith, his access to the great and powerful such as Dundas was clearly useful mainly as a means of securing small favours, often for colleagues or acquaintances or indeed for their wives and families after the decease of their breadwinner. To many Scottish graduates who were never likely to hobnob with Pitt or Dundas, the British realms still offered very great opportunities for personal advancement, and of no group was this more true than the medical graduates. Equally, the existence of such opportunities was bound to affect the structure of Scottish educational provision, and of this the development of the Edinburgh medical school is an outstanding example.

There had long existed in Glasgow a chartered Faculty of Physicians and Surgeons and in Edinburgh a College of Physicians and an Incorporation of Surgeons. Medical qualification was usually achieved by an apprenticeship of some years to a practitioner, though the corporate bodies of physicians and surgeons (to whom apothecaries and barbers remained attached until the late eighteenth or early nineteenth centuries) normally provided some measure of academic instruction. Those Scots who sought formal university courses in medicine had long gone abroad to French or German universities and latterly to those of the United Netherlands. However, the eighteenth century saw the rapid creation of substantial schools of medicine in Scottish universities. No fewer than eleven medical chairs were established in the University of Edinburgh between 1685 and 1807, but the decisive moment was probably the appointment in 1720 of Alexander Monro (1697–1767) as Professor of Anatomy. Alexander Monro had studied medicine in Edinburgh, London, Paris and Leiden. The solid support of Edinburgh Town Council, which ruled over the town's college it had founded, secured him against damaging demarcation disputes with the Faculty of Surgeons. It also helped to provide vital facilities such as a new anatomical lecture theatre and access to the infirmary which was established in 1738. Thereafter the build-up of staff and facilities was supported by manifest success in attracting students. Between 1720 and 1790 roughly 12,800 men passed through the Edinburgh medical school.

Edinburgh could expand its university teaching of medicine much faster than Glasgow, where an effective medical school only began to function from about 1750. Dr William Cullen, who moved from Hamilton to Glasgow in 1744 and began to lecture on medicine outside the university, was the key figure in Glasgow. By 1746 he was lecturing within the university. By 1747 he had persuaded the university to fit up a chemical laboratory where he taught chemistry with the aid of John Carrick, assistant to the Professor of Anatomy. In 1748 Cullen also began to teach *materia medica* and botany and in January 1751 he was appointed Professor of Medicine. One of the problems facing medical education in Glasgow was the continuing conflict between the Faculty of Physicians and Surgeons and the university. It was gradually overcome and with the opening of Glasgow Royal Infirmary in 1794, where classes in clinical medicine and clinical surgery were being held under university auspices by the end of the century, Glasgow built up individual medical classes of 200 students. Few of these graduated. Most were qualifying by apprenticeship. The improving facilities of the university were being used by them to supplement a more traditional training. Crown initiative led to the creation of no fewer than five regius chairs (in natural history, surgery, midwifery, botany and chemistry) between 1807 and 1818, but these underlined another peculiarly Glaswegian problem. Decisions of the Court of Session in 1771–2 had confirmed that the government of the University of Glasgow was a closed corporation consisting of the Faculty or the holders of the thirteen then-established chairs plus the principal of the university. Regius professors were excluded from not only the governance of the institution, but also from examining. Nevertheless, Glasgow's medical school was the second most important in Scotland. The two Aberdeen universities had no systematic teaching of medicine, though each maintained on its staff a mediciner, and each exercised the right to award the degree of MD, after due payment of fees. A conjoint medical school was to have been one result of a proposed union of the universities in 1786, but that union aborted. From 1818 a joint supervisory committee from Marischal College and King's did successfully manage a programme of medical instruction, but between 1826 and 1839 King's awarded only four degrees in medicine, and Marischal twenty-five. St Andrews had from 1722 a Chandos Professor of Medicine and Anatomy whose main function was to vet candidates for MD degrees. He had no other significant function for he had no medical colleagues and the shoals of St Andrews MDs evoked bitter criticism from Edinburgh, though they were all in theory established medical men and included leading Edinburgh medical figures as well as such exotics as Jean Paul Marat, the future French revolutionary.

Careers lay at the base of rapid expansion of medical education in Edinburgh and to a lesser extent Glasgow. Scotsmen were already outstanding figures in the medical world of London around 1750. Three Lanarkshire men in particular stand out. The first to make his name was Dr William Smellie, the leading London obstetrician of his day and author of a celebrated textbook on midwifery which was revised by another Glasgow medical man, the novelist Tobias Smollett (1721–71), who went to London in 1739 and discovered that his vocation lay in the picaresque novel rather than the medical scene. The two other Lanarkshire doctors were William and John Hunter. William had worked with William Cullen in a country practice near Hamilton but his ambition led him to London, where he stayed first with the hospitable Smellie and then established himself as a private teacher of anatomy. His brother John joined him in that most competitive field in which he rose to astonishing eminence. The last twenty-five years of John Hunter's life were spent as surgeon to St George's Hospital. He died in 1793, loaded with honours: Surgeon-General to the Army, Inspector-General of Hospitals and Surgeon-Extraordinary to the King. William Hunter had already perpetuated their joint names in 1781 with the princely bequest of collections and cash to the University of Glasgow which led to the creation of the Hunterian Museum.

Such careers were not without precedent. Dr John Arbuthnot (1667–1735), a graduate of Marischal College in arts and a St Andrews MD, had been physician to Queen Anne and an intimate friend of Pope and Swift two generations before. What the later eighteenth century offered to the medical entrepreneur from Scotland was unprecedented scope. Dr James Graham, born in Edinburgh in 1745, can serve as an (extreme) example for many. After studying medicine in Edinburgh, he made a fortune by practice in England and America. Returning to Edinburgh in 1783, he delivered public discourses on health illustrated by the nubile charms of 'Vestina', his female assistant who posed on a pillar and later became Admiral Nelson's Lady Hamilton. Sadly, Dr Graham did not live to see 'Vestina's' later triumphs. He died in 1794, after being declared mad in 1788. Rogues and charlatans are natural accompaniments of opportunity. In the Peninsular War against Napoleon, Sir James McGrigor, who rose to be Director General of the Medical Department of the British Army, was rightly much appreciated by the Duke of Wellington and laid the modern foundations of his profession, but another Edinburgh doctor under his command, Alexander Lesassier, was mainly interested in self-advancement and copulating with local girls. Lesassier subsequently practised unsuccessfully as an obstetrician based on Picardy Place in Edinburgh. He made love to a disturbingly high percentage of the ladies he attended before finally retreating back to the army, this time in India where he died but not before his long-suffering wife finally abandoned him, returned to Edinburgh acccusing him of blatant 'carnal dealings with a native female', and divorced him. Lesassier had good looks but was hardly a good doctor.

Medicine was unusual in being a profession with a very buoyant demand for its services. There were comparatively few such professions in eighteenth-century Scotland. The Kirk was chronically over-subscribed, partly because access to its divinity schools cost little or nothing, apart from a frugal subsistence during academic terms. Would-be incumbents could, of course, eke out a living as tutors or schoolmasters while they waited for a favourable conjunction of parish and patron. Nevertheless, the 'stickit minister' who never was able to call a pulpit his own was already a problem in the eighteenth century, long before he became a stock figure in the prose of the sentimental 'kailyard' writers of the nineteenth century. Law, as we have seen, involved an expensive training and was dominated by the upper classes who tended to view the Scottish legal system as virtually their own private domain. This did not prevent individuals from among the upper echelons of Scottish society from carving out highly successful legal careers for themselves in England. The best example is William Murray, the fourth son of David, fifth Viscount Stormont. Educated at Westminster School and Christ Church Oxford, Murray made much of his Scottish connections to gain his first briefs at the English bar. Once established, his intellectual capacity and silver tongue carried him upwards. Though a valued ally of the Duke of Newcastle when an MP, he found the pressure of political conflict wearing and escaped gratefully to the position of Lord Chief Justice, being ennobled as Lord Mansfield, in 1756. Notably liberal on Roman Catholic emancipation, Mansfield struck a great blow for negro emancipation by his judgement in Somersett's case in 1771, which freed any slave in Britain. Yet on central political issues like the social order, the American Revolution or the French Revolution, Mansfield was soundly conservative. His greatness lay in his development of English mercantile law.

Scottish universities were themselves a buoyant field of professional enterprise. There was plenty of nepotism in them. Alexander Monro *primus* was succeeded in the Edinburgh Chair of Anatomy by his son Alexander Monro *secundus* (1733–1817), who was duly succeeded by his son Alexander

Monro *tertius* (1773–1859). St Andrews, which was not particularly distinguished in this era, was at least outstanding in the
scale of the nepotism sponsored by its dominant figure, George
Hill, Professor of Greek from 1772 and Principal of St Mary's
College between 1791 and 1819. As the acknowledged leader of
the Moderate party in the General Assembly after the retiral of
Principal Robertson, Hill necessarily worked hand-in-glove with
Henry Dundas, who served as Chancellor of the University from
1788 to 1811. Though such a chancellor was of some assistance
to the institution and its students, particularly when they were
looking for jobs, Dundas did not fail also to advance his own
interests and those of his ally Hill, whose relatives at one stage
held six out of thirteen places on the St Andrews Senate. In all
Scottish universities professors tended to view their chairs as life
freeholds and failure to perform the most minimal of teaching
duties was quite common. Adam Smith's view that the system of
class fees as a major element in professorial incomes in Scotland
was a guarantee of application to teaching duties was obviously
an over-simplification, but one which contained a large element
of truth.

Class fees were never very high. Most divinity courses were
free. Even as late as 1826 three to four guineas was about as
much as anyone expected to pay for a university class in
Scotland. Just how much it cost a student to survive the six-
month academic term from autumn to early summer is not easy
to say, for it varied from institution to institution and from
person to person, but £14 to £20 was a range which would
include most careful if not penurious students. Professors whose
subjects were compulsory, such as moral philosophy in the Arts
Faculty, and professors whose subjects were popular, could and
did make a lot of money from their large classes. Dugald Stewart,
Professor of Moral Philosophy in the University of Edinburgh
from 1785 to 1811, was fortunate both in the status of his
subject and in his talents as 'one of the greatest didactic orators'.
A pupil of Thomas Reid, he actually succeeded his own father
as Professor of Mathematics in Edinburgh a decade before he
moved to the vastly more appropriate philosophical chair.

Though no original thinker, hc popularised the philosophical tradition of Reid, both by lectures and by writings such as the *Elements of the Philosophy of the Human Mind*, whose first volume appeared in 1792, to become at once a standard text in the colleges of the United States, as well as influential in Britain. In lectures on political economy Stewart popularised the main conclusions of Adam Smith. When the French war drove young English aristocrats such as the future Lords Lansdowne, Palmerston and John Russell off the Grand Tour and into his lecture theatre, Stewart improved the shining hour by boarding them at £400 a boarder per session. Stewart was an academic entrepreneur behind a lectern.

To some extent this was what would now be called extramural lecturing: instructive entertainment which made major academic developments available to non-specialist audiences in very simplified form. Indeed Thomas Charles Hope, Professor of Chemistry in Edinburgh for over forty years from 1799, abandoned pure research to polish the demonstration techniques which kept numbers in his spectacular and popular regular class as high as 500. Extra-mural lectures to a wide variety of audiences ranging from the Faculty of Advocates to fashionable ladies yielded him annual fees for a single class as high as £700. Edinburgh University regularly tried to poach outstanding staff from other Scottish universities. Prominent Glasgow professors such as William Cullen and his successor Joseph Black, for example, moved across to Edinburgh chairs and one of the incentives was undoubtedly the attraction of fees from large classes.

In a more profound sense the Scottish university system in this era happened to be in a phase of rapid expansion at the very end of a long phase of contraction in the universities of most of western Europe. The late sixteenth and early seventeenth centuries had seen a huge expansion in matriculations at Oxford and Cambridge. Imperial Spain, at the height of its Golden Age, had no fewer than forty universities within its world empire. By the end of the seventeenth century this 'education revolution' had run its course. Everywhere in the western world student numbers tended to decline for about a century or more. England shared this experience, but not Scotland where a unique if fading cultural heritage, and the profit motive, moved a minority of professors to generate a dynamism which was further fuelled by the relatively favourable opportunities offered by an expanding British political and economic system to educated men. The frustrated and therefore alienated intellectual was unimportant in eighteenth-century Scotland. This was a most significant fact, for student numbers increased steadily in every university except St Andrews where there were some 150 students in 1730 and not many more in 1824. Edinburgh, however, had 400 students around 1700, about 1,300 in 1800 and 2,300 in 1824. Glasgow rose from 400 in 1702 to 1,240 by 1824. The two Aberdeen universities had a combined total of 257 students in 1776 and about 730 by 1824.

On the other hand, cultural shock and identity crises were prominent features of the late eighteenth-century Scottish literary landscape. This was hardly surprising when the leading Scottish intellectuals were so obviously bent on joining the headlong movement towards a profitable integration into the British world ruled from Westminster. The slow rhythms of agricultural life in a still predominantly pre-industrial society and the ingrained, if waning, cultural heritage of an older, independent Scotland inevitably resisted the Gadarene rush towards anglicisation spearheaded by the nobility and well supported by the professors. The central figure in the early revival of Scots vernacular poetry was the elder Allan Ramsay, who came to Edinburgh from Leadhills in Lanarkshire around 1700 and who died in 1758. His life and work underline the paradoxes and tensions of his mental world. Co-founder of the Easy-Club in 1712, he aped the manner of the Augustan wits of the court of Queen Anne, adopting the soubriquet of 'Isaac Bickerstaff', which he exchanged for the very Scottish 'Gavin Douglas' in 1713. Always capable of Augustan English verse of little merit, which he could even use for strongly patriotic Scottish themes, Ramsay is important for his use of the contemporary vernacular and for his editing of selections of Scottish songs and ballads, and of the great poetry of late-medieval Scotland. His collection of Scots songs for *The Tea-Table Miscellany* was part of a patriotic cult which culminated in the remarkable achievement of Robert Burns in this field. His cavalier editorship of poets like Dunbar and Henryson in *The Ever Green* was as significant for the survival of a distinct Scots literary tradition as it is infuriating to modern scholars. At his best, he could use the vernacular in poems about Edinburgh characters in a way which fixed people like Maggy Johnston, John Cowper and Lucky Wood like flies in amber. At his worst, he displayed an uncertain, arch and even patronising attitude towards the Scots tongue which underlined its ambiguous and confused literary status.

Incomparably greater as a poet of the vernacular revival, despite his short life, was Robert Fergusson (1750–74). Born in Edinburgh and possessed of a brilliant mind, Fergusson was educated at the High School of Edinburgh, Dundee and at the University of St Andrews, which he left with no degree because his father died and an attempt to secure financial support from a landed branch of his family proved abortive. A life of quill-pushing drudgery as a commissary clerk was diversified by the social revels of the Cape Club, a typical Edinburgh drinking club with intellectual as well as alcoholic interests. Fergusson always had a streak of unreconstructed Scottish nationalism in him, as his lines indicate:

> Black be the day that e're to England's ground
> Scotland was eikit by the Union's bond

This did not prevent him from writing indifferent verse in Augustan English, but his use of Scots to reflect the teeming urban life of the Edinburgh he knew so well was far more assured as well as more skilful than the similar exercises of Ramsay. It is appropriate that Fergusson's masterpiece is generally considered to be his substantial poem on Edinburgh entitled 'Auld Reekie'. Fergusson published a single volume of verse in 1773, from which he seems financially to have reaped about twice what Robert Burns made out of his own Kilmarnock edition. Yet in a deeper sense the publication failed, for it attracted no flattering reviews, no upper-class patronage. By 18 October 1774

Fergusson was dead of a complex mixture of alcoholism, depressive mania and physical trauma, yet it is important to remember Burns's comment on this tragedy. Burns always revered the memory of Fergusson; indeed it was he who placed the headstone on Fergusson's grave, and Burns was clear that it was lack of patronage which drove a great poet to an early grave:

> My curse upon your Whunstane hearts
> Ye Enbrugh gentry!
> The tythe o' what ye waste at Cartes
> Wad stow'd his pantry!

The great figure of Burns himself never lacked patronage of a sort after the publication of his first collection of verse, but his career illustrates fully the multiple crises of identity which haunted the Scottish literary scene of his day. He was the son of an Ayrshire tenant farmer who hailed, like Fergusson's father, from the north-east of Scotland. Despite inadequate fare, frugality and cripplingly hard work which probably permanently undermined the constitution of the young Robert Burns, the family never managed to make an economic success of its tenancies. The rents demanded by some Ayrshire landlords in the two decades after the birth of Burns in 1759 clearly outran prospects of practical improvement, especially on poor soil. Robert Burns even entered into partnership with a rascally flax-dresser in the Ayrshire port of Irvine, in the hopes that the growing and preparing of flax might offer a chance of prosperity, but the episode ended in farce and frustration. However, it must be said that Burns was well schooled and quite prodigiously well read. He could write correct standard English, and apparently speak it with less of a Scottish accent than the philosopher Hume. After toying with the idea of emigration to Jamaica, Burns launched upon the world in 1786 the famous Kilmarnock edition of *Poems, Chiefly in the Scottish Dialect, by Robert Burns*. The Reverend George Lawrie, minister of Loudon, sent a copy to Edinburgh, and Burns was famous overnight.

He was lionised and patronised by the self-appointed arbiters of literary merit in Edinburgh, of whom perhaps the most dominant in 1786 when Burns came to the city in person was Henry Mackenzie (1745–1831), the master of the sentimental novel. Mackenzie made his name in 1771 by the publication (originally anonymously) of *The Man of Feeling*, which went through nine editions by 1800 and thirty more by 1824. So successful was it that an unhappy English clergyman, Mr Eccles of Bath, tried to exploit the work's original anonymity by claiming to have written it. Burns read two copies of the book, claiming to revere it next to the Bible. To modern taste it is a depressingly humourless collection of stock situations designed to elicit pathos and pity. Yet Mackenzie was a central figure in Edinburgh intellectual life to the end of his days, which came the year before the demise of his close friend Walter Scott. In a periodical called *The Lounger* in December 1786 Mackenzie wrote the first important criticism of Burns, praising his 'unimitable delicacy' and 'rapt and inspired melancholy'. Though the literati including Hugh Blair, the Reverend Professor of Rhetoric, and Dugald Stewart, the philosopher, responded enthusiastically to the very misleading image of Burns as 'the unlettered ploughman' (which he was not, despite his own and Mackenzie's publicity on this theme), they were hostile to the Scots tongue and would have turned Burns into a sentimental spouter of neo-classical English. James Beattie produced in 1787, when Burns was in Edinburgh, a list of Scotticisms to be avoided.

It is the measure of the genius of Burns that though he did write undistinguished English verse, he continued to use Scots in a sophisticated range of density which made him the first and last man in the eighteenth and nineteenth centuries to apparently surmount the two great linguistic crises facing Lowlanders. One was the disintegration of standard court Scots into a series of regional dialects after 1603. The other was the divorce between the language of the head, English, and that of the heart, Scots. His vast range of styles is all the more impressive in a man whose last years of creative activity were largely given up to a tremendous work on Scottish songs. Through much of his work runs a strain of iconoclastic radicalism. His own ambiguous and fragile role in the company of his betters gave an edge to his social satire no less keen than that on his biting Juvenal-like attacks against the more hypocritical and illiberal side of the Kirk. For politicians there is nearly always a note of contempt. Burns was an open admirer of the French Revolution, being cut by upper-class friends as a result.

Yet even Burns represented no real threat to the social order or Dundas ascendancy. Security for Burns and for the large legitimate and illegitimate brood he loved was his job as an Excise Officer in Dumfries, a job which he openly acknowledged he owed to the benign patronage of James, Earl of Glencairn and patron of Kilmarnock parish. Before he died of rheumatic heart disease in 1796 he had recanted his pro-Revolutionary views to keep his Excise job. After 1793 he penned patriotic anti-French verse. His eldest son attended both Edinburgh and Glasgow universities before embarking on a distinguished civil service career. His second and third sons, William Nicol Burns and James Glencairn Burns, were to be colonels in the armies of the Honourable East India Company. Burns may never have gone to the West Indies, as he once proposed, but his brood rode the accelerating current of globalisation that could carry contemporary Scots to the United States and Canada, as it did in great numbers, as well as to every other continent, whether under the auspices of the Union flag or not. History tends to remember only the eminent and successful, but those who died or just failed are essential to a balanced picture.

The engineer officer, Captain Bruce, who organised and led the escalade of the virtually impregnable Maratha stronghold of Gwalior in India in 1780, and then foiled Mádhava Ráo Sindhia's counter-offensive by a surprise night attack on his camp, was a brother of the Stirlingshire laird James Bruce, consul in Algiers and Abyssinian traveller. However, James died embittered and mocked as 'the great Abyssinian liar' because his realistic account of the Ethiopians in his *Travels to Discover the Sources of the Nile* (1790) was deemed a farrago of invention and absurdity. Scots may have been among the most successful entrepreneurs in the competitive and fluid Indian military labour market, but they could be disastrous entrepreneurs in other fields. The lawyer Henry Low, who showed outstanding talent as a golfer, went bankrupt (with many others) in Fife in 1825, Australia in 1830 and Calcutta in 1833 before dying in Burma, one hopes in the arms of an amiable Burmese lady, for there can have been little satisfaction in the rest of his career. With a white death rate running at 10–12 per cent per annum in the Caribbean in the eighteenth century, and probably much higher in India, one has to see failure or death as a price paid by many Scots for their participation in new global networks.

6

The Melvilles and their System
under the Pressures of War 1793–1815

The outbreak of war with Revolutionary France in 1793 and the continuation of conflicts, first with a revolutionary French republican regime and then with the Napoleonic Empire that succeeded it, at first simply consolidated the grip of the Dundas system on Scottish political life. It was already formidable and much of what appeared on the surface as spontaneous expression of opinion by the county elites was probably studied sycophancy with ulterior motives in view. When, for example, it became clear late in 1793 that Dundas was not prepared to promote the son of Sir Robert Anstruther from a lieutenancy to a captaincy in the Royal Navy the indignant father, who carried much electoral weight in the Anstruther Easter District of Burghs, claimed of himself that 'no one has been more ready in promoting every address, subscription, and other county measure which was supposed acceptable to the ministry'. Certainly, Dundas was fierce and vigilant in protecting and expanding what he saw as his electoral interest at by-elections, crushing ruthlessly signs of disaffection by the Marquis of Tweeddale in Haddingtonshire in 1795 and wresting Kirkcudbrightshire from the control of the Earl of Galloway, with the aid of a flood of patronage, in the same year. However, it was really the declaration of war early in 1793 by the French Convention on Great Britain and Holland that opened the way to the apogee of the Dundas ascendancy in North Britain.

Though himself a natural conservative clear that the Glorious Revolution of 1688 was the last British revolution he wanted to hear about, and even then preferably in terms of studied vagueness, Dundas hardly welcomed the war. Nevertheless he more than any other individual ran it at the administrative level, first as Home Secretary and then as Secretary of State for War until Pitt's government resigned in March 1801. Control over the vastly expanded armed forces could only massively enhance the patronage at his disposal. Pressure of business at the War, Home and India Offices compelled Dundas to transfer the detailed management of Scotland to his nephew, Robert Dundas of Arniston, a tactful, amiable mediocrity who served as Lord Advocate. His task was easy, for virtually the entire membership of the ruling classes of Scotland rallied to the regime under the twin pressures of patriotism and social panic.

The French republic, like the new American one, had an ideology which talked much about Liberty. The French, like the Americans, asserted a right to define it and 'help' other people achieve a version of this universally desirable blessing authenticated by their support, if necessary in arms. It was potentially an extremely aggressive ideology, and like the Americans the French soon set out to create an 'Empire of Liberty' by raping a continent. They faced much more formidable opposition than the Americans, but their abolition of social and legal privilege and opening of careers to talent did gain them extensive sympathy in radical middle-class circles, including anglophone ones. Writers like Thomas Paine, the English champion of both the French and American revolutions, were indeed advocating very radical social and political change, and his *Rights of Man* (1792) was widely read in Scotland. Everyone in politics in 1793, when war with France broke out, was a Whig. Pitt and Dundas were mainline Whigs, but increasingly they were denied the name and dubbed with the name of the long-dead Tory party of Queen Anne to underline their refusal to endorse the more radical doctrines of the reformers inspired by the idealism of the French Revolution.

In retrospect it is clear that the activities of radical activists were primarily a great help to Dundas. The French Revolution certainly helped to stimulate political awareness in Scotland. In 1782 there were eight Scottish newspapers. By 1790 there were twenty-seven and more were established in 1791–2. In July 1792 the first society of Friends of the People in Scotland met in Edinburgh. By 1792 similar societies were spreading all over Scotland. In September 1792 the Dundee Friends of the Constitution constituted themselves. The Glasgow Associated Friends of the Constitution and of the People came into existence about the same time. Though led by radical lairds and lawyers, these Scottish societies had low subscriptions and had more in common with the populist London Corresponding Society than with the London Friends of the People, which had a high sub-scription and consisted of very upper-class men bent mainly on emasculating any popular political movement by appropriating its leadership. Dundas himself seems to have shared the general alarm among the possessing classes in Scotland that a movement which encouraged political mobilisation among the lower orders might lead on to effective demands for political and social reform. Spies were employed to infiltrate radical organisations. Money was disbursed to writers on papers like the *Edinburgh Herald* and *Caledonian Mercury*, and the official government line rapidly hardened into denouncing anyone who wanted any reform at all as a 'Leveller', 'Republican' or 'French Democrat'. Moderate clergymen like the Reverend Dr Hardy, who had earned his spurs writing in defence of ecclesiastical patronage, now denounced in print the 'system of pillage' advocated by Thomas Paine.

The year 1792 saw the first General Convention of the Friends of the People in Scotland. Thomas Muir, the son of a Glasgow merchant who had become an Edinburgh advocate, was promi-nent at it and insisted on reading an address from the Society of United Irishmen which many delegates regarded as far too violent. The Convention itself, despite the backing of a move-ment full of radical shopkeepers and artisans, was extremely traditional in demanding equal representation in frequent parliaments. This had been a platitude of reform politics for gen-erations. The Septennial Act of 1716 had rendered elections offensively infrequent and the franchise was so irrational as to raise doubts as to whether it made any sense at all. From January

1793 the Crown law officers embarked on a series of sedition trials designed to discredit and intimidate the reform movement. Muir did not help his cause by visiting Paris and Dublin before his trial on exceedingly dubious charges of sedition. With the Lord Justice Clerk, Robert MacQueen, Lord Braxfield, openly baying for his blood he was sentenced to fourteen years' transportation. Next month Thomas Fysche Palmer, the Englishman who ministered to a small Unitarian congregation in Dundee, was condemned to seven years' transportation on charges of writing an address against the war. In fact he probably only helped revise it, but a career which for him began as a schoolboy at Eton ended in Australia at Botany Bay.

Undaunted by such trials, which continued intermittently until 1820, and secured the transportation of, among others, William Skirving, the moving spirit in the third and last General Convention of the Friends of the People in Edinburgh in 1793, the tiny minority of active radicals continued along increasingly desperate paths. Their programme of annual parliaments, universal male suffrage and an end to the war had virtually no support in the country at large. The French government persistently deluded itself that Scotland, like Ireland, was panting to throw off the English yoke. It was not true. There was no equivalent in Scotland of the political mobilisation in Ireland which in 1798 produced a radical Presbyterian rising in Ulster and a Roman Catholic peasant rising in the south. Even on Ireland, the French were misled on the levels of support they could expect for an invasion and rising by their chief informant Wolfe Tone. Like most political exiles, he had a tendency to gloss over awkward realities in the pursuit of his goals.

Nevertheless, what made the response to the French Revolution in Scotland so alarming to the authorities in kirk and state was the way in which it involved groups well below those social levels which were traditionally expected to take an interest in politics. Weavers rioted quite seriously in many Scottish towns in 1773–4, threatening to emigrate 'to the colonies' unless they gained the points they were fighting for, but these were essentially traditional, acceptable riots concerned with material issues. Political militancy on such subjects as burghal and parliamentary reform was almost entirely confined to quite small groups composed of lawyers, merchants and the odd disgruntled landowner. The Incorporated Trades of the Scottish burghs also tended to support agitation for parliamentary and municipal reform in the 1780s, thereby expressing an hostility to the town councils which ran back into the medieval period, when the merchant oligarchs first established a stranglehold on municipal government. Events in France in the early 1790s certainly interested these groups. The Friends of the People societies set up after 1792 tended to be led by merchants, lawyers, manufacturers and teachers, but as the French Revolution became bloodier and more aggressive externally, the original leadership in the Scottish societies shrank back. From an early stage they had appealed for support from the skilled working class prepared to pay 3d. a quarter subscription. Now the lower middle class and these same skilled craftsmen, above all weavers, moved to the forefront.

Alienation among the traditional elites was instant and total. The Conveners' Courts which were the normal spokesmen for the political views of the Incorporated Trades in Dundee and St Andrews, for example, simply dropped their previously active support for reform until after 1815. As the government systematically persecuted the Friends of the People out of sight, governmental warnings of social subversion became a self-fulfilling prophecy. In industrial towns in the west of Scotland and in commercial towns in the east it was the skilled working class which resisted the government's political offensive and formed the much more militant United Scotsmen. Immigrant weavers from Ulster were active in this body. Indeed, almost everyone accused of sedition in Scotland between 1797 and 1803 was a weaver. Only in textile counties with a high proportion of Seceders was there serious support for the United Scotsmen. By 1803 it was clear that this second radical wave had failed as completely as the first. It never had the least chance of success. Given the social and power structures of the time, radical weavers were about the last group capable of seizing power, and these precociously literate and articulate men merely reinforced the iniquities they denounced by helping to frighten everyone else into the conservative patriotic camp. Radical demands seldom went beyond the purely political, but invariably raised the spectre of social levelling.

The great bulk of the active males in the better-off classes rushed to display their military zeal by joining the numerous Volunteer Corps which sprang up all over Scotland to resist a French invasion. Robert Burns was a Royal Dumfries Volunteer, while the young Walter Scott was Quartermaster, Secretary and briefly Paymaster of the Royal Edinburgh Light Dragoons. It is true that a measure for embodying a militia of 6,000 men in Scotland in 1797 was only enforced after severe rioting in several places, rioting which cost lives before being crushed by Volunteers and regular troops. However, this was a perfectly reasonable act of resistance by the poorer classes (who alone were likely to be affected) against a system of conscription organised by the schoolmasters, who drew up the basic lists, and providing the government with a force only too likely to be drafted for regular service abroad.

The new radical group provided a continuing *bête noire* for the well-affected. George Mealmaker, the best-known United Scotsman martyr, was transported to Botany Bay in 1798. In 1799 the United Scotsmen were finally banned by name. They were never significant either in numbers or in personnel, being but a shadow of the United Irishmen they were so clearly influenced by, and even the United Irishmen, outside Ulster, had owed their mass support to being entered and effectively swamped by the Roman Catholic secret societies known as Defenders. The simple fact is that Scotland was in no way remarkable for politically-motivated opposition to the government at this period, and did not possess what did exist in Ulster – a disaffected Presbyterian community alienated by an Anglican Establishment. The Royal Navy, with its fleet mutinies at Spithead and the Nore in 1797, posed far graver problems for the politicians and put far more effective pressure on them to treat at least one section of the under-privileged with common decency. Characteristically, when the sailors returned to their duty it was a Scottish admiral, Adam Duncan, second son of Duncan of Lundie near Dundee, who led them to victory over the French-controlled Dutch fleet, at the battle from which he took his title of Viscount Camperdown.

Dundas himself approached the General Election of 1796 in a spirit of near euphoria. He had the obsession typical of the pure machine politician, even though he predated mass party machines – he dreamed of a monopoly of power in his defined precinct: Scotland. In June 1796 he told Lord Hobart, Governor of Madras, that he had been convinced 'that if I came to Scotland and exerted myself thoroughly, I might be able to prevent the return of any one Member for Scotland hostile to Government'. Sir David Carnegie MP for Forfarshire succeeded in defeating that ambition. He hated Dundas. About eight other Scots MPs were not quite totally in the Dundas interest. Otherwise '96 was a Roman Triumph for 'Harry the Ninth', the 'Scotch Dictator', the 'Satrap of Scotland' or, as others put it, 'the slee Dundas'. Socially conservative, but not totally averse to change if it made government easier or the executive more powerful without making it more responsible, the flexible Dundas had exploited the winds of change abroad in his world to create a unique position for himself. For the future his recipe was more of the lines of development he saw as wise. He supported Pitt's Union of Ireland and Great Britain in 1800 not just as necessary for the war effort, but as a further beneficent extension of the Union of Scotland and England in 1707, the foundation stone of his political universe. Scots MPs and peers were notably enthusiastic about the Union of 1800, holding before Irish eyes a vision of conciliation as well as that wider stage of profit and honour, on which they themselves had acted so successfully.

Yet by 1800 the self-confidence of the ruling groups was shaken. The wars that had so decimated the political opposition at first had dragged on too long. Over Roman Catholic emancipation the general sense of the ruling classes, on which Pitt and Dundas were ultimately so dependent, was against them. Pitt wanted it to rally Irish Catholics to the Union and the war effort. Dundas supported him but could not take religion

seriously and was an appallingly bad guide to its future significance in nineteenth-century British politics. George III, much
clearer than either Pitt or Dundas about the essentially confes-
sional basis of the political structure inherited from the English
past, dismissed the 'damned Scotch metaphysics' with which
Dundas plied him on the Catholic question. A government originally established to vindicate the role of the Crown as a vital
element in the sovereign body had no option when opposed by
the King on a central issue. In 1801 Pitt resigned. With him went
Dundas. War weariness was interlocked with resistance to
Catholic emancipation, and Dundas was on both counts no
longer acceptable in office. It was ironic that he who, like Pitt,
had by no means rejoiced at the outbreak of war, should suffer
when a long succession of military reverses allied to heavy war
taxation punctured the fighting spirit of the ruling classes.

That the Scottish aristocracy, with its well-established tradition of political advancement by troop raising, was originally as
bellicose as any other section of the British aristocracy is clear. It
is equally clear that even within the landed classes there was
always in Scotland a small and increasingly abused minority
which stood outside the consensus for war and paid the penalty
for presenting a rationally argued alternative to one of those dramatic swings of mental fashion which in times of stress tend to
be the characteristic reaction of the British Establishment. A
Stirlingshire laird, Robert Haldane of Airthrey, illustrates neatly
the strengths and weaknesses of these upper-class dissenters. He
was an ex-officer of the Royal Navy and like his former commander Admiral Lord St Vincent he regarded the war with
France as 'unnecessary, impolitic, and lamentable'. At first his
views were treated as a permissible eccentricity. Socially he
remained on good terms with Mr Secretary Dundas and other
Scotch Pittites such as the gallant Sir Ralph Abercromby and the
local magnate, the Duke of Montrose, who condescended to visit
Airthrey as late as the summer of 1794.

However, party spirit mounted as Revolutionary France
became to the Stirlingshire gentry a symbol of Godlessness and
Democracy. Robert Haldane had the great moral courage to

stand up at a county meeting presided over by the Duke of Montrose and oppose a proposal to raise a Volunteer Corps on the grounds that it was unnecessary for internal security and would inevitably be used to feed the war machine. He added, with dignity and insight, that the fanatical opposition to all change whatsoever characteristic of the supporters of the war struck him as singularly injudicious, and contrary to the basic principles of the Reformation. Evangelical religion as well as the rational analysis of the Enlightenment combined to form Robert Haldane's mind. Radical he was not. When in 1800 he published an 'Address on Politics' to vindicate his record he insisted that as soon as political societies embracing the lower orders were formed he opposed them as likely to inflame rather than inform the public. In any case, by 1795 he had abandoned politics for missionary religion, feeling called to witness in Bengal. East India Company hostility to missionaries blocked that scheme, so he and his brother James were diverted into evangelisation at home. Nevertheless, men like Robert Haldane and the Earl of Lauderdale upheld an alternative policy of seeking peace, which events made respectable again to all but a few unbalanced ideological warriors.

Specific individuals, faced with the dual challenge of external war and internal unrest, rushed to the paranoid conclusion that there was a vast and active plot to subvert the entire social order. John Robison, who held the chair of Natural Philosophy in Edinburgh for thirty years, published in 1798 his *Proofs of a Conspiracy against all the Religions and Governments of Europe* in which he claimed that he had first obtained hints of this devilish conspiracy by mixing in Masonic circles in St Petersburg in the 1770s when, like not a few Scottish professional men, he had sought advancement and profit in the service of the westernising government of the Russian Empire. Fear of social revolution had sent virtually all British politicians, including the weightier part of the former parliamentary opposition led by the Duke of Portland, into a tight phalanx around Pitt by 1794. From that date alone can the largely meaningless term Tory be applied without confusion to the party of government and the name

Whig be reserved to the rump opposition led by Charles James Fox. The great majority of Scottish members of the ruling classes rushed into the Tory camp if they were not there already, but by 1802 neither the confidence nor the solidarity of that camp was quite what it had once been.

The resignation of Henry Dundas with that of the Pitt government in 1801 caused a spasm of consternation among his well-drilled Scottish supporters, who had come to assume that office and Dundas were synonymous terms. However, it soon became clear that there was an uneasy, tacit deal between Dundas and Pitt's successor Henry Addington. At the General Election in 1802 Dundas supported the administration and secured the return of a squad of thirty-one MPs – twenty-two from the counties and nine from districts of burghs. This represented a marginal but unmistakeable erosion of the Dundas interest. It is difficult to be precise, but Dundas definitely lost control in Fife and Stirling, and his decline was further underlined by the election for representative peers, where five out of the sixteen chosen were his known enemies. In a by-election caused by the death of the Earl of Dumfries in 1803, Dundas even failed to return his man, Lord Kellie. Elevated to the peerage as Viscount Melville by Addington, Dundas came back into office as First Lord of the Admiralty in 1804 in Pitt's new administration formed after the renewal of war with France. He at once threw the weight of government patronage behind a counter-offensive in Fife, and by similar means ensured that Lord Kellie entered the House of Lords. Then in April 1805, as the result of revelations (in the 10th Report of the Commissioners of Naval Enquiry) about massive use of public funds passing through the Navy Pay Office for the purpose of private speculation by Alexander Trotter of Dreghorn, a Scots laird who was Paymaster of the Navy, Dundas was condemned by a vote of the House of Commons, forced to resign from the cabinet, and impeached. Money had never greatly interested the careless and generous Dundas, whose obsession was power, so his eventual acquittal was probably right as well as deeply gratifying to such supporters of the fallen minister as the future Sir

Walter Scott, but the death of Pitt in January 1806 finished Dundas as an active politician.

He had never been able totally to crush resistance to his power in Scotland, though he tried hard enough. Indeed the treasurer and party manager of the opposition group centred on Fox and the Duke of Portland was, after 1789, a Scots laird from Fife, William Adam of Blair Adam, a lawyer who was a member of the great architectural family. William Adam had little time in the end for his architect uncles whose megalomania and lack of financial sense had brought the family fortunes to the brink of total disaster with their grandiose Adelphi building scheme off the Strand in London in 1768–74. William was a cautious politician, a supporter of Lord North, who even fought a duel with C. J. Fox before succumbing to the compelling charm of that wayward man. Thereafter he was the anchorman of the Foxite Whigs, protected to some extent from the wrath and fury of Pitt and Dundas by the reversionary interest and patronage of the Prince of Wales. He was appointed Solicitor-General to the Prince and endeared himself to the self-indulgent heir to the throne by his sustained efforts to redeem the usually dismal and scandalous state of 'Prinny's' finances. Long after 1800 Prinny and his equally scapegrace brothers, the dukes of York and Clarence, were recurring themes in William Adam's correspondence, almost always with reference to their financial straits. After the split between Fox and Portland in 1792–4, William Adam, who had tried very hard to avert it, stubbornly and skilfully managed the business of the Foxite Whigs, especially in Scotland. There had always been an element among the nobility and gentry that could not stomach the subservience demanded by Dundas. On this rock Adam could build a small but vocal opposition. Nor should the issue be seen as purely one of personalities. In the eighteenth century it was a commonplace that it mattered less how a member reached the legislature than that he should there represent with manly independence the varied interests of the localities.

James Maitland, eighth Earl of Lauderdale, a violent-tempered, clever nobleman with a strong Scotch accent and a taste for political economy, was typical of the conservative wing of the Foxites. A representative peer who strongly opposed the war with France and the restrictions on personal liberty in Britain which accompanied it, he was excluded from the Lords by Dundas in 1796 and 1802 for his pains. Even an arch-conservative (though he called himself a Whig) like the second Earl of Fife, who died in 1809 at the age of eighty, was at times very unhappy about the dictatorial strain in Dundas, despite the fact that he supported most of his policies, including the French war. Fife was a most conscientious supporter of his own region's interests and he remarked in 1794 that:

> I wonder the Country does not see how much it is in their interest to support independency, you know what trouble and expense it cost me to support this principle. Mr Dundas wants to put down every independent man, and to annihilate that character as much as possible.

'Independency' against the odds seemed to reap its reward early in 1806 when the death of Pitt compelled George III to accept a 'Ministry of all the Talents' with Fox prominent in its ranks. Lauderdale was made a peer of the United Kingdom. His nomination as Governor-General of India was effectively black-balled by the Honourable East India Company, but he became Keeper of the Great Seal of Scotland and was sworn of the Privy Council. Henry Erskine, the brilliant Whig lawyer who had been removed from his position as Dean of the Faculty of Advocates on 12 January 1796 by a notable display of partisan rancour on the part of the Tory majority in that body, was appointed Lord Advocate for Scotland for the second time in his career. The 'manly patriots', numbering thirty-eight in all, who had voted for him in January 1796, and who had been toasted at Whig social gatherings ever since, seemed vindicated. Henry's facile but absurdly vain youngest brother Thomas, who had not seen Scotland since 1764 when he left it to join, briefly, the Royal Navy, even achieved the gown of Lord Chancellor on the strength of his career at the English bar.

Alas, in April 1807, with little positive achievement in Scotland, the government fell. The Whigs had already experienced the fickle nature of the Prince's friendship. Thomas Erskine had been dismissed as Attorney General to the Prince of Wales in 1792 for characteristically reckless support for the radical publicist Tom Paine, who was accused of slandering the royal family. He should have been less surprised than he was when the Prince ratted decisively on his Whig friends once he became Prince Regent with full powers in February 1812. After April 1807 the Dundas regime was to all intents and purposes restored in Scotland. Now led by Robert Saunders Dundas, Melville's only son, it emerged from the 1807 General Election rather battered with only twenty-four MPs, but its grip on the peerage election was impressive. Their Lordships only dared return one name not on the list of Dundas candidates hawked round by the Duke of Buccleuch. Henry Dundas died in 1811 after an extraordinary career based ultimately on his ability to manipulate the admittedly inadequate representation of Scotland at Westminster and to ensure that it raised no serious demands for attention from His Majesty's Government. His early zeal for administrative reform had long preceded him to the grave. Robert, second Viscount Melville, had already succeeded smoothly to his regional political empire, and now succeeded in many of his offices, down to the chancellorship of the University of St Andrews.

His arch-opponent, William Adam, reached Parliament by means of an English constituency. The only chancellorship he ever held was that of the Duchy of Cornwall, in the gift of the Prince of Wales. Nevertheless, he believed his own political cause would triumph over a long haul, by making himself the spokesman for the ever more important commercial and manufacturing middle classes. Like so many theories, this one contained a vein of shrewd insight but was overall too simple by half. James Loch, the brains behind the Sutherland clearances, who was one of Adam's regular correspondents when 'hunting Dundas' was the favourite Whig sport in 1805–6, was a living illustration of the inter-connections between land and industry, and between the middle classes and the ruling aristocracy. The Sutherlands and Adams tended to be Whigs. Most Scots landed and political dynasts were Tory. The Tory ascendancy ultimately fell more from internal fission than from external attack, and its collapse in England was bound to trigger even more violent change in Scotland. The longer it postponed changes perceived as overdue, the harder it was going ultimately to fall, and then opposition ideology would seriously influence policy.

That is why the intellectual climate among the educated classes was so vital. Dugald Stewart, who succeeded Adam Ferguson as Professor of Moral Philosophy in Edinburgh in 1785, was, despite his lack of philosophical originality, therefore a very important figure, for this eloquent, charismatic teacher was not only the supreme exponent of the Scots 'Common-Sense' school of philosophy stretching back in impeccable social respectability to Thomas Reid, but also a convinced Whig. If he was the most cautious of Whigs, capable of cringing apology to a Noble Lord for having inadvertently mentioned an infidel French philosopher like Condorcet in one of his writings without explicitly condemning him, that too merely enhanced the influence of a man whose books were accepted at once, in the United States of America as much as in Britain, as an authoritative summary of the philosophical school which had given the lie to the atheistical Hume. Certainly Dugald Stewart's class in Political Economy was a common bond between the four young men behind the *Edinburgh Review* whose first number appeared in October 1802. The four were Sidney Smith, an English parson serving as a tutor in Edinburgh; Francis Jeffrey, son of a Deputy Clerk to the Court of Session; Francis Horner, son of a merchant and grandson of a Writer to the Signet; and Henry Brougham, son of an English squire and a Scottish lady who was the niece of Principal Robertson. Both Horner and Brougham were called to the Scottish bar. Both rapidly abandoned it for lusher pastures in London. Horner died prematurely in 1817. Brougham rose from being 'a briefless barrister on the Scottish Southern Circuit' to being Lord Chancellor of England, in the Whig interest. Before 1808 *The Edinburgh* was, however, not a politically partisan journal. Its remarkable impact was due to the fact that in politics and literature it offered a sharp and at times iconoclastic vein of criticism for which English-speaking opinion was ready. In 1816 the London *Times* had a daily circulation of only 8,000. *The Edinburgh* had a subscription list of 12,000 in 1813 and Jeffrey, its editor, was surely right in arguing that this represented at least 50,000 readers.

It was Brougham, a passionate humanitarian devoted to alleviating the lot of such human chattels as the negro slave or the British soldier, but in all other respects an unprincipled and conceited careerist, who pushed *The Edinburgh* over the top late in 1808 with an article (jointly written with Jeffrey) in which it was said that 'reforms in the administration of our affairs must be adopted, to prevent more violent changes'. In a sense, the question is why such a performance should have elicited so violent a Tory response. Brougham would cheerfully have enlisted under the Tory banner, if offered advancement for doing so. Accusations by a Tory MP in a pamphlet entitled *Remarks on the Jacobinical Tendency of the Edinburgh Review* were more or less routine and not at all convincing. The sheer lunacy of the more extreme forms of the 'Jacobin' parrot-cry as a means of smearing all opponents of the ruling clique was becoming obvious. By 1815 John Robison's theory of universal malignant conspiracy against all the decencies was being referred to with something akin to levity in the pages of the *Transactions of the Royal Society of Edinburgh*. Henry Dundas, to the very end of his life, automatically accused anyone in Scotland who would not knuckle under his political will of embracing the unmentionable excesses of the French Jacobins. It was a charge doubly hollow when applied to a member of the ducal house of Hamilton at a time when Britons were fighting a conservative military dictator, Napoleon Bonaparte. Whigs were not Jacobins. Brougham's wilder statements of near-democratic theory were every whit as offensive to the conservative wing of the Whigs as to the Tories.

Yet Walter Scott, culturally the rising hope of the stern, unbending Tories, found the defeatism of *The Edinburgh*'s comments on the British campaigns in Spain unendurable and not only withdrew from occasionally contributing to it, but also sponsored the launch in 1809 of the rival, militantly Tory, *Quarterly Review*, backed by many of the staff of an ultra-rightwing paper, the *Anti-Jacobin*, that had ceased publication in

1798. Scott, the son of a Writer to the Signet and the eldest daughter of John Rutherford, Professor of Medicine in the University of Edinburgh, was nothing if not committed to the Tory cause. Called to the Scots bar in 1792, he married the daughter of a French Royalist refugee in 1797, and in 1799 was preferred, through the influence of the Duke of Buccleuch, to the post of Sheriff-Depute of Selkirkshire, a job which left plenty of free time for literature. The years 1802–3 saw the publication of the three volumes of his superb *Minstrelsy of the Scottish Border*, which brought to fulfilment his obsession with Border balladry. Long narrative poems of high adventure like *The Lay of the Last Minstrel* (1805), *Marmion* (1808) and *The Lady of the Lake* (1810) sold astonishingly well and made his literary name. In 1811 Scott purchased the beginnings of the estate on the Tweed he called Abbotsford. He was fatally tempted to build up an extensive estate, less as an economic investment than as the appropriate background to a neo-feudal lifestyle as a Scottish laird well in with the Melville regime.

The Scotch Whigs were by comparison out in the cold. Their old leader Lauderdale was drifting steadily to the right at a rate of knots calculated to carry him out of the Whig haven altogether. Such was the state of Whiggery in North Britain that for several years its leading public figure was an Irish earl, Lord Moira. Like William Adam, he was an intimate of the Prince of Wales, to the point of having been his second in a duel. He was appointed Commander-in-Chief Scotland in 1803 and in 1804 married a Scottish heiress, Flora, Countess of Loudon, in her own right. They lived at Duddingston House and were deservedly popular. Moira had commanded a Loyalist unit, the Volunteers of Ireland, in the American war, emerging from it alienated from a Westminster government he denounced as first neglecting the Loyalists, then expecting too much from them, before finally betraying them and, inexcusably, trying to transfer blame for the debacle onto them. After failing to achieve high political office in 1807 and 1812, Moira, a good administrator and better soldier (though financially chaotic like most of the Prince's set), was given his big chance in 1813, when he went off to achieve lasting fame as Governor General of India and Marquis of Hastings. In 1806 Walter Scott, with backing from the Buccleuch interest, was appointed one of the principal clerks of the Court of Session. Henry Erskine's last hopes of legal preferment evaporated in 1811 when Charles Hope was appointed Lord President of the Court of Session over his head. 'Harry' Erskine had had enough. He retired to the solace of his country seat, his garden and his violin. What then did the Tories fear? Fundamentally they seem to have sensed what Henry Cockburn, a relative of Dundas but a Whig, described in his *Memorials Of His Time* as 'a great though as yet a silent change' in the 'mind of the lower, and far more of the middle, class'. Peace, with its economic problems and release from the wartime pressures for patriotic support for the King's government, could only accelerate that change.

The conservative reaction in Scotland had been too successful for too long. It was part of a general British revulsion from the radicalism of the French Revolution which found its supreme expression in the Irishman Edmund Burke's *Reflections on the Revolution in France* (1790). Burke there argued from the prescriptive rhetoric of the Common Law tradition, defending the status quo on the ground that its survival proved its worth. He virtually, if not absolutely, closed the door to conscious reform, though not to cumulative piecemeal adaptation. James Mackintosh, a young Scot educated at Aberdeen and Edinburgh universities, produced in 1791 in *Vindiciae Gallicae* a brilliant refutation of Burke which, among others, deeply influenced Robert Haldane of Airthrey. Yet Mackintosh, like Haldane, subsequently withdrew from articulate opposition to the sharp swing to the right among the ruling classes. Inevitably that swing went to extremes. In a world where the Dundas interest seemed to have obliterated serious opposition, Lord Braxfield was so foolish at the trial of Thomas Muir in 1793 as actually to say that government was 'just like a corporation; and in this country, it is made up of the landed interest, which alone has a right to be represented'. Given the infamous state of Scottish municipal corporations, which belied even the most ingenious attempts by government sycophants to argue that parliamentary representation in some mysterious way reflected the property and intelligence of the land, it was a singularly injudicious analogy.

Of course, Braxfield's concept of what central government did would have been very limited. In the localities he assumed that the aristocracy and gentry would govern. Scots tradition still allowed specialist bodies to legislate in their own fields, so in 1756 the Court of Session had by an Act of Sederunt introduced procedures which simplified and facilitated the removal of tenants, sub-tenants and their dependants. It might seem that this confirmed the total dominance of Braxfield's landed interest, but in fact in a traditional society like rural Scotland there was a built-in sense of reciprocity, best expressed in the baron courts that were so important in regulating rural society, where the laws and customs of the barony were ultimately defined by the suitors to the court, that is the substantial tenants, and the baron was deemed subject to the laws and above all the customs of the barony. Attempts to use the court to discipline tenants in order to stop them from damaging innovations like commercial forestry plantations could prove difficult to enforce. The fact that colliers and saltpan workers in Scotland were technically hereditary serfs or slaves did not mean that decisions were just imposed by their masters. Colliers could be awkward and expensive, as the Duke of Buccleuch discovered when he tried to use his Lothian workers to open a new pit at Canonbie in Dumfriesshire in 1768. In the end he sent them home as more trouble than they were worth and used local colliers.

Rioting was more or less built into the traditional system, which lacked the means, other than calling in the army, which was easier said than done, to suppress it. Women were often prominent in riots, as in 1755 when the agents of Lord Findlater, trying to transfer a traditional market from Keith to his lordship's planned village of New Keith, were beaten up and chased off by a mob of women. Above all, the lower orders were in the period before the American Revolution developing the threat of emigration as a negotiating weapon. There was an unprecedented volume of emigration to the provinces of British North America in the early 1770s, when Scotland was one of two major sources of emigrants. The other was in southern England. When in 1773 ringleaders of an unlawful combination of weavers striking in Paisley for higher wages were tried, the judge was clearly moved to conciliation by giving lighter sentences on those convicted than he could have because of his fear that the weavers' threat 'to go off in a body to America' might be implemented. Exporters of corn in time of local dearth were either subjected to riots, as in Dumfries in 1772 and Dundee and Fife in 1772–3, or to individual intimidation. The fact that he was a sometime Lord Provost of Aberdeen did not exempt Alexander Livingston from going in fear of his life in 1753 when local rumour blamed him for a doubling of the price of meal in the city. The Presbyterian communion was far from monolithic by the late eighteenth century and dissenting Presbyterians often generated violence over attempts by patrons to insert unpopular nominees in kirks. Sailors' strikes in Greenock in 1773 and Port Glasgow in 1776 needed troops from Glasgow to suppress them.

'The orthodoxy of passivity' is therefore as indefensible in Scotland in this era as it would be in any other western European early-modern society. What will not do is an attempt to create a vision of late eighteenth-century workers and peasants struggling against the impact of a bourgeois capitalist 'revolution' that some Marxist historiography has argued occurred in Scotland in the two generations before 1745. Even the best of this school has to admit that it was an odd 'revolution' in comparison with events in Europe on which they paste the same misleading label. Far from seeing the violent creation of a new state embodying 'bourgeois nationalism', as theory demands, it saw the dismantling of an old one and its incorporation in another. Such historians under-estimate the degree of social negotiation through violence that was quite normal in early-modern society and present in Scotland if anything more abundantly in the first half of the eighteenth century than in the second. Social and economic change was bound to undermine a system as narrowly based and static as that of the first Viscount Melville, and the wars between 1792 and 1815 did see unprecedented ideological threats to the social order, but they also called forth a patriotic

Scottish conservative reaction against foreign aggression that penetrated far deeper into the masses than any republican ideology could hope to unless it could attach itself to a pre-existing, preferably sectarian, cause. The second Viscount Melville could run a modified version of his father's system in Scotland after 1804 and beyond 1815 partly because of the way the French Revolutionaries and Napoleon effectively rallied support for the Melvilles' conservative but 'improving' version of Scotland.

Arrogance was depriving the authorities of their capacity for some of the central techniques of the British Establishment, such as the avoidance of confrontation, the use of urbane prevarication rather than open refusal, and above all the making of ambiguous or inconsequential concessions in order to preserve their grip on the significant decision-making process. As the agitations of the 1780s resumed after 1815, it was to become clear that only the Whigs had the ability fully to deploy such weapons in defence of the established social and political order. English Tories did indeed try to adopt a more flexible, empirical attitude from the early 1820s, but paid a heavy price in terms of internal conflict and fission. Scots Tories, always an extreme case, inhabited a world in which politics had been reduced to interlocking patronage rackets and social hysteria. Flexibility was beyond them. Immediately after the outbreak of peace Henry Cockburn unerringly identified the emerging swing of opinion among the propertied classes. Radicalism of the United Scotsman type might be dead but Whigs were now emerging 'from despised dissenting congregations, from half liberated corporations, from shops, from the law, even from medicine, and the best symptom of all, from the aristocracy of the lower orders'. To such people the Whigs offered a prospect of reform of the more outrageous and indefensible abuses in Scottish public life without any accompanying threat to property rights or the principle of hierarchy in social relationships.

7

Change:
The Underlying Time Bomb 1790–1815

Within the framework of order provided by the landed ascendancy, Scottish society was changing rapidly by the late eighteenth century, and changing in ways which ultimately were to erode the bases of that ascendancy. Fully to understand what was happening, it is essential to look more closely at the forces changing the face of the Lowlands and convulsing parts of the Highlands, where Gaelic society was to pay a heavy price for its almost total subordination to Anglo-Saxon values. Fortunately we have, in *The Statistical Account of Scotland*, a unique contemporary source sponsored and organised by the improving laird and politician Sir John Sinclair of Ulbster (1754–1835), whose estates lay in the northern but not Highland county of Caithness. Using his own resources and the help of the clergy of the Church of Scotland, he produced twenty-one volumes of a survey, as well as a digest of those volumes, and more specialised surveys of agriculture.

From these works, it is clear that from about 1770 onwards change had become fairly general in the countryside and that the prime mover in this complex process was nearly always landlord demand for higher rents, related initially more often to a simple need for money to sustain higher standards of living than to any systematic investment in improvement as such. Sinclair reckoned the landlord class as encompassing well under 8,000 individuals. He calculated that there were 396 persons owning large properties worth £2,500 sterling or more in rent per annum; 1,077 proprietors of estates worth between £600 and £2,500;

and some 6,181 proprietors of small estates worth less than £600 of annual rent. This gave a total of 7,654 estate owners, to which had to be added 144 estates belonging to corporate bodies. Though in certain areas, such as the small county of Kinross, there were significant concentrations of working farmers who were owner-occupiers, most of Lowland Scotland had the 'three-decker' rural social structure characteristic of most of England. Below a small owner class the land was worked by tenant-farmers and their families, usually with the aid of a low-status class of labourers.

The world of the labourers was itself hierarchical and complex. Their origins varied enormously from one region to another. In the Lothians, where commercial farming was most highly developed, the skilled labourer or hind was landless but was paid half or more of his wage in grain. This inflation-proof element was supplemented by a money wage which to a skilled ploughman in 1815 might be £15–20 a year. On the other hand, the unskilled 'day labourer' was physically segregated from the regular workforce in a hut or bothy and paid purely in cash. Many small farmers in hill areas like the Sidlaws or Ochils seem to have lost their holdings in the course of landlord consolidation of farms; to have lacked the capital to set up on their own account; and to have ended up as labourers, either on improved farms in fertile areas or in towns, where they could still move out seasonally to take agricultural work such as reaping or shearing. In Aberdeenshire, where there was a substantial Scots-speaking crofter population, it was traditional for the crofters to send bachelor sons to be living-in servants on the improved farms. Elsewhere, in fertile areas such as the Carse of Gowrie on the north side of the Tay or the Carse of Stirling, there were significant concentrations of people known as cottars. They had a house and garden, but not enough land to live off. Rather, they had a dwelling and a means of occupying themselves during the quieter periods of the agricultural year while keeping themselves available for unskilled labour at the busy seasons. Robert Burns, himself an Ayrshire tenant-farmer, immortalised and sentimentalised such a household in his poem 'The Cottar's Saturday

Night', but like other small tenants cottars seem to have been increasingly squeezed out in favour of hired hands as the eighteenth century progressed.

By 1814, after twenty years during which landlords undoubtedly had invested quite heavily in their estates, it was reckoned that the land-rent of Scotland was increasing by a steady £100,000 to £200,000 per annum, but Scottish landlords would not have been able to obtain these continually higher rents as leases fell in and were renewed by public auction if prospective tenants had not been confident that they could expand their output and yet receive good prices for their produce. Throughout much of previous history increased output simply meant lower prices, at least in local markets. One explanation of the new confidence in farming was population growth. After being probably no higher in 1755 than in 1690, the Scottish population entered a phase of steady expansion, increasing by a quarter by 1801, when it was on the threshold of even more rapid retained growth. The next decade saw an annual population increment averaging 1.5 per cent, and that was the highest ever seen, before or since. The usual natural checks, which had reversed or flattened population growth curves in all previous time, ceased to operate. The years 1740–2 had seen Scotland come close to a major famine, but effective steps had been taken to avert catastrophe. In 1782 there was a severe food shortage over much of Scotland due to harvest failure. However, those extensive regions of Scotland affected by the shortages simply coped, without famine, political convulsion or the panic emigration so common in previous eras. Malting could be abandoned by agreement, thus releasing significant grain stocks for consumption. Stores were of course consumed. In some counties increases in mortality rates of up to 13 per cent among the lower orders cut the demand for grain, while early reaping and substantial imports eased the final stages of the crisis. Imports were particularly significant, because they were evidence of accumulated capital which could be used to stave off demographic collapse.

Scottish farming, which had probably reached its climatic limits of expansion under existing techniques by about 1750, had clearly passed through a major transition to more intensive farming sustained by increasing commercialisation and higher levels of investment. Investment was much encouraged by the effect of war after 1793. In 1795, for example, a poor harvest and restrictions on imports of grain from Europe led to a leap in wheat prices from 50 shillings to 81s. 6d. a quarter in some Scottish markets. In 1796 prices as high as 96s. a quarter can be found, while in 1812 payments for wheat as high as 126s. 6d. a quarter occurred. The role of wheat must not be exaggerated and overall statistics are usually confounded by the partial nature of our records and the scale of regional variations, but it is quite clear that the war gave a great stimulus to agricultural prices in many different sectors of production. The droving trade in cattle to English markets is an excellent example. War had always been good news for it, mainly because it implied a huge government demand for salt beef for the Royal Navy, and the French Revolutionary and Napoleonic wars were extremely protracted. In 1786 the average price of beasts crossing from Skye to the mainland was £2 to £3. In 1794 it went up to about £4. Towards the end of the war in 1814 prices peaked at as much as £18 a head.

Market mechanisms were thus transmitting the effects of high protective barriers and soaring state expenditure to individual farmers. So profitable were markets that landlords were willing to invest in social overhead capital for its indirect effect on their rent rolls. Though coastal shipping should never be under-estimated, turnpike roads were a prime example of the landlord contribution to the creation of an improved transport system. These toll roads were largely funded by the landed interest at a construction cost estimated to be in the region of £5,300 a mile. In the twenty years up to 1814, between £2 million and £3 million sterling was sunk in Scottish roads in this way. Between 1750 and 1814 as much as 3,000 miles of new roadway may have been built. Yet by 1821, with a few exceptions like the Inverurie turnpike in Aberdeenshire, Scottish turnpikes were financially in a mess, usually barely capable of servicing interest and upkeep charges, quite incapable of repaying the large debts representing initial construction costs. Over-optimism during the turnpike boom is only a partial explanation of this situation. The gains expected from turnpikes were always in large measure indirect and measured in enhanced rents for agricultural land or quarries, as much as in dividends.

Another example of this kind of landlord investment was the planned village. Hundreds of them were built by enlightened landlords in Scotland between 1730 and 1830, and the tradition of establishing such new nucleated settlements only died with the stagnation of agricultural rents in the so-called 'Great Depression' of the late nineteenth century. From early examples such as Ormiston in East Lothian, laid out by John Cockburn of Ormiston around 1740, a whole range of types of village developed. Many represented the clearing of an old village from the vicinity of a noble seat. Thus, between 1803 and 1808 the Earl of Mansfield not only completely rebuilt Scone Palace outside Perth, but also erased Old Scone village, and built New Scone a mile and a half off. The dukes of Argyll had been engaging in a similar operation at Inveraray from the 1740s, albeit with far higher architectural standards for the new burgh of Inveraray. Other planned villages were meant to be centres of industry and population, facilitating the commercialisation of surrounding agricultural areas. Some failed totally. Others flourished.

Until cheap tile drains were introduced on a large scale by such innovating landlords as Sir James Richardson of Pitfour in the Carse of Gowrie near Dundee in the 1820s, the absence of efficient low-cost drainage was a grave problem. Huge quantities of lime were used on the fields to sweeten and fertilise the sour, wet soils. The latter half of the eighteenth century saw a spectacular expansion in lime production and the creation of lime quarries and kilns on a scale never seen before. An expert (Robert Bald) writing in 1808 remarked that the lime industry 'may be said to be only in its infancy'. Lothian with its coal, advanced agriculture and carboniferous limestone had many lime kilns. A battery of kilns on the Earl of Morton's estate at Raw Camps near East Calder was producing up to 20,000 bolls of lime annually around 1800.[1] By 1837 there were more than two dozen large commercial limeworks in the region around Edinburgh. Nor was this sort of development limited to Lothian. The parish of St Cyrus on the Angus coast south of Montrose had two very large commercial limeworks.

Though some aspects of agricultural change, such as the gradual spread of potato culture after 1750, were relatively cheap, most forms of improvement required significant invest-ment. Reorganisation, including abolition of runrig or farming on strips of land, amalgamation of tenancies and improvement of layout on larger farms, involved heavy costs, including, sur-veying costs. Indeed between 1740 and the coming of the Ordnance Survey a century later lay the golden age of the land surveying profession in Scotland. Yet tenant-farmers as well as landlords were latterly willing to invest in new methods, which is why improved implements such as James Small's lightweight horse-drawn swing plough with iron wearing parts spread so rapidly after 1763. Farmers could obtain credit to embark on improvements because of the sophistication of Scottish banking.

Due to a chronic shortage of specie, Scottish banks had by 1750 encouraged the use of notes far further than in any other European country and had made of them the dominant element of the money supply. Adam Smith remarked that by the 1760s Scotland had new banking companies in virtually every consider-able town 'and even in some country villages'. Credit had always been available on the security of heritable landed property, but after the suspension of cash payments by banks in 1797, credit accounts for tenant-farmers became common. Fewer farmers pro-duced more food which sold at higher prices. The principal victims of radical reorganisation were those displaced from the land; the *Statistical Account* of Perth described their fate:

> The poor are very numerous. Some of the heritors maintain any who may be upon their estates. The great resort of the poor, from all parts of the country, is to Perth. Some of them make a shift, perhaps for

---

[1]   A boll was standardised at 10 stones or 140 lb by 1824. Prior to that date it varied by region and commodity.

3 years, to maintain themselves, and then when they fall into distress, or their cart horses die by which they gained their daily bread, they apply to the public for relief.

At least in the Lowlands there were expanding towns like Perth capable of absorbing displaced rural population, and the economic structure of farming was in the long run strengthened by the changes taking place. The Highlands were a very different story and perhaps a classic illustration of the inadequacy of any theory of economic growth which suggests that rational organisation and efficiently enforced property rights are by themselves adequate guarantees of long-term development. The lack of development in the Highlands was a matter for concern for bodies like the Commissioners for the Forfeited Annexed Estates and the Highland Society of London (established in 1775) long before 1800. Publicists like Dr James Anderson were arguing with passion in the 1770s and '80s that Highland development, especially in fisheries and the woollen manufacture, ought to be a priority. With the swing to internal colonisation after the loss of America, this view gained ground and the London Scot John Knox elaborated in several books a whole programme of improvements ranging from establishing towns to transport facilities such as the future Caledonian and Crinan canals. Gone was Adam Smith's cautious scepticism as to whether the Highlands could be successfully modernised on a commercial basis.

In 1786 'The British Society for extending the Fisheries and improving the Sea Coasts of this Kingdom' was founded in London, patronised by Highland magnates like the Duke of Argyll and Lowland lairds like George Dempster of Dunnichen. Contemporaries were very anxious to stop what they saw as an alarming wave of emigration which set in after 1770 when many tacksmen preferred to sell up and emigrate, with their dependants, rather than be continually rackrented. At least 12,000 left the Highlands between 1782 and 1802, despite bodies like the British Fisheries Society which tried to develop new fishing towns in the Highlands and Islands. Despite limited success at Tobermory in Mull, it was clear by 1806 that the Society was never going to effect a major economic transformation. To an aristocratic regime increasingly paranoid about social upheaval, the loss of 'simple', 'loyal', Highland peasant stock was an unfortunate development underlined by the obvious inability of the region after 1793 to produce the regiments it had supplied for previous wars. The fact that Highland regiments also had a distinguished tradition of mutiny stretching from 1743 to 1804 was conveniently forgotten in loud lamentations about the need to keep up Highland units with Lowland recruits.

But as the embodiment of the image of the 'Noble Savage' the Highlander marched on, for that image fed on a cult of the primitive and an optimism about the inherent moral potential of mankind that were pervasive in polite circles in Europe in the eighteenth century. That historian's abstraction known as the European Enlightenment contained many intellectual strands, some of which had been present in previous ages, and many of which were hardly consistent with one another. Alongside the cultivation of universal and classical values there went, in the later eighteenth century, a rising tide of enthusiasm for folk poetry. In the English-speaking world the best-remembered literary milestone along this latter road was the publication in 1765 of Thomas Percy's *Reliques of Ancient English Poetry*, with a dedication written by Dr Johnson which stressed that the poems were presented 'not as labours of art, but as effusions of nature, shewing the first efforts of ancient genius'. Dr Johnson was less impressed by a young Gaelic-speaking schoolmaster and tutor from Ruthven near Kingussie who had rocketed to fame several years before as the 'translator' of alleged Gaelic poems admired on similar grounds.

This was James Macpherson, a burly, sour and ambitious man from a family with strong Jacobite connections who secured introductions to leading literary figures in Edinburgh through another Gaelic-speaker, Professor Adam Ferguson. In June 1760 he published there a flimsy pamphlet, *Fragments of Ancient Poetry*, allegedly translated from Gaelic originals collected in the Highlands. Nothing better demonstrates the disintegration of social and moral structures in the Highlands than the career of

James 'Fingal' Macpherson, as impudent a rogue as the Celtic Twilight ever sent to plague Anglo-Saxon complacency before the rise of David Lloyd George in the twentieth century. He was encouraged by men like John Home, the clerical author of the now unreadable tragedy *Douglas*, who introduced him to an important future patron in the shape of Lord Bute, who was interested in Scottish culture and at the time of the introduction George III's leading minister. Above all, he was taken up by Reverend Doctor Hugh Blair, a literary critic panting for an ancient Scottish epic comparable to Homer's. His hopes that Macpherson could be the key to its rediscovery were shared by the Reverend Doctor Alexander 'Jupiter' Carlyle, not to mention David Hume and Principal Robertson. His fellow Gael Adam Ferguson talked with him in the early 1760s while agitating for a Scots militia. So, pressured by the expectations of friends, Macpherson foisted on the world what purported to be transla-tions of two ancient Gaelic epics by the poet Ossian, *Fingal, an Ancient Epic Poem, in Six Books* (London and Edinburgh, 1761), and *Temora, an Ancient Epic Poem, in Eight Books* (London, 1763). Though Macpherson did use some authentic Gaelic traditional materials, he fleshed these out with a mass of banality. By 1763 the two 'epics' had been translated into Italian and went on to be translated into most European tongues. To Macpherson the whole operation appears to have been primar-ily a means of gaining access to the patronage which would lift him from poverty and neglect to fame and fortune. Basically he was well aware of the way social and economic change was destroying his native culture, which added an edge of unscrupu-lousness to his attempt to seek consolation in the heart of the new English-speaking ascendancy in London. As he said: he hated John Bull but loved his daughters. Fornication and politi-cal mischief-making soon absorbed him.

Temora was too much for many even of his supporters. David Hume experienced grave doubts, while a strong school of opinion in London denounced Macpherson as a shameless forger, despite the stout defence of him mounted there by Tobias Smollet, nov-elist and a Lowlander who intermittently despaired of English willingness sincerely to embrace an additional British identity. Welsh and Irish historians were infuriated by Macpherson's arrogant dismissals of their own Celtic heritages. He brazened it out with all and sundry save the formidable Dr Johnson, who forced the pretentious Caledonian to crawl away from a literary dogfight with all the dignity of a well-beaten cur. The Highland Society of Edinburgh was still publishing an elaborate report on the Ossianic controversy in 1805, long after the real author of that bard's works had been laid, with great pomp, in 1796 in his grave in Westminster Abbey, near to the tomb of the irascible, and presumably rapidly rotating, Johnson. After 1765 Macpherson turned to history and politics, becoming an MP and plunging deep into the seamier aspects of imperial politics, from west Florida to India. He was at one stage London agent for the Nawab of Arcot, an Indian potentate whose debts and shark-like British creditors were one of the great contemporary scandals. He helped his kinsman, Sir John Macpherson, another ambiguous and privately alienated Gael, to shuffle his way into the position of Governor General of British India.

In Europe, Voltaire cackled with malevolent insight over the whole Ossian episode, but in France, Italy and Germany the impact of the Ossianic literature was widespread and profound, reaching writers of the stature of Goethe and Herder. Goethe's silly, mawkish early novel *Die Leiden des jungen Werthers* ('The Sorrows of Young Werther'), was deeply influenced by the 'Ossian' it carried with it as it swept Europe. Napoleon was an Ossianic enthusiast, while in America Thomas Jefferson rated that bard the greatest of all poets. Macpherson was always something of a wry commentator on contemporary social and intellectual appetites, succeeding because, pre-programmed by Blair, he gave people what they wanted. He eventually retired to a Highland estate which had belonged to the Macintoshes of Borlum. He had Robert Adam build his mansion, and derived satisfaction from making the local lairds treat his children, every one a bastard, as equals. It was worth doing so to get invitations to his parties. Macpherson was a good Highland landlord, eulogised in genuine Gaelic laments on his death. Self-hyping even

then, it was fitting he return in death to the international metropolis where so many displaced Scots of his time reinvented themselves or at least learned to play their roles, often with barely
suppressed irony, behind an acceptable mask, or masks.

Government action was directed mainly towards roads in the
Highlands. For half a century expenditure on military roads
there had been a recurring feature of the state budget, and the
mileage created by General Wade before the '45 was expanded
up to about 1,000 miles by his successors, but these were purely
military roads, useful to Bonnie Prince Charlie in 1745, but not
really designed to facilitate commercial intercourse, and the 800
miles or so of them still usable towards the end of the century
were increasingly dilapidated and neglected. The British
Fisheries Society employed as its surveyor Thomas Telford
(1757–1834), perhaps the greatest of all civil engineers. He had
started out a Scots apprentice mason in the service of the Duke
of Buccleuch, moving as building booms attracted him from
Edinburgh to London and then to Portsmouth Docks. The
patronage of Sir William Pulteney, who had been born a
Johnstone of Westerhall in Dumfriesshire and had changed his
name when he married the heiress to the Earl of Bath, helped to
make him surveyor of public works in Shropshire. Like the architect Robert Adam, Telford returned to Scotland with a reputation made outside it. In 1801 the Treasury commissioned him to
survey the potential for road, canal and fishery development in
the Highlands.

An Act of 1803 created a Commission, funded by public
money, 'for making Roads and building Bridges in the Highlands
of Scotland'. Under its aegis, with the Commission paying half
the cost and local heritors the other half, the modern road pattern
of the Highlands was laid down as 900 miles of road were created
between 1803 and 1821 and another 300 miles of road substan-
tially upgraded. Strategic bridges were a vital part of the achievement and their construction endorsed the insight of the
Commissioners for the Forfeited Annexed Estates, who had latterly directed their funds towards, among other objects, bridges.

In 1802 Telford recommended the construction of the

Caledonian Canal from Inverness to Fort William, along the line of the Great Glen. Opened belatedly in 1822 with a mere 12 feet of water in the cuts, 15 in the locks, it was a financial white elephant useful mainly for fishing boats. The Crinan Canal across the Mull of Kintyre opened in 1801 with a modest 10 foot depth, but by 1817 financial straits had placed it under the commissioners responsible for the Caledonian Canal. Though by 1750 some Highland lairds were said to have 'screwed their rents to an extravagant Height', the traditional agriculture of the Highlands simply could not compete with improved Lowland farming. Specialisation rather than general development attracted proprietors whose patriarchal qualities showed more in London ballrooms than on estates which they saw mainly as sources of rent.

Demand for wool and mutton was so buoyant around 1800 that Blackface and Cheviot stock sheep, managed by southern graziers, had already displaced black cattle as the main surplus Highland product south of the Great Glen, and as wool prices continued to soar extensive sheep farming spread inexorably into Inverness-shire, Ross-shire, Sutherland and the Hebridean islands. Extensive reorganisation of farming and tenurial relationships was essential to create big commercial sheep farms. Cleared from the interior, the old tenants were to be settled on small plots or crofts near the shore whence, as the surveyor who planned the much-resented reorganisation of Lord Macdonald's estates in Skye and North Uist around 1800 remarked, 'immense sums may be drawn, equal at least, if not passing, the produce of the soil'. The reference was to the kelp manufacture, a process of collecting and burning seaweed in simple kilns to produce an alkaline extract used in soap and glass manufacture. Kelp prices had been just over £2 a ton in the 1760s, soaring to about £10 a ton in the 1790s when the war cut off imports of Spanish barilla, the main rival industrial alkali, and briefly doubling thereafter. It was believed in the early 1800s that Hebridean landlords alone made a profit of £70,000 on an annual export of 15,000–20,000 tons of kelp.

Paying as they did a mere pittance to their labour force,

Highland landlords naturally tried to preserve and expand it. They supported the Passenger Vessels Act of 1803 which they hoped would obstruct emigration by raising shipping standards and therefore costs. Social constraints on early marriage were dissolved. Between 1801 and 1821 population soared by 20 per cent in Argyll, by 24 in Inverness-shire, by 29 in Caithness and by 22 in Ross and Cromarty. Kelp alone does not explain all this. Population rose in Skye, where kelping was less important, and in Shetland by 30 per cent, partly due to the stimulus of the labour-intensive 'haf fishery'.

Seen against this general background, the obsession of many historians with the clearances on one utterly atypical estate may appear deeply misleading. The ducal house of Sutherland was in the early nineteenth century the richest noble family in Britain. Elizabeth, Countess of Sutherland in her own right, married in 1785 the heir to the vast landed and industrial wealth of the Marquis of Stafford in the English Potteries. With over a million acres, comprising most of the county, the Sutherlands set out with the guidance of their principal man of business James Loch, a kinsman of the architect Adams of Blair Adam near Kinross, to transform Sutherland into a profitable, viable estate.

The programme was a variation on the standard one. The Sutherlands were mildly Whiggish in politics. Loch was an Edinburgh intellectual, a friend of Edinburgh Whigs like Henry Brougham and Henry Cockburn, and a devotee of Smithian political economy. His policies were more articulate than most. He even wrote a book in 1820, *An Account of the Improvements on the Estates of the Marquis of Stafford*, to defend them, but his policies were compounded of cocksure current dogmas. As his local enforcers of change, pushing landward tenants out to make way for sheep, and trying to compel people to be industrious crofters on the shores instead, two Morayshire capitalists William Young and Patrick Sellar became obnoxious to contemporaries and historians alike. As one local minister could see by 1818, the whole enterprise failed to create a more viable economy. It was not worth the cost to the landlords, nor the trauma to the people, but at least the Sutherland concept of development was not a reckless over-expansion of population and kelping. Like the Reverend T. R. Malthus, Loch had an obsession about the tendency for population to outgrow the means of subsistence.

Elsewhere, and especially in the Hebrides, the collapse of kelping before foreign imports and synthetic substitutes after 1820 led to new waves of clearance and emigration. By then Gaelic culture had been severely weakened, ironically just when a slightly more enlightened approach to the Gaelic language was becoming acceptable. The Society in Scotland for Propagating Christian Knowledge (the SSPCK) had been the body most concerned for education in the Gaelic Highlands after its founding in Edinburgh in 1709. Its subscribers established charity schools, aided by a small royal grant. It was a pioneer of more widespread literacy in the Highlands, but exclusively in English. Its mainly male pupils were taught in English and forbidden to use Gaelic between themselves. Though the thinly spread parochial schools in the Highlands were also exclusively anglophone, the SSPCK was not unswerving in its ban on the Gaelic language, especially when it produced a Gaelic New Testament in 1767 of which it printed 15,000 copies. The SSPCK went on to publish a Gaelic Old Testament in four parts between 1783 and 1801. It also from 1766 adopted a policy of teaching English through Gaelic. The result was greatly to facilitate the learning of English. Societies were set up in Edinburgh in 1811, Glasgow in 1812 and Inverness in 1818 to promote Gaelic schools, partly to increase readership for the Scriptures in Gaelic, but they also taught English. A complete Gaelic Bible was available in one volume from 1807. A revised edition of 1827 judged the text away from archaic classical Gaelic towards the vernacular but by then the language was retreating in border parishes in the Highlands, and though it survived strongly as a domestic tongue, it became disproportionately the language of women and of religion, especially religion in the passionately Evangelical revivalist form that was becoming widespread in the Highlands by 1825.

Gaelic-speakers wanted to learn English. That was a problem for those anxious to preserve Gaelic, as indeed it was to be for governments promoting a weakened Irish Gaelic tradition in the Irish Free State and Republic in the twentieth century. Despite, or perhaps partly because of, their strong sectarian and political motivation, they failed to reverse its decline. In the eighteenth-century Highlands there was still a big core of monoglots speaking no English and a distinct, if threatened, cadre of small lairds and tacksmen who were bilingual and who patronised poets. Though collected oral 'folksong' is fashionable and politically correct among modern academics, and was a significant element in Gaelic culture in the eighteenth century, what is striking is the continuity within change. The old hereditary professional bards using classical metres and an archaic vocabulary generally common to Scotland and Ireland, of whom the Mac Mhuirich family was the greatest example, were admittedly all gone by 1746. With the collapse of the bardic schools it was possible for two of the great poets of the new school, Donnchadh Bann and Robb Donn, to be non-literate, but many poets knew a good deal about their predecessors and were part of one of the oldest literary traditions in Europe. The classic case is the outstanding poet of the century, Alasdair Mac Mhaighstir Alasdair, the son of an Episcopal minister. While working for the SSPCK he produced in 1741 the first Gaelic dictionary in the shape of a Gaelic–English vocabulary. His work made him aware of the threat to his culture, producing a defensive reaction that carried him into active Jacobitism and Roman Catholicism. Despite the counter-productive impact of the failure of the '45, he went on to publish a collection of poems in 1751 that was the first book of secular poetry published in Gaelic. Even in adversity, Gaelic poets were innovative and dynamic.

Much the same happened to the musical culture of the Gael. The tradition of the professional harpers or clarsairs, playing the small wire-strung (as distinct from gut-strung) harp and employed by chiefs, was in decline after about 1750. It was to revive much later under very different circumstances. The hereditary piping dynasties such as the MacCrimmons, who served Macleod of Macleod, found themselves in the same position as their 'kindly' tenancies given in exchange for their music were converted to cash rents which were then relentlessly raised. Emigration to America was not unheard of in these cases. Piping itself fared rather better, though at the cost of much misunderstanding of the nature of the Scottish achievement on the bagpipes, an instrument which far from being uniquely Scottish can be found all over Europe. Like 'Highland dress', the bagpipes became part of the Scottish national identity forged by romantic culture in the first half of the nineteenth century, greatly assisted by the popularity of British army pipers, and formal competitions organised by the Highland Societies of London and Scotland in this period. Under acute Ossianic influence a great deal of nonsense was spouted about the spontaneous simplicity and wildness of the ancient music of the hills, when in fact *ceòl mòr*, the classical music of the pipes, was not rude and ancient but an extremely sophisticated and evolving art form. It was better that some of the great achievements of Gaelic culture should survive, even on other peoples' terms, rather than perish.

The fact was that all Scottish landlords, Highland and Lowland, were becoming dependent on the changing pattern of demand generated by a new industrial society, a society that ultimately was to undermine the political ascendancy of the landed classes, but without whose buoyant demand the latter could scarcely have weathered the huge burden of war taxation between 1793 and 1815. Industrialisation in Scotland in this period was undoubtedly textile-led, though other non-agricultural activities such as coal mining also throve. Heavy investment in machinery in the linen trade, the first spectacular growth area in Scottish textiles, was long confined to the finishing stages of manufacture, so for several decades industrial growth was closely linked with dispersed cottage industry.

The spread of mechanisation, because initially it was dependent on good water-power sites, did not at first break this pattern of interwoven industrial and agricultural developments. Vertically mounted, water-powered, four-bladed rotors were invented to scutch flax by breaking the woody parts of its stem prior to their removal by heckling or combing, and by 1772 there were 252 of these lint mills in Scotland. Much more significant was the opening in 1788–9 of the first water-powered roller spinning mill for linen yarn in Scotland, at Brigton in Angus. By 1760, with the general adoption of the 'flying shuttle', one hand loom weaver needed five or six hand spinners to supply him. Now the spinning bottleneck was broken. Already linen had totally outstripped the traditional Scottish woollen manufacture, though a small commercial woollen trade survived in Clackmannan, Stirlingshire and Aberdeenshire, and woollen tweed manufacture was by 1800 expanding in Border towns like Jedburgh, Hawick and Galashiels. However, the scale of linen manufacture may be judged by the fact that in 1778 there were 4,000 linen looms in and around Glasgow, as well as another 1,360 in nearby Paisley. Dundee at that time had some 2,000 linen looms weaving mainly coarser fabrics.

The truly explosive growth sector in Scottish textiles after 1780 was cotton. The first cotton-spinning mill was set up at Penicuik in 1779, followed by one at Rothesay in 1780. By 1834 there were 134 cotton mills in Scotland and apart from some big ones in Aberdeen and one at Stanley on the Tay near Perth, they were almost all in Glasgow or within a 25-mile radius of that city. Great noblemen like the Duke of Atholl, landlord of Stanley, tended merely to lease land to cotton spinners, but lesser lairds were often active partners in cotton mills, as were Clydeside West India merchants, who imported the original sea-island long-staple cotton. By 1812 Sir John Sinclair believed that the Scottish cotton industry employed 151,300 people, many working in their own homes, and was producing £6,200,000 of output per annum.

Mechanising the delicate weaving process proved more difficult. Indeed, steam power was applied to spinning long before mechanical weaving became practical. Urbanisation of industry was the inevitable consequence of the coming of steam power, however incompletely. There were, of course, exceptions such as the Scottish paper industry which remained in rural surroundings, albeit usually near places like Aberdeen, Glasgow and Edinburgh whose demand helped it to grow from 9 per cent of UK output in 1800 to 22 per cent in 1850. Few manufacturers needed so many millions of gallons of water as paper makers.

The not-very-efficient Savery and Newcomen pumping

engines developed in England had been slowly adopted by Scots mines for drainage work. Only with the invention of the separate condenser by the young Glasgow instrument maker James Watt was the efficiency of the steam engine dramatically increased. Watt's breakthrough seems to have owed less to the academic theories of his Glasgow mentors, such as Professor Joseph Black, than to patient empirical experiment, both in Scotland and in Birmingham, where Watt went into partnership with the English industrialist Matthew Boulton. To Watt's separate condenser were added a centrifugal governor and a device furnishing rotary motion. Though widely used in mines, the despatch of Boulton and Watt engines, in small numbers, to Scottish textile mills in the 1780s and 1790s was most significant. When Watt's patents expired after 1800, the manufacture of improved engines became widely dispersed throughout Scottish foundries, and the early 1820s in particular saw a surge in the rate of installation of engines in urban works.

One consequence was an additional stimulus to the rise in coal prices which were already soaring under pressure of domestic and industrial demand. Between 1790 and 1795 coal in Glasgow went from 5s. 5d. to 10s. 10d. a bag. After 1780 there was a boom in coal mining, with rapid growth of the waggonway systems along whose wooden rails horses pulled coal trucks to navigable water. Despite their servile status, men faceworkers in the pits doubled their wages between 1715 and 1785, and more than doubled them again by 1808. By 1799 collier and salter bondage had been abolished, to encourage cheap labour to flood into the pits.

Close connections with England, and marginal but decisive cost advantages, explain a great deal of Scottish industrial growth around 1800, but the Scottish iron industry is rather an exception. Had not transport costs protected its domestic market from Welsh competition, it would almost certainly have been in dire trouble. Eric Svedenstierna, a Swedish official who visited Britain in 1802–3 and toured the major Scottish ironworks, has left an account of them. He visited the Wilsontown works in Lanarkshire wholly owned by John Wilson of London.

Svedenstierna could see that it was the scale of production of iron and steel spades mainly from scrap metal which made the Cramond works outside Edinburgh so competitive, but he could also see that David Mushet (1772–1847), the foundry manager at Calder Iron works near Glasgow who in 1801 identified huge native resources of black-band ironstone in central Scotland, was congenitally incapable of the precise costing needed for commercial success. Svedenstierna could not see as clearly as historians can in retrospect that the under-capitalised Scottish ironworks were desperately dependent on war demand. Carron works was founded during the Seven Years War, Wilsontown during the American war, and four more just before and four during the Revolutionary and Napoleonic wars. By 1820 overcapacity was an acute problem.

Only in the chemical industry can it be convincingly argued that the academic teaching of science in Scotland was a necessary though not of course by itself a sufficient cause of early nineteenth-century industrial growth. The textile industry's need for bleaching agents more efficient than sunshine and sour milk led to the establishment of the Prestonpans sulphuric acid works in 1749. By 1815 a dozen or so establishments around Edinburgh and Glasgow were producing the acid. Its commercial use had been publicised by the lectures and writing of academics like Dr Francis Home (1719–1803) of Edinburgh. Key entrepreneurs had usually learned the indispensable minimum of chemistry at lectures in Scottish university medical schools. However, it was with Charles Tennant's success in taming the new gas chlorine by combining it with lime to produce bleaching powder that Scottish chemical manufactures really made the decisive leap forward.

Tennant established the St Rollox Works in Glasgow near the Monkland Canal. By 1830 the works covered 10 acres and produced bleaching powder, sulphuric acid, soaps and industrial alkali. Though patented by Tennant, the chlorine powder had actually been invented by Charles Macintosh, son of a dyestuff manufacturer. Charles joined the Glasgow University Chemical Society which had been founded under the inspiration of

Dr William Irvine, who held conjoint lectureships in Chemistry and *Materia Medica* between 1769 and 1787. Several other members joined Macintosh in his first independent venture – the manufacture of the mordant required to 'fix' textile dyes, from aluminous shales in Renfrewshire near Paisley.

In what was undoubtedly a bonanza atmosphere around 1800, the chemical industry inevitably spawned eccentrics like the ninth Earl of Dundonald who tried to repair a ravaged family fortune by distilling coal tar, pioneering gas lighting, synthesising salt and industrial alkali, and even manufacturing cheap bread from potatoes. Financially, if not chemically, he was a failure, but he had his revenge on respectable mediocrity with his son Thomas, Lord Cochrane, later tenth Earl of Dundonald. Inventor, swashbuckling admiral and pugnacious Whig MP, Lord Cochrane went off to be a hero of Latin American independence after being convicted in 1814 of participation in a stock-exchange swindle. He was almost certainly rightly exonerated later. His villainous uncle Andrew Cochrane-Johnstone seems to have misled and manipulated him.

Any country producing members of the ruling class like the Cochranes was unstable as well as vital. The Britain of which Scotland was a part was moving along a path of inflation, growth and cyclical economic instability. Between 1780 and 1815 urban and agricultural wages were said to have grown two and a half to three times. Generalisation is misleading, but that increase rather outstripped the overall rise in food costs. However, there were many less fortunate, as well as the fortunate. Between January 1799 and April 1800 Edinburgh meal prices went from a shilling a peck (one sixteenth of a boll or about 9 lb) to 3s. 7d. – a 358 per cent price rise in fifteen months. Meal riots were, hardly surprisingly, endemic in Scottish burghs between 1783 and 1813. Industrial strike action was not unknown, especially among weavers and seamen. The Commander-in-Chief Scotland, Lord Adam Gordon, was clear that riots in Ross and Sutherland in 1792 proceeded not from political radicalism, but well-founded fear of expulsion in favour of sheep. Even the isolated Highland tenants whom the eighth Earl of Selkirk

(1771–1820) considered ground down by greedy landlords and ruthless factors, to the point where he encouraged them to emigrate to Canada, did occasionally riot against clearances.

Selkirk is an interesting example of a radical Scots Whig who could see that the Dundas ascendancy and in particular the Highland landlords who had such an important part in it were generating precisely that social upheaval in and emigration from the Highlands that they so disliked and tried to check by restrictive legislation such as the Passenger Vessel Act of 1803. Like his father, Selkirk campaigned relentlessly against the scandal of government manipulation of Scottish Representative Peer elections. His campaign for reform achieved little except his own election. Experience of corrupt and aggressive demagogic politics in both France and the United States dulled his originally quasi-republican populist enthusiasms. He became an exponent of the need for a mobilised but hierarchic society to defend traditional British values against both the French and the Americans. Impressive in stature and with serviceable Gaelic, this red-haired Lowlander enraged the political establishment by buying Canadian land and encouraging the emigration they detested.

He started by talking with people like Father Alexander MacDonnell, the chaplain to the Glengarry fencible regiment, who was trying to secure government assistance for his people to emigrate. In the end Selkirk lost a lot of money by buying land, Hudson's Bay Company stock (for he needed the Company's cooperation in his settlement schemes), and above all in developing the first significant Canadian settlement in the west in the Red River area, against considerable opposition from the rival North West Company. The two companies amalgamated in 1821. Both had disproportionately Scottish personnel, but being fur traders they had no real enthusiasm for settlers. Selkirk remains an important figure in Canadian history, not least by helping ensure Canada survived in the face of rampant American imperialism greatly encouraged by the sell-out peace of 1783 to think that the usual combination of manipulative whining and threats might persuade Westminster to give up even more in North America for nothing but the usual insincere assurances about 'reconciliation'. In Scotland his activities underlined the unwelcome truth that despite a surge of government expenditure after 1803 on public works in the Highlands specifically designed to stabilise population there, it was in the nature of the conservative Dundas system to dig its own grave by creating runaway levels of social change.

The lower orders looked back to a patriarchalism their betters preached but with the odd exception like Selkirk did not practice. In 1812 Glasgow weavers did secure a court ruling that the local JPs had a statutory duty to fix adequate wages. The JPs refused to enforce the wages they set at a time of falling wage rates, and secured repeal of the relevant legislation in 1813. A massive weavers' strike in the western Lowlands in 1812–13 failed completely. The ability of the ruling groups to force the principal victims of change to pay much of the price for it remained, as did the self-righteousness of the propertied. Paranoia, however, could move the propertied classes not only to mindless resistance, but also to contemplating the need for a degree of timely change before social tensions reached explosive levels. Quite vitally, the propertied classes were divided, with more and more of them not within the very narrow ranks of the landed and urban patrician elites who manned the ramparts of the old order. Above all, the scale of mobilisation and government expenditure was bound to plummet on the outbreak of peace. Scotland had experienced dramatic agricultural change and decisive industrial change and urbanisation between 1792 and 1815 in a context of heightened protectionism due to the choking off of many import trades, and what modern economists would call turboprop Keynsian economics, due to a huge government input into the economy.

In 1789 there were 40,000 men in the British army. By 1814 there were a quarter of a million. The Royal Navy went from 16,000 in 1789 to 140,000 in 1812. Supplementing these men there was a vast structure of half a million or so men organised in part-time or volunteer units used mainly for home defence. Over 800,000 mobilised men could not be sustained for any longer than was strictly necessary, and nor could the cost of the massive wartime government orders for food, goods and services continue to be funded. Traumatic deflation was bound to accompany peace. War had been good to many. It had enabled the Carron Iron Founding and Shipping Company, whose works were near Falkirk, to find a market for the carronade, a very short light carriage gun firing a heavy shot with a light propellant charge for use as a 'smasher' at short range. Introduced in 1799 as a supplement to main ship armaments, it did not count in the number of guns determining the 'rate' of a Royal Navy warship until 1817, but it was sold in large quantities to both merchantmen and warships between 1799 and 1815. Not far across the Forth from Carron Ironworks lay the estate of Tulliallan, bought by Admiral George Keith Elphinstone, Lord Elphinstone, in 1800. He was a great fleet organiser who never won a major fleet action but who was central to British naval achievement in the Napoleonic wars, and the Royal Navy's greatest exponent of amphibious operations, as he showed in the successful invasions of Egypt and the strategically vital Dutch colony at the Cape of Good Hope.

Elphinstone made more than £100,000 in prize money alone, supplemented eventually by a full admiral's salary. In 1754 his family had been reduced to selling its sixteenth-century ancestral tower house on the south side of the Forth directly opposite Tulliallan to the earls of Dunmore. Their Georgian castellated mansion of 1820–5 is long ruined, but in one of its walled gardens still stands The Pineapple, built in 1761, an astonishing stone show-off garden pavilion in the shape of the fruit. By 1820 the Dunmores were outshone, not just by Lord Elphinstone's accumulation of estates in several Scottish counties but also by the huge, symmetrical but somewhat whimsical neo-Gothic castellated mansion built at Tulliallan for him between 1817 and 1820 to the designs of William Atkinson. It eventually was to become the Scottish Police College. Elphinstone could well afford to contribute to the development of the nearby small port of Kincardine, and to land reclamation on the shore.

So much did his Highland and Lowland clients benefit from the regime of Henry Dundas that they honoured him like a deceased

Roman emperor. He had a country house at Dunira near Comrie where he mostly lived after retirement. In 1812, the year after his death, there was raised a couple of miles to the east of Dunira, on the 840 foot knoll of Dun More in Glen Lednock, a massive masonry memorial column just north of the Highland Line. Also, between 1821 and 1828 in Edinburgh a Dundas doric memorial column was erected in St Andrew's (later St Andrew) Square. It was modelled on Trajan's Column in Rome and crowned by Dundas's effigy. The only objection came from local householders who worried that the 136 foot column might fall on them, so architect William Burn was advised by the lighthouse specialist Robert Stevenson over the foundations. Ironically, by 1828 social, economic and political tensions had risen to a pitch which ensured that the foundations of the political ascendancy Henry Dundas had built and his son sustained were much shakier than those of his Highland and Lowland monuments.

8

The Last Hurrahs of the Old Regime 1815–1827

The celebrations in Edinburgh that marked the overthrow of Napoleon in 1814 and in 1815 (after his attempt to return in 'the hundred days') were the first of two public last hurrahs for those who hoped that spontaneous patriotic or loyal enthusiasm could be manipulated to help underpin the existing social and political order in Scotland. The other was the cultural circus accompanying the visit of George IV in 1822. The patriotism these celebrations encouraged had a very strong Scottish tone. Tartan tokens were encouraged. Among the artists and literary figures who jumped at a chance for self-advertisement in the celebrations were Alexander Nasmyth, a major landscape artist who designed illuminations for the occasion, and James Hogg. Hogg, the largely self-educated 'Ettrick Shepherd', was, with the help of patronage from Walter Scott and the Duchess of Buccleuch, busy reinventing himself as a literary original and exponent of the Gothic supernatural tale, which fitted with the tone of the novel that was to be his masterpiece, *Confessions of a Justified Sinner* (1824), which in many ways prefigures Robert Louis Stevenson's parable on the complexities of identity, *Dr Jekyll and Mr Hyde* (1886). Scottish identity was a major theme of the 1814–15 and 1822 celebrations. The attempt to reduce Scotland and England to North and South Britain, explicit in the Act of Union of 1707, had at the level of nomenclature failed, less because the Scottish ruling class rejected North Britain than because their English equivalents simply could not swallow South Britain.

The incorporation of the Loyal and Brave Highlander into officially countenanced mythology was so complete that the white cockade of the Jacobites was worn in Edinburgh as a symbol of the white lilies of royalist France in celebration of the return to their throne of the exiled Bourbons (who had recently lived in Edinburgh in Holyrood Palace). The Bourbons owed much to the Black Watch (the 42nd Regiment of Foot) who had fought heroically throughout the Napoleonic Wars from Egypt under Sir Ralph Abercromby; to Corunna in Spain in 1809 under another famous Scottish name, Sir John Moore; to the final climacteric of Waterloo where they fought under that long-nosed Irishman driven by his cult of Duty to the Crown, the Duke of Wellington. Savagely pounded by Marshal Ney's cuirassiers at the battle of Quatre Bras two days before, the Black Watch did not bear a prominent role at Waterloo, but they lined the hedges through which the Scots Greys galloped in a famous and destructive charge, encouraged as they went by the Black Watch shouting, 'Scotland for Ever!'

Nobody embodied the Scottish cultural cross-currents of the period in more intriguing form than the man who arranged a dinner for the Black Watch in the Assembly Rooms after their triumphant return to post-war Edinburgh. That man was Walter Scott, who had on 7 July 1814 published anonymously and hugely successfully his first novel *Waverley* with its Jacobite theme. Hogg was subsequently to publish his own *Jacobite Relics of Scotland*. Scott has been perceptively described as 'a great novelist with a weak aesthetic conscience'. He had been willing to acknowledge his authorship of poetry but the anonymity with which he masked his relationship with *Waverley* was an expression of a deep-seated doubt whether scribbling novels was compatible with the dignity of a landed gentleman or a man of business.[1] Yet *Waverley* is a great novel and a milestone both in Scott's personal career, and in the history of world literature. That the novel is about the '45, the last Jacobite rising in Scotland, does not render it in any way

---

[1] He first publicly acknowledged his authorship of the novels as late as 1827.

parochial, for like all the greatest of Scott's novels it is essentially a study of social and ideological conflict, as reflected in the dramatised lives of specific individuals. On the other hand, the Scottish context was quite vital for Scott to find full scope for both his enormous antiquarian erudition, and for the perhaps not always fully articulate tensions and contradictions within his personality which gave urgency and complexity to the major themes of the work. The idea of exploiting national characteristics and traits in dramatised prose was something Scott always generously admitted he had derived from a study of the work of his friend the Irish novelist Maria Edgeworth, whose first novel *Castle Rackrent* had appeared in 1800.

Scott produced the less successful novel *Guy Mannering* in 1815. In 1816 he published the first two titles in his 'Tales of my Landlord' series, *The Black Dwarf* and *Old Mortality*. His writing underlines the extent to which man was for him a social animal. *Old Mortality* is one of his greatest books, while the tale of the misanthrope dwarf is a disaster. He returned to the Jacobites again in 1818 with *Rob Roy*, producing also in the same year his most ambitious novel *The Heart of Midlothian*. The year 1819 saw *The Bride of Lammermoor*, his most overtly political novel in which the Whigs are the villains of the piece, and *A Legend of Montrose*. By 1820 *Ivanhoe*, a 'rattling good yarn', skilful and lively but stuffed with clichés and pseudo-medieval nonsense, gave warning of worse to come, though as late as 1824 in *Redgauntlet* he could revert to his most impressive vein. Written usually in three volumes (of which the third was often blatantly padded to reach the required length), the novels were sold in quite unprecedented numbers to a predominantly middle-class market. The three small duodecimo volumes of *Waverley*, for example, were priced at a guinea (21 shillings) and the first thousand went in under a week.

In itself the market for the forty-odd novels Scott produced was an irony. Scott, the arch-Tory despiser of the bourgeois virtues of thrift and caution, made his money out of the bourgeoisie. Then there was the additional irony that by his achievements in both verse and prose Scott was seen in retrospect as a

Father of European Romanticism. The very term Romantic is so imprecise as to create doubts about its usefulness, but in practice it is one of those unsatisfactory terms which must be used because to eschew it would be to commit the folly of refusing to recognise a major shift or series of shifts in the sensibility of modern man. Romantic literature sprang from the new liberal, secular view of man evolved mainly in pre-Revolutionary and Revolutionary France, though it could derive inspiration as much from revulsion against the implications of that view as from sympathy with it. Above all, Romanticism shifted the emphasis from man as a social being to man as an individual, man wrestling with his emotions, be they in his own heart or the result of communion with nature. Naturally Romantic writers were attracted by extreme forms of emotional experience. None of this fits Scott. So uninterested was he in depicting the raw emotion of sexual attraction that a reconciliation between a hero and a (usually insipid) heroine in his pages almost invariably symbolises a compromise between major historical processes. Although Scott repeatedly called himself an 'incorrigible Jacobite', there is precious little savouring of maudlin emotion for its own sake in his major Jacobite novels. They are extraordinarily sensible, fair and balanced. They shame the appalling excesses of those nineteenth-century Romantic propagandists in the American South or Nationalist Ireland who thought of themselves as literary disciples of 'the Wizard of the North'. They expressed their extremism in a parody of Scott's 'big Bow-Wow strain', but their simplistic and intolerant outlook in no way reflected his complex response to the concept of nationality.

Scott was an eighteenth-century man in terms of his formal values. Extremists in his works all die or retire into monasteries or convents. It is always the reasonable man in the middle, who can see both points of view, who survives, and survival is implicitly recognised as a major virtue. It is true that Scott is emancipated from one major delusion of the neo-classical Augustan school of literature which dominated the eighteenth century. He could see that no society could claim final validity for its culture or standards, and that cultures change over time, creating different psychological types in different generations. He admired the feudal virtues of loyalty and panache, but he dreaded the tradition of anarchic violence which he thought accompanied them. For him the defeat of the Jacobites, with all the traditional virtues of which some of them were capable, was inevitable, and the triumph of the house of Hanover was right and a step forward in human history. Ardent supporter of the Act of Union that he was, Scott jumped at the chance to express his Toryism, his monarchism and his Unionism, as well as his antiquarianism, by stage-managing the visit that George IV paid to Edinburgh in a typical foggy, wet and windy Scottish August in 1822. The former Prince Regent had lost none of his zest for expensive and exotic clothing, buying no less than £1,354 18s. worth of Highland dress and accoutrements for the trip. The second Viscount Melville, who had been strongly in favour of the visit, was, like Scott, quite delighted at its success in countering the spread of radical ideas by evoking 'determined and deep rooted monarchical feeling'.

Yet the visit also obviously evoked a heightened sense of Scottish identity on the part of all participants. Had this not been so, it is difficult to see why George IV bothered to drape his portly figure in the kilt, or why his millionaire crony and companion Sir William Curtis did the same, even if the pink pantaloons worn underneath the kilt rather spoiled the total effect. There was a heavy stress throughout the proceedings on the Highlands, with what were assumed to be their traditions of clanship and loyalty. Sir Walter, who had been instrumental in restoring to the light of day the long-mislaid Honours of Scotland (the Scottish crown jewels), even arranged a royal procession from Holyrood to Edinburgh Castle along the Royal Mile 'for the purpose of calling up, as exactly as might be, the time-hallowed observance of "the Riding of the Parliament"'. Given that one of the objections raised in 1780 to the proposal to establish a Society of Antiquaries in Scotland had been that it was not 'consistent with political wisdom, to call the attention of the Scots to the ancient honours and constitution of their independent Monarchy', times had clearly changed. Or had they?

Partly, the explanation for this heightened sense of Scottishness was the way in which Scottish national characteristics had ceased to constitute a serious political problem and had become, with changing artistic fashions, a source of visual or literary stimulus. Scott's novels were the best example of this, but a similar trend can easily be discerned in the visual arts. Sir Walter's baronetcy had been the first creation of the reign of George IV who, with all his faults, was a munificent and discerning patron of the arts who sincerely admired Scott's work and who had commissioned a portrait of the novelist by Sir Thomas Lawrence, the greatest painter-diplomat that Europe had seen since Rubens in the seventeenth century, for the great gallery of Windsor Castle. Also present in court dress at Holyrood House when George IV held court there as the first Hanoverian monarch ever to do so was the painter David Wilkie. A good friend of Sir Walter Scott and an artist whose use of Scottish materials offers parallels with Scott's literary career, he was the third son of the Reverend David Wilkie, Minister of Cults, a parish on the River Eden in Fife.

Wilkie was a product of the Drawing Academy set up in Edinburgh in 1798 under the auspices of the Board of Trustees for Manufactures and Fisheries in Scotland and taught mainly by the history painter John Graham. Previous Scottish academies of fine art such as the Academy of St Luke in Edinburgh between 1729 and 1731, or the Foulis Academy in Glasgow between 1753 and 1775, had been financially unstable and had failed to establish a tradition. Graham, though working on a shoestring, proved a great teacher, producing among his earliest students David Wilkie and William Allan and in the years up to his death in 1817 a remarkable percentage of the main names in Scottish art in the next generation. Wilkie was a more than competent portrait painter but he made his name as 'the Scottish Teniers' which implied, correctly, that he had much in common with the Dutch and Flemish genre painters of the seventeenth century. He attracted the attention of his first aristocratic patron, Lord Mansfield, with his picture of *Pitlessie Fair* and despite his poor health and shy manner he went on to a glittering career which progressed through an acquaintance with the Prince Regent, for whom he painted *Blind-Man's-Buff*, one of his best-composed genre pieces, to the companion piece *Penny Wedding*, completed in 1819 when George IV was already on the throne. By 1822 it was Wilkie who was chosen to record the royal junketings in Edinburgh in a canvas only finished much later, *The King's Entry into Holyrood*, which finds a prominent place for Walter Scott. Limner to the King for Scotland from 1823, Wilkie became in 1830 'Principal Painter in Ordinary to the King' in England and was so close to the Tory leadership (Sir Robert Peel was a personal friend) that it was considered a mark of grace on the part of a Whig administration to sponsor his knighthood at the hands of William IV in 1836.

Wilkie resented being categorised as merely a genre painter. He could present spectacularly an iconic vision of a state occasion like the King's jaunt to Edinburgh. Equally, he could commemorate the battle of Waterloo in a picture of Chelsea Pensioners receiving the news of the victory, a subtle device reminding one of the fleeting nature of all reality and especially of violent reality. Yet this was the picture Wellington bought, albeit in cash so that, as he said, his banker would not know what a damn fool he was. Wilkie's attitude to the fast-fading distinctively Scottish peasant society which he loved to paint is therefore significant. Scott had precious little sensibility in the field of painting, but in the Scots dialect of the peasant dialogues in his novels he was doing exactly the same – trying to render permanent by his art something vanishing swiftly before his eyes. This sense of loss was very widespread in articulate circles in Scotland. Mrs Grant of Laggan, writing from Edinburgh to a friend in Glasgow in 1812, remarked how profoundly anglicised Edinburgh was as compared with Glasgow, and then added that 'our spoken nationality decays so fast, that I feel a kind of pain at its departure'. Despite Scott's lack of discrimination in the pictures on his dining room walls at Abbotsford, he was important in involving artists in the task of fixing images of the Scottish past. William Allan is a good example. Returning from an extended stay in Russia in 1814, Allan was all set for a career as a painter of exotic subjects, producing fascinating canvases full of Circassian princes and captives, not to mention Turkish bashaws. However, he was employed by the publisher Constable to illustrate Scott's novels when they were issued as a set in 1820 and, encouraged by Scott and Wilkie, he developed into a history painter specialising in Scottish topics like *The Murder of Archbishop Sharpe* or *Knox Admonishing Mary Queen of Scots*. He never abandoned his exotic interests but when in the 1840s he turned to battle scenes *Prestonpans*, the Jacobite victory of 1745, preceded *Waterloo*, and he died with *Bannockburn* unfinished in his studio.

Incomparably the best example of linkages between literary and pictorial artists in the common endeavour to preserve lively images of a way of life clearly threatened with extinction was the novelist John Galt (1779–1839), who began to write in 1813 a book which eventually appeared in 1821 as *Annals of the Parish*. What makes him such a good example is his self-consciousness. After seeing Wilkie's *Village Politicians* and *Blind Fiddler* at a Royal Academy exhibition in London, Galt had written to Wilkie on 12 May 1807 virtually associating himself with a campaign to delineate the traditional Scottish peasant world before it altogether vanished.

Born in Irvine in Ayrshire, Galt was brought up after the age of ten in the busy port of Greenock, where his father was in the West India trade. Educated for a commercial career, Galt moved to London in 1804, seeking wider opportunities of which he singularly failed to take advantage, for he failed miserably and repeatedly in business. He survived by becoming a successful hack writer, using numerous pseudonyms. Another venture into business as the Gibraltar agent for the great Glasgow merchant Kirkman Finlay, who maintained an elaborate organisation for smuggling British goods into Europe past Napoleon's attempt to exclude them by his Continental System, necessarily came to an end with the war. Only as a writer was Galt ever much of an entrepreneur, but it was his good luck in 1819 to establish a special relationship with one of Scotland's most enterprising publishers – William Blackwood. Like that other thrusting Tory publisher Archibald Constable, who produced the *Quarterly*

Review, Blackwood went into periodical publication with *Blackwood's Magazine* in 1817, partly as a counterweight to the appearance that year of the pro-reform newspaper *The Scotsman*. By 1819 Galt was contributing regularly to *Blackwood's*, and indeed a series of connected articles he started to produce for it grew into a major novel, *The Ayrshire Legatees*. In 1821, when Galt was entrenched at the heart of the Tory reaction, *Annals of the Parish* deservedly made his literary name for him. The next two years saw a burst of high-level creativity such as Galt never again matched and which gave to the world books such as *The Provost, The Entail*, and *Ringan Gilhaize*.

As late as 1832, Galt produced an important political novel, *The Member*, based on his characteristically unsuccessful experiences when he was employed by the directors of the Edinburgh and Glasgow Union Canal to lobby at Westminster on behalf of a bill which was to have empowered them to raise more funds. Like Scott, Galt's supreme ambition was to live the life of a country gentleman, an ambition all the more tantalising in that he actually achieved it temporarily in the 1820s in Canada as the resident agent of a predictably unsound Canadian land development company. However, it is the achievement represented by the six novels in Ayrshire Scots which Blackwood kept in print for a hundred years as 'The Works of John Galt' which has left an enduring mark on Scottish letters. The free use of dialect rather shocked the Edinburgh literati, not excluding Walter Scott who found some of Galt's language 'vulgar'. *The Last of the Lairds*, a not altogether successful novel which Galt published in 1826, was thoroughly bowdlerised by Dr D. M. Moir, at Blackwood's request, before publication. The original text only appeared in print as late as 1976.

Henry Mackenzie, by sheer longevity, survived to be puzzled by the new acceptability of all things Scots. He claimed that he could not even understand the language spoken by Galt's characters. Mackenzie had not moved with the times. Scottish national consciousness symbolised by the broadswords of Jacobite gentlemen as late as 1746 had threatened the status quo. Tamed, provincialised and apparently fading, a vernacular culture could in 1820 be used to buttress the status quo. Galt's half-remembered, half-invented Irvine was a stable hierarchy, threatened by radical influences from outside, but ultimately unshakeable under shrewd, pawky Tory leadership. Not for nothing had a Mr Brown of Dundee so commended himself to Henry Dundas in the 1790s by an anti-reform pamphlet archly entitled *Look before Ye Loup*, that Dundas promptly made him editor of a new government-sponsored newspaper entitled the *Patriot's Weekly Chronicle*. The first decades of the nineteenth century were in fact the period when Carolina Oliphant, a retiring member of Sir Walter Scott's Edinburgh social circle, wrote many of the 'traditional' Jacobite ballads like 'Wi' a hundred pipers' or 'Will ye no come back again'. They were sung with approval in circles devoid of a flicker of disloyalty to the house of Hanover. Indeed in 1822, on the occasion of the visit to Holyrood duly recorded by Wilkie, George IV was presented with a petition drawn up by Sir Walter Scott praying him to restore the titles of attainted Jacobite families which, unlike their estates, had not been returned, and it was the granting of this request by legislation of 1824 which turned Carolina Oliphant or Nairne into Lady Nairne, when her husband Major Nairne, an Irish Assistant Inspector of Barracks, became Lord Nairne.

A logical corollary of this change in the attitude of the ruling elite towards Scottish culture was a new attitude towards the Scottish past. The old distrust of Scottish history, the feeling that it should be discountenanced 'for fear of awakening the Old National Grudge, that should now be sopited and industriously forgotten', as Francis Pringle the Professor of Greek in St Andrews said in 1736, had long passed. Principal Robertson had found Scottish history a convenient vehicle for the launching of his career, though he jettisoned it with his usual urbane egotism when he wished to become an international celebrity. Robertson had little time for emotionalism. He even thought Burke's *Reflections on the French Revolution* excessively emotion-charged. By 1790, when the *Reflections* appeared, Robertson was out of step with official opinion. Sir Walter Scott believed that there was strong practical utility in studying the continuity of the Scottish historical past. With his prodigious energy and zest in the tradition of convivial clubmanship which was so central to the eighteenth-century Edinburgh social and intellectual scene, Walter Scott was able to institutionalise his concern for the Scottish past by being instrumental in the foundation in 1823 of the first of the Scottish historical publishing clubs, the Bannatyne Club.

Scott was not, of course, conjuring new forces into creation when he helped to found the Bannatyne. There had always been a strong antiquarian tradition already several centuries old running alongside the grand 'philosophical history' tradition of the eighteenth century. Writers like David Hume simply assumed that human nature and indeed human society, in every aspect save the purely technological, were essentially unchanging. As Hume put it in his *Enquiry Concerning Human Understanding*, 'The same motives always produce the same actions, the same events follow from the same causes'. The antiquarian tradition was far readier to study the past on its own terms, and as a result had a vastly great interest in the study of primary sources. It was scholars in the antiquarian tradition like Thomas Innes and James Anderson who had by 1740 introduced all that was best in European developments in palaeography and diplomatics into the stream of Scottish scholarship. It is no accident that Scott gives a sympathetic if humorous portrait of the old scholar Jonathan Oldbuck, the eponymous hero of *The Antiquary*. However, in the work of Sir David Dalrymple, Lord Hailes, a law lord who lived from 1726 to 1792, the purely antiquarian and the more philosophical traditions in Scottish historiography came together in a fashion which enabled Walter Scott to describe Hailes as 'the father of national history'. The principal work produced by Hailes was his *Annals of Scotland from the Accession of Malcolm Canmore*, in which, as well as in a number of tracts originally published separately, he subjected the sources of medieval Scottish history to salutary scrutiny. When William Creech, the most important Edinburgh bookseller of the day and an old friend of Lord Hailes, published the latter's collected works in three volumes in 1797, he could compare them favourably with Voltaire's *Annales de l'Empire*, saying that they had 'all the philosophic reflection of the latter, with a superior acuteness of critical investigation'. It was no mean boast, even if it has not worn well.

Scotland was already by 1788 endowed with the earliest purpose-designed record repository in Britain in the handsome shape of Register House in Edinburgh, designed by Robert Adam in a unique blend of Roman Imperial grandeur and neo-classical Palladian taste. It was this commission which confirmed Robert Adam's reputation in Scotland. In London the appearance of a similar complex, Somerset House, designed by his deadly rival Sir William Chambers (himself the son of a Scottish merchant trading in Sweden), almost instantly over-shadowed Adam's achievement. It was in Edinburgh, with Register House, Charlotte Square and his work for the University of Edinburgh, that Robert Adam left a monumental mark on a metropolis. However, a fine repository is not necessarily a guarantee of a flourishing 'national history'. It was equally important that after the bulk of the national archives had been transferred from the Laigh Parliament House to the new depository, they be made accessible to historians by the creation of a repertory and catalogues, and by the publication of the more important series in scholarly editions. The official legally responsible for the oversight of the Scottish records was the Lord Clerk Register. In 1806 the holder of this post, Lord Frederick Campbell, earned the eternal gratitude of historians by appointing a Deputy Clerk Register in the shape of a young advocate who was a former secretary to Lord Hailes, and a close friend of Walter Scott. This man was Thomas Thomson who, under the absentee but benign sway of the Lord Clerk Register, laid the foundations of modern Scottish archival methods. Thomson succeeded Scott in the presidency of the Bannatyne Club and in association with men like Robert Pitcairn and Cosmo Innes assumed a leading role in its publication work. In fact Thomson was careless in accounting for public moneys and incorrigibly dilatory in producing volumes for publication in such official series as the *Acts of the Parliaments of Scotland* (left incomplete when he left office in

1841), with the result that he demitted office under a cloud, but the foundations of scholarship he laid well.

There was a broad spectrum of support for all these efforts to make the sources of Scottish history available. Geographically, it became clear that the Bannatyne, with its considerable social status connected with a limited membership, would be imitated outside Edinburgh when in 1829 the Maitland Club was established in Glasgow. It shared members, like Scott and Pitcairn, with the Bannatyne, but was predictably more mercantile in membership than its lawyer-dominated Edinburgh counterpart. As the nineteenth century progressed, other Scottish cities were to participate in the historical publishing club adventure. Whigs as well as Tories were founder members of clubs. Yet politics did creep into the hotly contested elections for membership to these rather exclusive bodies. In 1830 Scott was furious when the normal sequence of candidates coming up for election to the Bannatyne was overturned to admit the Whig MP for the Ayr burghs, Thomas Kennedy of Dunure, in preference to Scott's friend the Tory Lord Medwyn. Cosmo Innes, a great record scholar of the generation after Thomson, was so strong a Whig that the passing of the Reform Act of 1832 represented a major career opportunity for him. Under sympathetic governments he was appointed Lord Advocate Depute in 1833 and Sheriff of Moray in 1840. Nevertheless, it is not going too far to argue that the core of the revival of interest in Scotland's past was unmistakeably Tory. The protean genius of Scott lay at the very heart of the movement. The only substantial multi-volume *History of Scotland* which emerged in this period (its first two volumes came out in 1829) was that of Patrick Fraser Tytler, who literally boasted of not having a drop of Whig blood in his veins. His fine scholarship failed to compensate for his hostility to post-1832 governments, which cost him every official post he aspired to.

A new emphasis on the old and the local was part of the response of the traditional ruling classes of Scotland to what they saw as a mounting threat to their long-entrenched political ascendancy. They had been shaken by what they saw as the corrosive

impact of cocksure Jacobin radicalism on the social and governmental structures of the France of the *ancien régime*. After 1815
they saw a similar threat in the increasingly strident and confident
Whig propaganda against the existing pattern of political power
in Scotland. There was a growing conviction in circles in Scotland
opposed to significant political change that the superficial ratio-
nalism inculcated in the elementary classes in Scottish universities
might well prove the solvent of those bonds of deference on which
their prescriptive right to rule rested. That there was truth in some
of the conservative strictures on the Scottish universities, and
merit in the new directions which the conservative reaction could
give to intellectual enquiry, is amply demonstrated by the career
of another friend of Walter Scott, the Seceder clergyman John
Jamieson. Born in Glasgow in 1759, the son of the pastor to one
of only two Seceder congregations then established in that city,
Jamieson was predestined to the priesthood of his denomination
more or less from birth. His higher education was therefore
absurdly premature. Admitted to the first Humanity (Latin) class
at the University of Glasgow at the ripe age of nine, he studied
logic at eleven, and sat at the feet of the venerable Thomas Reid,
the 'Father of the Common Sense School', a year later, at an age
which Jamieson himself thought rendered the exercise ridiculous.
The Associate Presbytery of Glasgow admitted him a student of
theology when he was fourteen, and licensed him to preach at
twenty. Settled, not very happily, at Forfar, he became friendly
with George Dempster of Dunnichen, and married the daughter
of a local laird. It was at Dempster's residence that he met the
Icelandic Professor of Antiquities Thörkelin who persuaded him
to embark on his great *Dictionary Of The Scottish Language*,
of which two quarto volumes appeared by subscription in
Edinburgh in 1808, and two comparable volumes modestly
described as *Supplement* in 1825. Latterly Jamieson had been
translated to a charge in Edinburgh. He was a regular visitor to
Scott's Abbotsford and pursued his hobby of angling in Border
streams until his death in 1838.

Apart from the accident of belonging to a Seceder Levitical
dynasty, Jamieson was a well-integrated, if relatively humble,

member of the ruling group in Scotland, with all that implied in terms of access to patronage for his seven sons. Alas, the dreadful mortality of the period ensured that only one of them outlived him, but it is significant that three of them died in the corn kist of Scotland, India. An even more remarkable example than Jamieson of Scott's ability to patronise creatively a very Scottish character of humble origins and to build him into the Tory literary establishment was James Hogg, the son of a shepherd in a remote part of the Borders.

After a few months of formal schooling, Hogg educated himself by sheer determination and labour, becoming well read to the point where his longer poems contain substantial echoes of Milton and Pope and his *Poetic Mirror* contains inspired parodies of, among others, Scott, Byron and Wordsworth. Though he was familiar with traditional Scots balladry and not ignorant of the late-medieval Scots poets known as the Makars, Hogg was also steeped in the formal English of the Authorised Version of the Bible. His lifelong friendship with Walter Scott dated from 1802 when Scott contacted him during researches for the third volume of his *Minstrelsy of the Scottish Border*. By 1810 Hogg, an unsuccessful farmer, had become a professional writer in Edinburgh, achieving overnight fame in 1813 with his poem 'The Queen's Wake'. By 1815 he was in possession of a life tenancy rent-free of a farm in Yarrow on the Borders on the Buccleuch estates. The gift mitigated the effects of Hogg's financial mismanagement, which, like Walter Scott's, remained chronic.

It was felt in aggressive Tory circles that the *Quarterly*, for all its merits, was too soft on the iniquities of the Whig *Edinburgh Review*, so in 1817 William Blackwood, a Tory bookseller-publisher who had taken the unprecedented step of quitting the old haunts of his profession on the High Street for Edinburgh's fashionable New Town, launched in April his *Edinburgh Monthly Magazine*. Having lost two uninspired editors, Blackwood stepped into the breach himself, supported by a group of friends including John Gibson Lockhart, the future son-in-law and biographer of Walter Scott; James Hogg; and John Wilson, better known by his soubriquet of 'Christopher North' and a future Professor of Moral Philosophy in the University of Edinburgh. With its seventh issue renamed *Blackwood's Magazine*, affectionately known as *Maga*, broke through. It savaged Archibald Constable, the rival printer who had suborned the original *Maga* editors; Francis Jeffrey of the *Edinburgh*, and indeed most of the city's leading Whigs, in mock Old Testament language in a very funny article entitled 'Translation from an Ancient Chaldee Manuscript'. Deemed so blasphemous that it had to be omitted in reprints of the number, the piece produced exactly the sensation needed to make people buy future numbers. From 1822 to 1835 *Blackwood's* ran an extraordinary series of articles in the form of imaginary conversations between 'Christopher North' and others including a figure obviously based on Hogg. They were subsequently collected as the *Noctes Ambrosianae*. Wilson's was the master-hand among several behind it, and his condescending treatment of Hogg a twisted literary triumph. Hogg himself was a complex character, writing four versions of an autobiography, none very reliable. His masterpiece *The Private Memoirs and Confessions of a Justified Sinner* (1824), arguably the most compelling exposition of the power of evil in the literature of the English-speaking peoples, was published anonymously and the posthumous edition of 1837 (by which time the authorship was known) was expurgated to appease High Calvinist opinion.

Hogg greatly assisted the *Blackwood's* group in attacking the Whig leadership, amusingly, but at times unfairly, viciously and vulgarly. Whig newspapers like *The Scotsman* and the *London Magazine* protested that Hogg's stature as a 'true national poet' was being prostituted to serve the purposes of 'the guilt and filth' of *Blackwood's*. The levels of animosity generated by such abuse became lethal. John Scott, the young editor of the *London Magazine*, was actually killed in a duel with Lockhart's friend Christie. It is therefore hardly surprising that when in 1819 John Gibson Lockhart produced his *Peter's Letters to his Kinsfolk*, an extended commentary mainly on the Edinburgh scene, he made serious efforts to tone down the personal bitterness in his writing and even to apologise indirectly to some, like the rising Tory divine Thomas Chalmers, whom he had attacked recklessly and mistakenly. Nevertheless, *Peter's Letters* scored a considerable *succès de scandale* when it appeared, partly because, despite the less acerbic tone of its prose, it was permeated by a strongly partisan tone, and partly because in making sure that the Whig dogs had the worst of it Lockhart necessarily developed a critique of polite Edinburgh culture which was both serious and significant. For years Walter Scott had been the only Edinburgh literary figure of stature who was also a committed Tory. Now Lockhart, fresh from enjoying at Abbotsford, in the company of Scott and the second Viscount Melville, a neo-feudal lifestyle which was nothing if not intensely Scottish, could point out that the Whig tradition as embodied in the *Edinburgh* was blind to some of the most important cultural developments of the day, notably to the greatness of Wordsworth and to the theme of nationality which was so central to the work of Scott.

Romantic Toryism drew strength from cultural currents running far beyond the shores of Britain, and notably from Germany. In the early 1790s Walter Scott himself had become 'German-mad'. The first signs of serious interest in German literature in Scotland followed Henry Mackenzie's 'Account of the German Theatre' read to the Royal Society of Edinburgh on 21 April 1788, and published in its *Transactions* two years later. Alexander Fraser Tytler, the father of Patrick Fraser Tytler, had translated Schiller's *Die Räuber*. Scott never achieved the exact scholarly knowledge of German possessed by, say, his friend James Skene of Rubislaw, who had lived in Saxony, but he acquired enough of the language to plunge deep into German ballads and to translate pieces by Burger and Goethe. With the coming of the French Revolutionary wars, German *Sturm und Drang* literature was increasingly identified in Britian with radicalism and godlessness. Indeed the Reverend James Macdonald, minister of Anstruther Wester in Fife from 1799 to 1804, and a man who had lived in Germany, and who not only propagated a knowledge of German literature in Scotland but also pioneered the introduction of the poetry of Burns to German readers, was moved to try to organise criticism of John Robison's *Proofs of a*

Conspiracy against all the Religions and Governments of Europe around 1800, on the grounds that it stoked a needless and irrational prejudice against German culture. In practice, romanticism had no necessary political bias. It could be used to serve the end of either reaction or radicalism. Its only inherent hostility was to the aesthetics of neo-classical culture. After 1815 it was therefore natural for conservatives in Scottish cultural life to draw once more on the reserves of sympathetic material available in contemporary Germany. From 1817 to 1828 *Blackwood's Magazine* ran a series of 'Horae Germanicae' designed to widen its readers' acquaintance with German literature. Blackwood himself in 1817 financed Lockhart's summer holiday in Germany, in the course of which Lockhart went to Weimar and met Goethe. Blackwood also commissioned a work of translation from the German from Lockhart, and it is revealing that the latter chose to translate the *Geschichte der alten und neuen Literatur* of Carl Wilhelm Friedrich von Schlegel, who after a career as the *enfant terrible* of radical romanticism had swung to the opposite extreme. Converting to Roman Catholicism and the Austrian public service, he had acquired those nationalistic and reactionary views discernible in much of his later work, including the translated *On the History of Literature* which Lockhart published in 1818.

The cultural counter-offensive by the defenders of the political status quo in Scotland was a symptom of insecurity, but was impressive in its width, vitality and quality. Lockhart's *Peter's Letters*, that biography of a national culture, was probably justified in its claim that the great weight of talent in 1819 in literary circles in Scotland was on the Tory side. Yet it is clear that the erosion of the Tory grip on Scottish life continued, if not at a pace which threatened revolution, then at least at a pace which deeply disturbed Tories, and it is important to ask why this should have been so. The answer seems to lie in a combination of positive and negative factors. The latter may briefly be summed up as a set of reasons why the Tory reaction was more impressive than convincing, and to these reasons it is logical to turn first.

In a preface to his novel *Quentin Durward*, dated December 1831, Scott remarked that this book, set mainly in late-medieval

France, had proved more popular both at home and on the Continent than some of its predecessors. This was true. Scott rapidly reached a regular print run of 10,000 copies for the first impression of a novel and Lockhart reckoned his annual income from fiction, or 'works of mere amusement' as Scott called them, at £10,000, after the first four novels. However, increasingly careless and diffuse writing led eventually to well-deserved failures such as *The Abbot*, and once the magic spell was broken to undeserved failures such as *Redgauntlet*, which was poorly received, so it was obviously a fillip to Scott that *Quentin Durward* revived a measure of his old success, the more so as its implicit 'message' was so close to Scott's heart. The 'message' which Scott spelled out was the danger involved in the total loss of the feudal virtues of honour, constancy and loyalty in the face of the socially disruptive Machiavellian egotism of a ruler like Louis XI. Yet Scott's own neo-feudalism was bogus and unstable. Lockhart, whose biographical technique, polished on lives of Robert Burns and Napoleon, involved an artistic blending of the man and his myth, carefully concealed in the official biography of Scott the extent to which Scott was responsible for the financial disaster which overwhelmed both him and his business associates in 1826. Lockhart set up as the villains of the episode the Ballantyne brothers, who between them served as Scott's copy-editors, printers and literary agents, but in fact the Ballantynes and Archibald Constable, Scott's publisher, were the victims of the bad business judgement and total financial irresponsibility of Scott, with whom their finances were hopelessly and to some extent secretly intertwined.

Already, in a lengthy preface to *The Fortunes of Nigel*, Scott had felt obliged hotly to defend himself against the charge that he wrote too much too fast in an attempt to collect a maximum amount of copy money in a minimum time. The charges were perfectly true but greed was not the motive. Rather was it desperation to keep intact a bubble of credit which finally burst late in 1825. The collapse itself was in the long run clearly inevitable, but its dating was closely linked to a traumatic downturn in the business cycle in Britain which involved a run on the banks which was itself rendered more disruptive by a credit-squeeze imposed by the Bank of England. James Ballantyne and Company had been hopelessly insolvent for some time. When the crash came, Scott was responsible for no less than £116,838 11s. 3d. of debt, almost all of which had been contracted on his initiative. Archibald Constable and Company went bankrupt with a deficiency of £256,000, and their valuable assets had to be sold for a fraction of their true worth to satisfy desperate creditors. That Scott, with the assistance of generous creditors, coped heroically with this terrible debacle and literally buckled down to writing off his debts, to the point where he had drafted his last novel, unpublished before the twentieth century, during the Mediterranean holiday which ended in his death, was less significant than the collapse of his make-believe world.

Scott was by no means the only man living in that world, though he was by far the most remarkable inhabitant of a cosmos which Atlas-like he did so much to sustain. In the field of the visual arts Henry Raeburn also upheld a deeply romantic vision of Scotland. Raeburn's portraits of swashbuckling Highland chiefs like the MacNab, and that by no means dissimilar character Alastair Macdonnell of Glengarry, show all the penetration, masculine vigour and authority of which the painter was capable, though one has to remember that he could also produce stunning portraits of women, young and old. After 1798 Raeburn had no serious rival as a portrait painter in Edinburgh. He was of middle-class origin, the son of a textile manufacturer, and his portraiture was particularly effective when its subject was a member of the professional classes. His brush has recorded such academic figures as Professor John Robison. With the aristocracy he had a struggle to establish himself, and he failed in a tentative bid to set up as a fashionable London portrait painter in 1810.

Like Scott and Hogg, he was latterly hounded by problems of debt due to unsuccessful business deals. His career had been crucially assisted by marriage to a well-off widow twelve years his senior. It was her money that enabled him to take off for the two years in Italy that like Robert Adam's much grander tour gave him the credentials of a serious artist. Critics accused him of slapdash finish and deficient anatomical knowledge, so he had few official commissions for portraits in the Grand Manner, despite being willing to produce them at less than half the rate demanded by the leading London portrait painter of the early 1800s, Sir Thomas Lawrence. The critics may have missed the point. Raeburn painted a portrait of Thomas Reid, whose answer to Humean scepticism was essentially that the mind apprehended reality by instinct and not by rational analysis. The painter was also friendly with Dugald Stewart, Reid's main interpreter whose *Elements of the Human Mind* began to appear from 1804, with a first volume devoted to perception. Raeburn painted spontaneously with no prior drawing, manipulating paint and light into simplified units of perception, ultimately unique to him but communicable to others. He survived bankruptcy in 1808, at the cost of family turmoil, and died in 1823, having been knighted by George IV during that monarch's visit to Scotland, which in many ways was the final celebration by a virile but doomed provincial ascendancy of their extraordinary neo-feudal romantic self-justification, so compellingly limned by the brush of Raeburn in his Highland portraits, and so persuasively preached by Scott in his numerous novels. These were houses or rather castles built on sand, as the rickety entrepreneurial finances of so many of these men underlined.

Beneath the glamorous if sometimes gimcrack surface of events, the old ruling groups were undoubtedly losing their grip on Scottish society. High agricultural prices and rents during the Napoleonic Wars had enabled the aristocracy to indulge in massive building schemes. Their new residences, as befitted intellectual fashions in the best circles, were often in that castellated style first developed by Robert Morris at Inveraray and further developed by Robert Adam in a whole series of Scottish castles such as Mellerstain and Wedderburn in Berwickshire, Seton in East Lothian, Airthrey in Stirlingshire, and perhaps most spectacularly at Culzean in Ayrshire. At Abbotsford Sir Walter Scott and the architect William Atkinson created after 1816 the prototype building for the Scottish baronial style which was to sweep Scotland after the mid-century. Meantime, magnates like the

Earl of Breadalbane were building vast castellated palaces like Taymouth Castle in Perthshire which was begun by the architects Archibald and James Elliot in 1806 and extended by William Atkinson after 1818. Gothic revival was clearly in the air, a self-conscious cultivation of pseudo-medieval religiosity which made the Elliots call the arcade girdling the basement at Taymouth a cloister, and caused patrons like the Earl of Mansfield to build medieval touches into every room in the new Scone Palace built under William Atkinson's supervision between 1803 and 1812. At Crawford Priory in Fife, near Cupar, after 1813 a rising young Scots architect, James Gillespie Graham, recased an eighteenth-century house in 'ecclesiastical gothic'.

Yet the religiosity was as unconvincing as the feudal postures. Scott patronised Episcopalian churches occasionally to underline his dislike of the Presbyterian Kirk, but his real religious commitment appears to have been as tepid as that of the elder Dundas. The old Moderate ascendancy in the Kirk By Law Established was undoubtedly the most convenient arrangement for those who managed Scotland in the Dundas interest, but by 1820 it was clear that the peace in church–state relations created by that ascendancy was under threat from two irresistibly growing forces – Evangelical sentiment within the Church of Scotland and dissenting denominations without.

The Original Secession of the 1730s had been led by men of ability and character. Its cause commanded widespread sympathy because of opposition to lay patronage and fear that the fundamentals of the Faith were in danger from fashionable theology. Only the difficulty of furnishing qualified ministers for its congregations prevented very rapid expansion in its numbers. Nevertheless, by 1737 the original four Seceder congregations had increased to fifteen, and three years later to thirty-six. From 1742, Seceders were active in Ulster and by 1760 there were ninety-nine Seceder congregations in Scotland alone. To the considerable glee of their opponents, they were increasingly riven by faction, dividing in 1747 into Burghers and Anti-Burghers over whether they could legitimately accept the terms of an oath necessary for those assuming the status of burgess in Scottish burghs without violating their own theological principles. In 1795 a serious dispute over the standing of the seventeenth-century Westminster Confession of Faith further divided Seceders between Auld Lichts and New Lichts, and underlined the extent to which new currents of thought were disturbing them. Yet the very divisions of this cantankerous religious tradition led to expansion, especially in the towns where the Seceding groups made a very strong appeal to the manufacturing and commercial middle classes. They also appealed to lower middle class and artisan groups in town and country, and never lost a strong following among small tenant-farmers.

Much more radical before 1800 in both theology and in their approach to the church-state relationship were the members of a third Presbyterian tradition which in 1761 set up what was called the Relief Presbytery. It owed its existence to a very remarkable man, Thomas Gillespie of Garnock. Deposed from his charge in the Church of Scotland, he never exhibited any bitterness towards it, and indeed all his life shunned the very face of the religious controversy on which Seceders throve. He held communion with all sincere Christians of any denomination. For his day this was a very radical step. Gillespie opposed not only patronage but also the church–state connection. Despite this he was a reluctant member of what was to become the Relief Kirk. He would have preferred it to be just an autonomous presbytery and eventually urged his own congregation to return to the Church of Scotland, which they did. Yet the denomination which this unworldly and saintly man so reluctantly founded went on after his death, liberal in its theology, radical in its politics, and charitable in its tone.

As early as 1765 it had been said that 100,000 people in Scotland adhered to non-established denominations. In 1795 the Lord Advocate, Robert Dundas of Arniston, thought the figure was 150,000. Almost certainly he exaggerated. Dr James Hall, a Burgher minister in Edinburgh, was able in 1797 to exploit the Lord Advocate's neurosis to collect £300 a year, secretly, for acting as Westminster's 'agent' among the Scotch Seceders. Only in 1807 did a new Prime Minister, Spencer Percival, put a stop to this discreditable confidence trick. Seceders were not Jacobins. However, they were outwith the scope of positive management by the politicians, and they drifted in more rather than less radical directions with time. For example, the Original Secession left the Church of Scotland still committed to the principle of a state church. It simply objected to the precise nature of the relationship between church and state in Scotland in the early eighteenth century. By the early nineteenth century the bulk of Seceding opinion was moving towards the disestablishment principles expounded by the Relief Kirk. One result of this development was a further spasm of schism which gave birth to the greatest single achievement in the writing of ecclesiastical history in nineteenth-century Scotland, the *Life of Knox* (1811) and the *Life of Melville* (1819), in which Thomas McCrie, that most conservative of Seceders, demonstrated beyond any shadow of doubt that the absence of a religious establishment had never been acceptable to the Fathers of the Scottish Reformation.

The Reverend Doctor Thomas McCrie, to give him his full title, also turned his warm indignation against what he saw as Walter Scott's denigration of Scottish Presbyterianism in *Old Mortality*, to such effect that Scott felt obliged to defend himself at length in an article in *The Quarterly Review*. Like Scott, McCrie was ultra-conservative. The inability of the two greatest Scottish men of letters of their day to agree was inevitable: they held radically antagonistic views as to precisely what kind of heritage needed to be conserved. At least their visions had this in common: neither was universally acceptable, though both had enduring emotional appeal. McCrie was wholly outwith the main currents of Seceder history, which in 1820 carried the two New Licht groups towards a union.[2]

More significant, from the point of view of the rulers of Scottish society, was the mounting Evangelical offensive within the Church of Scotland. Moderates disapproved in principle of the stress upon an intensely personal, emotion-charged conver-

---

[2]   Joined in 1847 by the Relief Church to constitute the United Presbyterian Church.

sion experience which was characteristic of the Evangelical school, but Evangelical and Seceder never became synonymous terms. The 'Cambuslang Wark' of 1742, a tremendous religious revival of a highly emotional kind centred on Cambuslang (a Clydeside parish with Covenanting traditions and on bad terms with its patron), owed much to the English Calvinistic Methodist George Whitefield, but it was associated with ministers of the Established Kirk. Evangelicals were bound to be unhappy about the implications for vital religion in a parish of an unbridled right of patronage in the hands of a patron whose commitment to the Faith might be tepid or non-existent. The Evangelical Party of the early nineteenth century was, until his death in 1827, under the extremely conservative leadership of the Reverend Sir Henry Moncrieff, Bt, of St Cuthbert's Edinburgh, but even at its most conservative that party was bound to want to restrict patrons' rights (never in Scottish ecclesiastical law deemed absolute), and from restriction to abolition was always a possible mental leap. Above all, Evangelicals had positive ideas about adapting the Established Kirk to meet the new challenges of a changing Scotland.

Of necessity this would have involved active cooperation and concessions from a state whose masters regarded Scottish politics as an exercise in buying individuals to ensure that Scottish problems were not even raised, let alone added to the long list of problems which Westminster was actively wrestling with, not always with success. It therefore added greatly to the potential difficulties of government when in 1809 the most dynamic and forceful personality produced by the Church of Scotland in the nineteenth century, Thomas Chalmers, experienced a conversion which turned this young minister of Kilmany in his native Fife from a typical Moderate into a conservative but bustling Evangelical. Evangelical revivalism was in the air in Scotland to the point where there was no emotional gap, as in England, for Methodism to fill, and this fact, allied to financial mismanagement by Valentine Ward, the leading Methodist preacher active in Scotland between 1811 and 1819, ensured that Scottish Methodism always remained small.

Lay evangelism which eventually contributed to the creation of Baptist and Congregational communities did exist and was sponsored between 1798 and 1810 to the tune of over £70,000 by the remarkable brothers James and Robert Haldane of Airthrey in Stirlingshire, but the main preoccupation of the embattled Moderates remained the duel with the Evangelicals during elections for representative elders to sit in the General Assembly.

During his tenure of a St Andrews professorship, Chalmers found he would never be returned to the General Assembly by either his ultra-conservative university or by the local presbytery. Forced to canvass his native burgh of Anstruther Easter, Chalmers had to pay the usual price in food and drink for the votes which returned him. Despite his election as Moderator of the General Assembly in 1832, the Moderate grip held until 1834. It was based on a landed and legal block in the Assembly which between 1820 and 1832 still accounted for about 80 per cent of the elders. Among the lawyers (50 to 60 per cent of elders in the Assembly in this period), 97 to 98 per cent were usually of Edinburgh provenance. However, the Moderate dam was clearly strained to breaking-point by the Evangelical pressure behind it before 1832, and this is all the more impressive in that the social composition of General Assemblies changed little.

Again and again the existing political ascendancy was falling foul of forces in Scottish life which represented the wave of the future, whether in the field of opinion, or in the changing balance of economic power. Nowhere was this more true than in the towns where the rapidly expanding commercial and manufacturing middle classes, very often Seceder or if Established Kirk then Evangelical in persuasion, were face to face with the oligarchical cliques which monopolised urban government. The management of burgh finances was always secretive, usually incompetent and not infrequently dishonest. By 1817 the long-moribund agitation for burghal reform had started to life again under one of its old leaders, Archibald Fletcher. A new reforming press had come into existence since 1800 and now strongly supported demands for a clean-up of an urban government system so disreputable that reformers of every hue were at one in denouncing it. *The Dundee Advertiser* was one of these radical papers and had been established in 1801. *The Aberdeen Chronicle* was another which had come into being in 1806. *The Scotsman* was born in Edinburgh in January 1817 as a direct result of the difficulties William Ritchie, an Edinburgh solicitor, had had in trying to publicise gross mismanagement in Edinburgh Royal Infirmary.

Burghal reform, to most of its supporters, was a common-sense rather than an ideological commitment, though their opinion of the London government inevitably declined when it became apparent that it was not prepared to countenance any meaningful reform. An old technique of securing a royal warrant for an election of the town council by a poll of all burgesses was reactivated in 1817 in Montrose by reform sympathisers who deliberately engineered irregularity in the council election, but the government soon made it clear it would issue no more such warrants. In 1819 Lord Archibald Hamilton secured a parliamentary inquiry which showed that Edinburgh, Aberdeen, Dundee and Dunfermline had been virtually bankrupted by corrupt practices. Between 1818 and 1821 petitions from the royal burghs of Scotland demanding reform rained in upon the House of Commons, which referred them to a select committee. Its *Report* (ordered to be printed 14–15 July 1821) admitted that the almost total breakdown of pre-1707 legal and accounting controls over the burghs had led to scandalous goings-on. It singled out Inverurie in Aberdeenshire as an extreme case of the improprieties generated by the practice of having absentee councillors, and Cupar in Fife as an infamous example of the sale of council office. Apart from the submission of public annual accounts and better audit procedures, the *Report* recommended no change, stating that any infringement of vested rights was too dangerous a precedent.

Yet in the burghs of Scotland the *ancien régime* was inexorably wasting away. Bankruptcy was staring Edinburgh in the face by 1825, when a further government loan of £240,000 was only secured by pledging most of the council's real-estate assets, including the docks in the subject port of Leith, on which great sums had been spent. Council plans to recover some ground by increasing already high port charges after selling the docks to a private company consisting mainly of councillors led to a major row. Subsequent legislation transferred control of Leith Docks to twenty-one commissioners, representing several interests as well as Edinburgh town council, which by 1833 was declared bankrupt. Dundee passed through a similar struggle as local textile manufacturers, acutely aware of the vital importance to them of dock facilities for coastal and other shipping in a pre-railway age, fought to keep control of harbour developments out of the hands of the urbane but rascally Provost Alexander Riddoch and his council cronies who undoubtedly hoped to impose increased levies on a growing flow of trade through an improved harbour, in order to service existing and dubiously acquired council debts.

Significantly, it was in the course of their struggle over the harbour that Dundee radicals like Robert Rintoul, editor of *The Dundee, Perth and Cupar Advertiser*, enlisted the support of local laird George Kinloch of Kinloch, a man of very strong character who in 1816 actually dared to oppose the main motion at a county meeting of noblemen and freeholders at Perth presided over by the Duke of Atholl. The motion roughly said that His Majesty's Government was making the best of a difficult job and that all reasonable men recognised that even its least popular policies were the only possible ones. Kinloch unsuccessfully suggested that the alternative to the only possible policy was to do something different and that in particular taxes were too high. William Maule, MP for Forfarshire and a member of an old aristocratic family long at odds with the upstart Melvilles, helped Kinloch and his allies to secure legislation establishing Dundee Harbour Commissioners. Kinloch had to flee abroad to avoid a charge of sedition in 1819 but he returned in 1822, was pardoned in 1823, and lived to serve briefly as Dundee's Whig MP between 1832 and his death in 1833.

With such support, reform could hardly be equated with anarchy, hard as the government tried. One of the few cards in government hands when the support of the bulk of the urban middle classes was at stake was the natural fear of 'the middling sort' for the social radicalism of 'the lower orders'. In certain cases this fear was well developed, almost to the point of paranoia. Kirkman Finlay, the Glasgow merchant-prince and cotton manufacturer, is a case in point. He was a notable opponent of the monopoly of the India trade held by the Honourable East India Company and after being elected MP for Glasgow in 1812 had the immense satisfaction of assisting in the destruction of that monopoly in 1813 (the Company kept its legal monopoly of British trade with China until 1833). Immediately, Kirkman Finlay freighted the first ship direct from the Clyde to India, the 600 ton *Buckinghamshire* which sailed for Calcutta. However, the great man's fear of revolution drove him in a steadily more conservative direction. The Glasgow crowd which had dragged his coach along the Trongate in triumph in 1812 to his house in Queen Street, returned in March 1815 to find him not at home, so they smashed all his windows to express their wrath at his support for the new Corn Law which, by prohibiting the sale of foreign grain in Britain until the home price reached 80s. a quarter for wheat and 40s. and 27s. respectively for barley and oats, aimed at keeping up domestic grain prices. It was only very marginally successful in so doing, but it became a great symbol of landed privilege, denounced by street orators as well as by academic economists like David Ricardo who believed in free trade.

By 1816 Kirkman Finlay was actively trying, in cooperation with a worried London government, to erect an intelligence network capable of penetrating any seditious radical conspiracies. There was certainly a lot of wild talk around in the Lowlands, where the period between 1815 and 1822 was one of sustained depression and hardship with few redeeming features for working-class Scotsmen. The singularly ungenerous so-called 'Old Scots Poor Law' had been firmly riveted on the countryside, though less successfully on the burghs. On the other hand, it was precisely in the burghs that the scale of the problem of poverty was becoming unmanageable. Nor was it mitigated by countervailing pressures from organised labour, for the failure in 1812–13 to sustain judicial settlement of wages by either legal or strike action took the heart out of any incipient trade union movement. Post-war depression came swiftly after 1815, exacerbated by massive demobilisation and a flow of poverty-stricken migrants from the countryside. Black cattle prices fell as soon as peace broke out, while kelp prices at once entered a long period of decline deeply debilitating to the Highland economy but inevitable due both to pressure from renewed imports of foreign organic-derived industrial alkali and to the competition of inorganic alkali produced by factories like the St Rollox Works in Glasgow.

Political awareness among hard-hit sections of the working classes was undoubtedly fanned by the activities of two Englishmen – William Cobbett, the journalist, and Major John Cartwright, a veteran radical agitator. Both men preached drastic parliamentary reform as a panacea for the troubles of the day. For Cartwright, who toured Scotland extensively in 1815 to promote the cause of radical Hampden Clubs, this meant annual parliaments, equal electoral districts, the secret ballot and payments to MPs. It was no accident that Cartwright went to important centres of the hand-weaving industry like Paisley, Dunfermline, Forfar, Perth, Dundee and Glasgow. Power looms were coming into use in Scotland. There were 1,500 of them in 1813, a figure which rose to 2,000 in 1820 and to 10,000 in 1829, but most of these were cotton looms in or near Glasgow. In 1833 Kirkman Finlay argued that the unsuitability of steam looms for fine weaving made hand looms perfectly competitive for many fabrics. Certainly in 1831 there were only 15,127 steam looms in and around Glasgow as compared with 32,000 hand looms. Wartime levels of income for hand loom weavers working on the plainer fabrics, and these were the vast majority of such weavers, fell sharply immediately after Waterloo and never recovered. Admittedly the wages of the most skilled weavers, such as those whose hand looms produced fine Paisley shawls, held up for another decade, but then they too fell.

A certain amount of secret oath-taking undoubtedly occurred in radical circles. Alexander Richmond, later demonised as 'the spy', a man who had been an active radical weaver in 1812, became drawn into the intelligence system operated by Kirkman

Finlay and his allies such as Samuel Hunter (1769–1839) who was a colonel in the Glasgow Yeomanry as well as editor of the violently conservative *Glasgow Herald*. The government, headed by Lord Liverpool since 1812, authorised state prosecutions of leading Scottish radicals arrested in 1817. The upshot was a fiasco. Truth and paranoid delusion were so confusingly inter-mingled that Whig lawyers like Jeffrey and Cockburn were able to secure acquittals or nominal sentences for the accused, and the principal state prosecutor, Lord Advocate Maconochie, looked so foolish that he had to be kicked upstairs as Lord Meadowbank by the already venerable tradition of appointment to the Court of Session as a reward for political loyalty, if not necessarily polit-ical intelligence. By suspending habeas corpus and passing further restrictive legislation known as the Six Acts, the govern-ment had heightened an already tense atmosphere which in Scotland finally erupted in the strangely pathetic 'Radical War' of 1820. That a minority of the unenfranchised were prepared to use violence to challenge the government is clear. In the 1830s champions of peaceful reform like the journalist Peter Mackenzie suggested that the conspiracies were entirely engineered by *agents provocateurs* like Richmond. This just does not seem to be true. Richmond was not employed as a government agent after 1817. What is clear is that only a tiny minority of reformers were ready to use physical force in 1820, when placards in Glasgow called on them to support a not very visible 'Provisional Government'. Weavers came out in a political strike, but a rising by radicals at Strathaven in Lanarkshire simply petered out, while a huge horde consisting of thirty-five Glasgow radicals marching on Carron was gallantly defeated by government cavalry – hussars and yeomanry – at Bonnymuir near Falkirk.

Apart from the trial of forty-seven men arrested and the exe-cution of three of them, that was the end of physical-force reform in Scotland and in most cases of any serious middle-class fear of revolution. The year 1819 had been the culmination of an appalling trade recession exacerbated by poor harvests, high grain prices and the most savage deliberate deflation by govern-ment in modern times. When in August 1819 a survey was made of an area, excluding Paisley, within a 5 mile radius of the centre of Glasgow, it revealed that of the 18,537 looms only 13,281 were working and 5,256 people were unemployed. Thomas Chalmers, who had been inducted to the crowded parish of the Tron Kirk in central Glasgow in 1815, had no sympathy with political radicalism, deeming 'the spirit of a factious discontent with the rulers of our land' to be 'unscriptural'. At various points he, as much as Walter Scott, was convinced that society was tee-tering on the brink of the abyss of revolution. Yet even Chalmers was by December 1819 convinced that the menace of political agitation was so reduced that 'the repeal of the Corn Bill' could be represented as a concession from strength. He insisted in a letter to his fellow-Evangelical the great anti-slavery campaigner William Wilberforce that repeal would in no way harm the landed interest and that nothing could be more effectual in 'recalling our people to loyalty and quietness'.

Chalmers was, as ever, over-optimistic. The rulers of the British state had shown considerable ability to mobilise mass support for the wars against Revolutionary and Napoleonic France, but the elites who had done this had opened a Pandora's box. Wars that demand mass-participation for victory usually leave a heritage of expectation for wider access to participation in public processes. The Napoleonic Wars were no exception, even if that participa-tion took the unusual form of passionate support for George IV's estranged spouse Queen Caroline, whom he was trying to divorce. 'Queenite' agitation peaked in 1820, varying from big petitions on her behalf organised by the middling orders of cities like Glasgow to traditional rioting on the part of, often female, members of the less fortunate strata of society.

From 1824 something like industrial warfare broke out in many industries, especially in and around Glasgow which was emerging as the crucible of Scotland's precocious industrialisa-tion. Tailors had organised and gone on strike, unsuccessfully, in 1823. Other groups, from miners to hand loom weavers, fol-lowed suit for the remainder of the 1820s. It was hardly surpris-ing. Initial gains in real wages up to the 1790s were being eaten away. Between 1810 and 1830 Dundee hand loom weavers' wages fell by about a third in real terms. Yet if radical industrial action was unsurprising, so was the defeat of its most militant exponents, like the hand loom weavers. With increasing mechanization, long-run trends were against them in an over stocked labour market fed increasingly by Highland and Irish migration to the Lowlands. Industrial Scotland was to be internationally competitive because, until the rise of 'modern' trade unions in the late nineteenth century, it was a relatively low-wage economy.

However, in the late 1820s many of the more skilled elements of the workforce in this industrialising society, like machine makers, millwrights and skilled foundry workers, began to benefit in real terms from economic growth and to differentiate themselves from 'rougher' elements, not least by active participation in organisations created by evangelical and educational outreach. They organised themselves in trade associations on a strictly male basis, using arguments about female 'fragility' to reduce potential competition from women. The trade papers that they sponsored began to preach the radical but non-violent amendment of the existing political system rather than its abolition.

Many modern Scottish historians of a radical disposition seem to have emotional difficulty in accepting that a revolution of the dispossessed was never a real possibility. Even in France those who benefited most from the French Revolution were those who had money to take advantage of opportunities it created. Reform of the Westminster system needed division within it and a willingness of some established politicians to call in a wider constituency, primarily to cement their victory over those who had for so long monopolised office. Nevertheless, the emergence of 'respectable' blue-collar reformers greatly assisted the creation of a wide consensus in Scotland for political change, a change seen as overdue and opposed only by the increasingly isolated and abused power-wielders of the old system who could no longer use paranoid fear of anarchy as a propaganda weapon to justify their retention of power.

9

Meltdown and
Reconfiguration 1827–1832

It is difficult to study the events leading up to the passage of the Scottish Reform Act in the summer of 1832 without seeing them through the distorting lenses provided by the writings of that most engaging of Scotch Whigs, Henry Cockburn. In the phrase of Thomas Carlyle, Cockburn, the son of a staunchly pro-Dundas father, was 'small, solid and genuine'. He was born in 1779. His father, partly owing to the influence of Dundas, rose to be a Baron of the Exchequer and a Judge Admiral. Despite the fact that his Whiggish proclivities were already known, Henry Cockburn was himself appointed Depute Lord Advocate by his imperious uncle Henry Dundas in 1807. Three years later, to his own relief, he was dismissed from the post for political insubordination. Cockburn was a conservative Whig who distrusted the wilder men of his party. He thought Brougham 'morally, as well as intellectually, mad'. Cockburn was in favour of extending the parliamentary franchise to the significant section of the well-off and the educated hitherto excluded, in order to avert the risk of revolution. In pursuit of his limited aims he was endearingly pugnacious. He was also a delightfully human character reflecting the many emotional and cultural currents of his period in a peculiarly graceful way epitomised by his regular journeys from his classical town house in Edinburgh to his beloved baronial retreat, Bonaly Castle in the Pentlands.

Oddly enough, Cockburn's literary reputation is almost totally posthumous. In his lifetime he published (in 1852) a competent two-volume *Life Of Lord Jeffrey With a Selection From*

His Correspondence, but the books on which Cockburn's fame rests, like the *Memorials Of His Time,* his so-called *Journal,* and his *Circuit Journeys,* were all published after his demise by his trustees. It is now clear that in selecting material to make up the *Memorials,* the trustees bowdlerised the manuscripts at their disposal. However, the *Memorials* derived from records which Cockburn began to keep about 1821 and the printed versions reflect accurately enough his tendency to depict the contemporary Scottish scene as a sharp dichotomy between two great political parties, the Whigs and the Tories. Naturally he saw himself and his fellow Whigs as striving to raise Scotland from the depths of political degradation, and at the very end of the *Memorials* (which close in 1830) stands the assertion that in this connection 'In the abuses of our representative and municipal systems alone, our predecessors have left us fields in which patriotism may exhaust itself'. Though true up to a point, this statement has done much to encourage a profoundly misleading perspective on the sequence of events which apparently culminated in 1832.

For a start, it insinuates an exaggerated view of the role of parliamentary elections in that decision-making process which may be described as the British political system. Certainly since the passing of the Septennial Act in 1717, which lengthened the permissible life of a Parliament to seven years, elections have never been intended to exert any serious influence over what historians call the 'High Politics' of major decisions. Secondly, Cockburn compounds this error by over-stressing a two-party model of contemporary politics which is itself over-simplified and which employs an extremely ambiguous nomenclature. To take the very last point first: such terms as 'Tory' have been used to describe political groupings in first English, then British politics over three centuries, but in fact the history of such groupings or parties is fragmentary and totally non-continuous. In Scotland in 1747 a Tory could either be a rank Jacobite or a throw-back to the English Toryism of the days of Queen Anne – an Episcopalian country gentleman of extreme conservative and 'country' views. By 1810 Tory in Scotland was a term of abuse applied by people like Jeffrey and Cockburn to supporters of the contemporary holders of power at Westminster, all of whom, incidentally, along with their Scottish supporters, would have ranked as rabid Whigs in terms of the politics of 1747 or indeed 1688.

Simply to give shape to the discussion, the terms Tory and Whig have been used in this present study from about 1794 when at least it can be said that the dichotomy between government and an identifiable, committed opposition is clear. The opposition called itself Whig for the same reason that modern southern Irish political movements literally fought one another over some dead hero's grave – to try to monopolise the prestige associated with a (usually specious) claim to continuity with an honoured name. However, to label the government and its supporters as Tory is to obscure the central and obvious fact that the administrations of the Younger Pitt and of Robert Banks Jenkinson, second Earl of Liverpool (1770–1828), who effectively succeeded Pitt as principal Man of Business to the British Establishment, were very much non-party 'broad-bottom' administrations endorsed in their heyday by all but a small, atypical, disgruntled minority of the ruling classes. The first major politician within the ruling consensus who was willing to call himself a Tory was George Canning. He too was desperate to establish himself as a representative of an historic and legitimate political tradition. The emptiness of his claims to be the natural leader of the ruling classes may be measured by the fact that his accession to power as premier in 1827, after Liverpool's resignation due to ill-health, marked the beginning of the end of the consensus so laboriously constructed by the Younger Pitt and the urbane, conciliatory Liverpool.

In Scotland, daily political life was dominated by the huge presence of the Melville interest, a political machine built on the sheer scale of the patronage at the disposal of the British government, and on the venality, even by eighteenth-century standards, of the Scottish ruling class, which was basically the landed interest and collaborating urban patricians, along with of course the large number of professional and commercial members of the middling orders who benefited from servicing their ever-expanding needs. However, partisan struggles in the constituencies did not imply, indeed at the British level hardly could imply, party government in any modern sense, where whipped 'Stalinist' parties could be used to transfer authority to their leaders and could reduce the Westminster legislature to an abject status that deprived it of any real capacity to monitor, let alone check, the executive. Unsalaried gentlemen of independent means refused to display the total subservience to the government whips characteristic of most modern MPs.

The seventh Lord Elgin, for example, was a Dundas man, even being educated at St Andrews under the eye of the youthful Professor of Greek, George Hill, a promising member of a Moderate dynasty of divines and academics wholly devoted to the Dundas ascendancy. However, when Elgin ran successfully for election as a representative peer in 1790, he stressed his objections to the total dominance of the election by a government list. Government was ultimately by negotiation with the ruling classes and Premier Pitt, though not willing to surrender to the faction led by lords Selkirk and Kinnaird that wanted to break all government control of the Scottish Representative Peer elections, conceded that four to six 'independent' peers were inevitable. Sir Ralph Abercromby, Elgin's neighbour and friend from Clackmannanshire, sent in his papers as Commander-in-Chief Ireland shortly before the 1798 risings there. The gesture solved nothing. Abercromby used the easy target of the Irish gentry, for whom he had developed a violent dislike while in Ireland during the American war (where his sympathies lay with the insurgent American Whigs), as scapegoats for the critical situation he left behind. Worse, he cleared the way for the brave but instinctively violent and insensitive General Lake to take over and deal with the crisis. Yet Abercromby was promptly appointed Commander-in-Chief North Britain in 1798 and went on to much higher commands. No gentleman lost status by sending in his papers if he was truly unhappy in the service. It was his right. Even at the height of his power, Henry Dundas made it his practice in wielding Crown ecclesiastical patronage to defer to the heritors or local landowners in a parish, intervening directly only when they differed. The autonomy of the local ruling class was real.

Cockburn might say that by the 1820s all that was best in the intellectual life of Edinburgh, apart from the bankrupt and ailing Scott, was Whig and of the Tories that 'their political influence now depended almost entirely on office'. Office was enough. There is absolutely no evidence that Cockburn or his friends, let alone any more radical and popular movement, were capable of shaking the political ascendancy built up by the Melvilles, itself essentially a re-creation of the sort of machine run by the Earl of Islay at an earlier period. Individual Whigs like Cockburn's friend Francis Jeffrey could show the weight of opinion behind the reformist impulse by being elected Lord Rector of Glasgow University in 1820 and again in 1823, not to mention Dean of the Faculty of Advocates in 1829, but he could penetrate the central political system only when it began to break up from within. That it was doing from 1827 onwards at Westminster level. Jeffrey became MP for Perth burghs in 1830 and became Lord Advocate (the senior political Scottish law officer) in Earl Grey's reforming government, but only after massive franchise extension was he returned for Edinburgh, which he held until he became a Judge of the Court of Session in 1834.

By then Scots Tories were paying for having held on too long without offering even minimal sops to legitimate complaints. By 1832 their reputation had already been comprehensively demonised to the point where they were to be quite incapable of returning to power after losing it. This was partly the result of cultural change which they could not control, like the penchant of the many early romantic poets for posing as violent opponents of the political establishment. Lord Castlereagh, perhaps the greatest of British foreign secretaries, and one who after 1815 facilitated the abandonment of the dog-eats-dog European international system for one with a real sense of enlightened community interest rising above mere state egotism, had the misfortune to attract hysterically exaggerated poetical criticism from Shelley, a significant poet who could also be an extraordinarily silly man. A poet like George Gordon, sixth Lord Byron (1788–1824), a man with Scottish antecedents like a foolish and unstable Gordon of Gight heiress mother, opened fire at an early stage against Scottish attitudes and individuals he found unsympathetic. Even conservative Scottish Whigs like Francis Jeffrey, editor of the *Edinburgh Review* until 1829, were alarmed by what they saw as the hints of anarchy in the new romantic poetry. As a result Jeffrey savaged the works of Wordsworth, Keats and Byron, earning from the latter a stinging reply in the powerful poetical satire 'English Bards and Scotch Reviewers' which denounced Jeffrey and 'his dirty crew'. Scottish Tories like the seventh Earl of Elgin fared much worse.

There was an increasing emphasis on the Greek side of the classical heritage of Western Europe towards the end of the eighteenth century. In the United Kingdom this trend was sharpened by the way the Napoleonic Wars effectively blocked the traditional Grand Tour with its focus on Italy and the (in truth much more relevant) Roman heritage. In the great wave of country house building that occurred in Scotland after 1750, neo-classical taste played an important role, drawing mainly on Roman architectural precedent, though Robert Adam, the outstanding neo-classical architect and interior designer of the late eighteenth century, had grasped during his study years in Italy the essential freedom and significant eclecticism of the best Roman practice. He could not afford a trip to Greece and always had an interest in the Gothic style. By the opening decades of the nineteenth century, however, neo-Grecian was all the rage in public architecture, especially in Edinburgh, the self-congratulatory 'Athens of the North', which was trying to repeat the confidence trick of ancient Athens within the Greek East Cultural Theme Park of the Roman Empire by hogging all the credit for cultural achievement, much of which in eighteenth-century Scotland belonged to rival cities. So it was proposed to build a memorial to the Scottish dead of the Napoleonic Wars in the shape of a replica of the Parthenon in Athens on the Calton Hill. The foundation stone was laid during the visit of George IV in 1822, but by 1830 money ran out and all that was achieved was twelve columns and a massive partial base of Craigleith stone standing curiously gaunt and appropriate to this day. Grecian Doric, however, went through fully to completion in Thomas Hamilton's stunning masterpiece of the genre, the Royal High School on Calton Hill, built between 1825 and 1829. What is now the Royal Scottish Academy on the Mound, originally the Royal Institution, is another example of Grecian Doric of the period. Thomas Hamilton's 1830 monument to Burns on the Calton Hill has a roof that is a literal rendition of an ancient Greek masterpiece, the choragic monument of Lysicrates.

Elgin, as ambassador to The Sublime Porte (Ottoman Turkey), famously removed a magnificent selection of sculptures from the frieze of the Parthenon. Byron was no social radical, indeed he was a crashing snob who could be boorishly condescending and brutal even when in his own eyes he was 'befriending' one of the lower orders like the great English clown Joseph Grimaldi. Yet it suited Byron's 'outsider' pose in 1811 to denounce Elgin in grotesque terms in his poetic masterpiece 'Childe Harold' as well as in the specially written 'Curse of Minerva'. Byron met a romantic poet's end, dying young of fever while fighting for Greek independence, and Elgin lived to be abandoned by his countess, imprisoned by Napoleon, and bankrupted, not least by the cost of saving the marbles which would otherwise have gone to the French or the ruin by neglect that awaited those not removed, so he lost the argument by definition. He was in due course supportive of Greek independence, but not such a fool as to think modern Greeks were ancient Athenians, though that was an image the Greeks started to build up as soon as they gained control of Athens in 1834. Byron was of course a gift for their propaganda. The whole question is complex, with arguments for and against Elgin, but it is absurd that it is still discussed in the crassly misleading terms laid down by Byron, who as one of his lovers Lady Caroline Lamb said, was 'mad, bad and dangerous to know'. Elgin continued to the end to lose money on rash industrial developments in Fife, but never seems to have grasped the connection between industrial and social change, which he promoted, and the franchise reforms of 1832, which he detested. Ironically, he had lost his first wife to the Whig Robert Ferguson of Raith who was returned MP for Kirkcaldy burghs in 1831, 1832 and 1837, when he also became Lord Lieutenant of Fife, probably the unkindest cut of all to Elgin.

Major turning-points in British politics, even after 1835 when formal party organisation became commoner and more publicly acceptable, tended to originate within ruling groups. Radical policy choices almost always involve party splits during high political manoeuvres which recast the ruling group or the patterns of thought fashionable within it. The decision-takers usually succeed in turning any electoral process into a confirmatory validation exercise after the big decision has been taken. The changes validated by the election which followed the passing of the Reform Acts had been in progress since 1822 and signs of the splits in the central political elite which heralded the coming of change had been apparent earlier than that.

Submerged social and political tensions can often find an outlet in a highly personalised form, which because of its stress on personalities obscures any incipient radicalism in the issue. Thus even James Boswell was able to surmount his usual panic-stricken social conservatism and support the 'popular' side in 'The Douglas Cause', a legal cause célèbre of the late 1760s when Archibald Douglas or Steuart, whose own paternity was not beyond question, successfully and to the great glee of the Edinburgh mob, asserted his right to succeed to the vast inheritance of the late Duke of Douglas, despite the furious efforts of the Duke of Hamilton to arrest the process of succession, on grounds of devious fraud by the father of the claimant, the rascally Jacobite Colonel John Steuart. The equivalent of this bizarre episode in the early nineteenth century, at a much higher level, of course, was the vulgar drama of Queen Caroline, whom George IV, her undutiful spouse, regarded with total loathing. Brougham had corresponded with her during her lengthy exile on the Continent, but when she elected to return to England in 1820 she rapidly came under the influence of the extreme London radical Alderman Wood. Brougham disapproved of her provocative behaviour, and stalled the announcement of his appointment as Queen's Attorney General as long as he could in the hope of being bought off by the government, but in fact his defence of his unsavoury client when George IV badgered his unhappy ministers into legal action against her was perhaps his greatest forensic achievement. Public opinion, alienated by a spoiled, self-indulgent monarch and his aloof, unsympathetic government, revelled in an orgy of Queenite enthusiasm, much of it violent and all of it spiced by the prurient details of Caroline's relationship with Bartolommeo Pergami, on which George IV hoped to build a case for divorce. A prince of cross-examiners, Henry Brougham more than any other man compelled the government to abandon its case in November 1820, and won for himself and his Whig aristocratic political associates a degree of popularity which they never quite lost.

The Queen's early death and George IV's partially successful counter-bid for popularity via provincial progresses, such as that to Edinburgh in 1822, eliminated Queenite agitation from the political agenda. However, an increasingly harried government was by 1822 embarking on a new course of liberalisation in economic policy associated with the name of William Huskisson (1770–1830), under whose regime at the Board of Trade freer trade, a simplified fiscal system and a new stress on economy became platitudes shared by the rival government factions headed by Canning and the Duke of Wellington. Such views did not, of course, win over radicals like the Scotch nabob Joseph Hume, who after making a fortune in India sat as a radical MP for Aberdeen (1818–30), Middlesex (1830–7), Kilkenny (1837–41), and eventually for Montrose burghs (1842–55). Opposed to the Corn Laws and obsessed with economy to the point where he virtually painted 'Retrenchment' on the Whig banners, Hume was irreconcilable and self-righteous, as his readiness to inflict speeches over three hours long on the House showed. However, government support was further fractured when it became clear that even the accession of Wellington to power as premier in 1828 marked no reversal of the gradual government drift towards economic liberalism, to which Wellington was every bit as committed as Huskisson.

The single most decisive development in the process whereby the heirs of Liverpool divided against one another without reconciling the hard core of the Whig opposition was undoubtedly the passing of Roman Catholic emancipation in 1829. In Scotland leading figures in pro-government and opposition circles combined to support the measure, alongside eminent divines like Thomas Chalmers, but even the sympathetic Cockburn had to admit that this legislation was profoundly unpopular. Twice as many Scots petitioned against it as for it. To some extent this may have been a reaction to the new stream of Irish Roman Catholic immigrants who after 1800 abruptly reversed the long, gradual decline of that communion in Scotland. In 1791 the immigration of Roman Catholic Highlanders into Glasgow had been encouraged by promises from local manufacturers of employment and facilities for worship. In 1793 in pursuance of the last promise, a distinguished Highland priest was established in Glasgow.

By 1831 it was said there were nearly 27,000 Roman Catholics in Glasgow and about as many again in the surrounding area, most of them of Irish origin. To employers they represented a vital reinforcement of cheap labour. So confident were radical political economists like Joseph Hume and Francis Place of the ability of market forces to make trade unions ineffective that in 1824–5 they were instrumental in securing the repeal of Pitt's 1800 Combination Act on the grounds that by adding the spice of illegality to their existence it was delaying the demise of unions. When a Catholic Schools Society was founded in Glasgow in 1817 it was supported by Protestant manufacturers like Kirkman Finlay who, in the teeth of popular Protestant resentment, persisted in his view that education was the least he owed to workers without whom his manufactures could not have been carried on.

Yet the feelings stirred by Roman Catholic emancipation ran much deeper than crude nativist hostility to immigrants. Sir Thomas Dick Lauder of Fountainhall, a friend of Cockburn and a well-known champion of the picturesque style of romantic taste, records an episode which underlines this. In his *Account*

Of The Great Floods Of August 1829, In The Province Of Moray (Edinburgh, 1830), he reported that a waterspout, a harbinger of the future massive floods, had on 12 July 1829 totally devastated the lands and crops of a hamlet in the parish of Contin in Ross-shire, and continued:

> This waterspout did not extend beyond two miles on each side of the village, a circumstance that led these simple people to consider their calamity as a visitation of Providence for their landlord's vote in Parliament in favour of Catholic emancipation.

The truth was that the curious political structure which governed Britain derived its, ultimately exorbitant, claims to sovereignty directly from the English Reformation under Henry VIII in the sixteenth century, and its claim for popular support on a vague but emphatically Protestant interpretation of freedoms secured by the Glorious Revolution of 1688. Politicisation could not be widespread in Scotland outside the major cities because of the restricted intellectual life of most of the country. While we perhaps tend to under-estimate the mental life of a provincial capital like Perth around 1800, with its very large printing industry (whose leading family, the Morisons, actually produced an *Encyclopaedia Perthensis*), the fact remains that as late as 1787 there was no bookseller between Aberdeen and Inverness. On the other hand, the humblest Highland peasant knew by the end of 1829 that the 'Protestant Constitution' he had been taught to revere was no more.

Also gone was any coherence in the groups which had supported Liverpool and Pitt before him. The second Viscount Melville was not prepared to swallow Catholic emancipation. He resigned, logically enough, for the political landscape was in full dissolution. The Earl of Lauderdale, no admirer of Queen Caroline and for a Whig unfashionably critical of some of the ideas of Adam Smith and Ricardo, had rapidly moved into a position of real influence with the government in the latter years of Liverpool. He also found the pace and direction of change more than he could take. For example, proposals to reduce the number of judges in the Court of Session, to use the salaries saved to enhance the remuneration of those left, and to reorganise the court in order to increase its efficiency, had provoked a storm of protest in the late eighteenth century, on the grounds that this constituted parliamentary violation of the Act of Union. Many critics opposed to yet another assertion of parliamentary aggression of a kind which had provoked both an American and an Irish crisis insisted that what was needed was rather an enhancement of the rights of juries in criminal cases in Scotland and the introduction of jury trial in civil cases. Even Walter Scott saw the need for reform of the procedure of the Court of Session which was carried through by legislation sponsored by the second Melville in 1808 and 1825. Civil jury trial was introduced in 1816, with Scott's friend the very conservative Whig William Adam of Blair Adam as the, outstandingly successful, Lord Chief Commissioner of the Jury Court. However, by 1830 legislation finally did reduce the Court of Session to thirteen judges, eight sitting as an Outer House and five in the Inner House. Lauderdale's last speech in the Lords in July 1830 was against the second reading of the Court of Session Bill. He voted by proxy against the second and third Reform Bills.

With Melville's resignation, the classic managerial regime in Scotland was in terminal crisis. As early as 1826, Sir Walter Scott had warned a correspondent in England against the dangers of permitting extensive liberalisation in Scotland on the grounds that 'Scotland, completely liberalised, as she is in a fair way of being, will be the most dangerous neighbour to England that she has had since 1639'. It was a curiously misguided comment. What was stirring was the second of three similar earthquakes in the political history of Scotland, all based on the paradigm of a Scottish political ascendancy so narrowly based that it had become deeply unpopular and dependent for survival on the existence of sympathetic and dominant allies in England. In 1688–9 the ascendancy of the Drummond brothers, lords Perth and Melfort, with their tiny inner clique of Catholic converts, survived only because of their capacity to manipulate King James VII and II. When he fell, they fell. The Melville regime in Scottish parliamentary politics, along with its tarnished urban patrician allies, was by 1830 staring at a similar fate. If they fell, they were going to fall hard. The third example came much later when the tiny Conservative minority of MPs and activists who monopolised Scottish offices and unelected appointed bodies in the late twentieth century was entirely dependent on perpetual Conservative majorities in Westminster and eventually fell so hard as to bring down the incorporating Union of 1707, clearing the way for extensive devolution of power to a renewed Scottish Parliament. In the early 1830s, however, there was no pressure for modification of the Union.

Scottish Whigs were modernisers who wanted to pull down what they saw as a uniquely narrow and intransigent Scottish *ançien régime,* not least so that Scotland could enjoy the same broader access to the parliamentary and municipal franchise as England. Change in Scotland would therefore inevitably be much more radical than in England, because there was such a leeway to make up. Even with Melville gone, and with the political elite in London deeply divided over the argument that some measure of meaningful reform was essential to eliminate the long-term danger of political and social revolution, pro-government candidates fared remarkably well in Scotland in the General Election of 1830. *The Scotsman* acidly remarked that in Scotland 'men would enlist under Beelzebub's banners, if he were First Lord of the Treasury'. The key to real change in Scotland lay in the Westminster legislature.

That change came with the fall of Wellington's administration in November 1830. Sheer insensitivity did more than anything else to bring the Hero of Waterloo down. As his most sympathetic and percipient biographer has remarked, geniality and willingness to make real concessions was something which he and his colleagues in government seemed to find natural only when dealing with foreigners. Even so, the eventual passage of the so-called Great Reform Bill by the government headed by an old champion of Queen Caroline, Earl Grey, was a saga involving a struggle with the House of Lords and with William IV. Agitation there certainly was all over Britain, reaching a crescendo in the wild Days of May in 1832. The burgh of Elgin was typical of all of Scotland, and much of England, in that the agitation only began with the process which culminated in the passing of the legislation. Isaac Forsyth, the local bookseller and antiquary, was prominent in the agitation despite the extreme hostility of his old friends the Duke and Duchess of Gordon, and he was assisted by such local worthies as Sir Andrew Leith Hay, the first MP for Elgin burghs after the passing of the Reform Bill, Admiral Duff of Drummuir and Dr John Paul. In Scotland there was no unconnected but contemporary upheaval like the wide-spread revolt of farm labourers which disturbed rural areas in southern and central England in 1828–30. These convulsions do not in fact appear to have been politically motivated but by coincidence they ensured that the political tension in England was heightened by all the horrors of arson, machine breaking and mobbing, culminating in ferocious repression directed by the Whig Home Secretary Lord Melbourne.

Lowland Scotland was a classic example of a mixed farming area and not a specialised cereal area like those parts of England where the labourers' revolt was at its worst. Because of the need for labour all year round, long hires were common in Scotland, where most farm servants were hired for six months or a year, and this stability was further enhanced by a substantial element of payment in kind in Scottish farm wages, which had the effect of minimising wage erosion by inflation. Though a system of housing single male workers in crude barracks known as bothies did exist in a few atypical areas such as Kincardineshire, the Carse of Gowrie or the Laigh (or coastal plain) of Moray, Scottish farmers did not normally keep the pool of under-employed, miserably paid, seasonal workers which existed in, say, Kent. Seasonal workers in Scotland tended to come in from the Highlands or Ireland.

Inevitably the bulk of attention at Westminster was bestowed on the English Reform Bill, to the relative neglect of the parallel Scottish and Irish measures. The Scottish measure, drawn up by Lord Advocate Francis Jeffrey, Solicitor General Henry Cockburn and their friend and ally T. F. Kennedy of Dunure, certainly pleased its authors. Cockburn insisted that the measure 'is giving us a political constitution for the first time'. Its overall impact could not but be dramatic once it became clear that Grey and his colleagues were bent on a franchise extension so generous as to stabilise the situation indefinitely and kill any further demand for changes which might affect the basic decision-taking process of government which Grey was determined to keep as secretive and aristocratic as ever. In 1820 there had been only 2,889 county electors in Scotland. Adding to these the burgh electors still gave a total of only 4,239, and of these only a fraction were truly independent. At the first reformed election in 1832 there were 65,000 voters. Quantitatively it was a much more drastic change than the one in England.

In the burghs in Scotland change was even more drastic. The franchise monopoly of the old town councils vanished. A £10 household franchise was uniformly applied instead. The number of burgh seats was increased from fifteen to twenty-three, a process which allowed a breach in the parliamentary monopoly of royal burghs by the granting of an MP to non-royal burghs such as Paisley and Greenock. Other burghs of this kind such as Falkirk were added to existing groups of burghs. Grouping sustained the average Scottish burgh electorate at a respectable average of over 1,300 voters each, even when Aberdeen, Dundee and Perth were withdrawn from their respective groups to return an MP apiece and Glasgow was similarly withdrawn to return two MPs. Edinburgh received an additional MP to match Glasgow with two. Obviously the self-perpetuating town council was doomed, and burgh reform legislation in 1833 introduced the £10 householder as the municipal elector. Already special commissioners for harbours and above all police commissioners, elected under private legislation to deal with a wide range of municipal functions including paving and lighting as well as the maintenance of order, had introduced the urban middle classes to the problems of voting for local government bodies. The great success of the Whigs in the Scottish constituencies in the election of 1832 rested mainly on urban votes. They not only swept the burghs but in the Scottish counties also it was often urban votes which tipped the balance in favour of Whigs, as in Selkirkshire where the reform candidate, Robert Pringle of Clifton, lost in the purely rural vote but won the county on the strength of his support in the small burghs of Selkirk and Galashiels. The Whig government owed the £10 householder his municipal franchise after 1832, for services rendered.

Whig or Liberal ascendancy in the Scottish burghs never really wavered before the British political system entered major crisis in the mid-1880s. Between 1832 and 1886 Tory or Conservative candidates (as they usually called themselves in Scotland) won only fourteen contests in Scottish burghs. This was what Cockburn and Brougham and Jeffrey expected. What was important about the Reform Act to them was that it rigged the franchise in such a way that the erstwhile Tory ascendancy was likely to lose elections in Scotland, for ever. The prosperous middle classes were enfranchised. They voted overwhelmingly Whig or Liberal. Nobody in circles which mattered in 1832 intended to enfranchise the working classes. *Chambers's Edinburgh Journal*, which was founded in 1832 by William Chambers, a staunch Whig supporter of the Reform Bill, was typical of Scots Whigs in eschewing any nonsense about democracy and offering the labouring classes not political power but political economy of the kind which lauded punctuality, assiduity and thrift and utterly deplored unions and strikes. James Stuart of Dunearn, another stalwart Whig who received and gave hard knocks in the approach to the Reform Bill, was a man of the same kidney. He actually shot and killed a scabrous Tory journalist (Sir Alexander Boswell, the son of the biographer of Johnson), but despite this and some little local difficulties over his bankruptcy, he achieved in 1833, with the help of Brougham who was now Lord Chancellor of England, his first government post. It was connected with the royal commission on the employment of children, and on that body, as in his subsequent career as an early factory inspector, Stuart displayed consistently bloody-minded prejudice in favour of employers. The millennium was meant to make the political world safe only for Whigs.

It was therefore a measure of the sheer incompetence of which the leading Whigs in North Britain were capable that they botched the job of fixing the county constituencies. The number of these constituencies remained at thirty, but the old practice of pairing small counties, with alternative right to representation, was abolished by accepting the need to fuse counties for electoral purposes. The new county franchise was supposed to eliminate the old jobbery inspired by a franchise based on feudal superiority and substitute the simple minimum criterion of effective control of property worth £10 per annum. Alas, the task of drafting a watertight definition of which tenants qualified under this rule proved quite beyond the authors of the bill. In December 1832 the Whigs romped home with forty-three out of fifty-three Scottish seats. Thereafter in the counties the old supporters of the Melville interest, like the Duke of Buccleuch, picked themselves up and realised that slipshod draftsmanship and the collapse of old checks on corruption had opened a marvellous vista on cut-price manipulation. As Sheriff John Cay said in 1838, 'never . . . had there been a statute vulnerable on so great a number of points, and those of so delicate a description'. With no secret ballot, and splendid opportunities to manufacture voters, the old discredited Tory magnates could count on their superior advantages in land, money and tenants to gradually regain the upper hand. By 1840 they had done so in all but a minority of constituencies where Whig aristocrats, using similar devious means, had established their own local ascendancy. Between 1841 and 1868 there were very few contests in Scottish counties. After 1832 what was by contemporary standards an infamous state of affairs in the Scottish burghs was rectified: power now roughly corresponded with property. In the counties, within a few years, remarkably little seemed to have changed except that voters were more numerous and cheaper. At Westminster the great majority of Scots MPs were still broadly in support of the government for, as the diarist Greville said at the end of the first session of the reformed legislature, 'matters remain pretty much as they were, except that the Whigs have got possession of the power which the Tories have lost.'

The decisive confrontation between Whig and Tory over parliamentary reform was in fact brief. For about three years before 1832 Scottish Tories tried to resist a strong current of opinion in favour of reform. Tory motives were largely self-interested. However, by 1831–2 pressure for change was overwhelming. In Glasgow even the Merchants' House, the seat of financial and social power in the city, petitioned for parliamentary reform in 1831. Virtually all other organised bodies in Glasgow, from the Incorporated Trades to the lawyers in the Faculty of Procurators, followed suit. Once defeated and relieved of their fear of social upheaval, Tories abandoned their opposition to changes the country clearly wanted. Inevitably Toryism paid a heavy immediate price for its selfish intransigence in terms of electoral defeat. Over much of rural Scotland the Tories' eclipse proved temporary, though they never recovered equally strongly in the Scottish burghs.

By 1832 Scotland was poised on the verge of momentous changes in her economic life. An era of industrial development based on water power and textiles was about to merge into a second wave of industrialisation based on steam power and heavy metallurgy. The first successful river steamboat in Europe was built and engined in Glasgow. This was Henry Bell's *Comet*, which in 1812 started to run on the much-dredged and deepened Clyde between Glasgow, Greenock and Helensburgh. In 1818 she opened the steamship route to Fort William via the Crinan Canal. On land the horse-drawn colliery or quarry waggonways started to evolve into locomotive-using railways like the Monkland and Kirkintilloch Railway, authorised in 1824 and opened in 1826. The eccentric Dundee and Newtyle Railway, which started in 1826 and was completed in 1832, lacked a mineral hinterland and was never very successful, despite a bold use of stationary engines and rope haulage to overcome severe gradients, but the Glasgow and Garnkirk Railway, which opened in 1831, proved that a railway could successfully compete with the nearby Monkland Canal.

Metallurgical expansion hinged on two discoveries. One was the discovery in 1801 by David Mushet of a vast reserve of raw material in the shape of black band ironstone near Glasgow. The other was the invention by James Beaumont Neilson, manager of the Glasgow Gas Company, of the huge saving in cost effected by heating the air blast sent through an iron-smelting furnace. Adopted by William Baird at his Gartsherrie works in 1828, hot blast was widely recognised as a success after 1835, and cheap iron became the foundation of an ever-expanding Clydeside heavy engineering complex.

Expansion and immigration bred problems and neuroses. In 1812 the Edinburgh authorities reinforced the social order by hanging three teenage youths who had beaten and robbed middle-class Hogmanay revellers outside the Tron Kirk. Another public execution in Edinburgh, in 1828, was that of William Burke, who with his fellow Irish immigrant William Hare had murdered many victims to supply dissection subjects for a third rising local entrepreneur, the anatomy teacher Dr Robert Knox. What is clear is that tensions were social and sectarian rather than nationalistic. As early as 1820 it became obvious that even the most radical of Caledonian reformers wanted to work closely with their English counterparts. The Reform Act of 1832 is best seen as an episode in a continuing debate in Britain as to the techniques and ideology best suited to the needs of the propertied classes in a rapidly changing industrial society. Francis Jeffrey, one of the framers of the Scottish Reform Act, said flatly, 'The real battle is not between Whigs and Tories, Liberals and Illiberals and such gentleman-like denominations, but between property and no-property – Swing and the law.' 'Captain Swing' was the mythical symbol of the revolt of the English farm labourers in the period 1831–2, a revolt much marked by incendiary attacks on property.

Curiously, the intellectual roots of the two rival ideologies competing to control the response of the British Establishment to 'Swing' were deeply embedded in early nineteenth-century Scotland. Presumably this fact, like other precocious aspects of Scottish social thought, derived from the stimulus provided by the experience of a dramatic and telescoped modernisation of Scottish society after 1750. Certainly by 1818 *Blackwood's*, the widest-selling of the quarterlies, was articulating a full-blown neo-feudal Tory aristocratic reaction against what it saw as destructive and excessive social and intellectual change. It held up a vision of a paternalistic, aristocratically led, vertically integrated society, and lambasted the tribe of liberal, free-trade, laissez-faire economists of the classical school as socially disruptive. *Blackwood's* vision of the conservative value of ancient loyalties was very much that of Walter Scott. It was Scott's social conservatism which made him so bitter about 'the late disposition to change everything in Scotland to an English model'. He defended the Scottish pound note in 1826 against attempts to abolish it with the same zeal he had supported the Dundas interest.

However, the rival set of values represented by what has been called 'the entrepreneurial ethic' was already well on the way to victory before 1832 set the seal on its triumph. The predominantly aristocratic ruling class was profoundly penetrated by commercial values and attracted by a school of classical political economists who rationalised a repudiation of responsibilities to the poor. Absentee landlords, Whig lawyers and collusive judges in the Court of Session had conspired by 1834 to write into the textbooks a largely bogus, and incredibly mean, 'Old Scots Poor Law' under which any attempt to lay on a local assessment to assist 'able-bodied labourers in time of dearth' was deemed illegal. Such legal chicanery was reinforced by white-hot Evangelical passion in the shape of that arch-Tory the Reverend Dr Thomas Chalmers, who in a famous experiment in his Church of Scotland parish in Glasgow tried to 'prove' that the poor could adequately be coped with by voluntary contributions, mainly from the poor themselves. In 1837, long after Chalmers had left Glasgow, his experiment was wound up as hopelessly inadequate.

Nevertheless, Evangelical religion, puritanical and individualistic, went well with a puritanical and atomistic social ethic. The increasingly confident and powerful middle classes could preach their gospel of self-help from more places than just the pulpit. They could preach through the press. J. R. McCulloch was not only a classical economist convinced that the working classes should abandon 'violent and unjustifiable proceedings' like strikes, but also a sometime editor of *The Scotsman*. Parochial education in Scotland was scarcely dynamic in 1832. Schoolteachers received their first pay rise since 1696 only in 1803, and then mainly as a reward for political conservatism. In

1836 the Reverend George Lewis of St David's parish Dundee published a pamphlet entitled *Scotland a Half Educated Nation*. By 1826 it had become clear that anachronistic constitutional arrangements were seriously obstructing the ability of the Scottish universities to respond to changed circumstances. However, a host of new educational devices ranging from lantern lectures to the Mechanics' Institutes set up in many towns propagated the ideology essential to the creation of that new and viable class society which was progressively ousting the old aristocratic ethos. Thomas Dick of Methven, Secession clergyman, popular author, pioneer of Mechanics' Institutes, saint and astronomer, summed up in himself many of the strengths of the new society.

That in the politics of the burghs after 1832 the Tories were often cast in the role of the Demon King in the recurring emotional pantomime that validated the new Whig or Liberal ascendancy, should not obscure the fact that the new order was based on a consensus over basic issues. The new '£10' voters, owners of houses, gardens and workshops with that minimum annual value, were the core of Whig urban support. These were often educated, reading men. Yet the harsh impersonality of a market society, shaped by class relationships, was hard for a man of imagination and sensitivity to stomach. Landscape painters like Alexander Nasmyth (1758–1840) and Sir Walter Scott's friend the Reverend John Thomson of Duddingston (1778–1840), limned a vision of Scotland as a non-industrial 'Land of the mountain and the flood'. Like Scott's evocation of a safely dead pre-Union Scotland, this vision was ultimately very seductive. Nevertheless, by 1832 power in Scotland was seated in its cities and industries. Until the late nineteenth century there was still a place for the landed interest as a junior partner, but there was to be no mid-Victorian age of balance between industry and land in Scotland. Industry and Whigs, and later Liberals, ruled with a heritage that included the peculiar vision of a unionist but distinct Scottish national identity that had been articulated under the Tory regime that finally foundered in 1832.

Conclusion: Enlightened Change?

1: 1746–1827, HEYDAY OF AN ANÇIEN RÉGIME

Between 1746 and 1832, after the elimination of any Jacobite threat and before the Scottish Reform Act, a stable and distinctive political system functioned in Scotland within the framework of the Union of 1707. Only from 1827 was it clear that the system was in terminal trouble. Operated by a ruling class which, widely construed, was probably under 3,000 strong in 1800, the system was compatible with very rapid change if there was a consensus for it within the elite. Striking developments occurred in Scottish economic as well as artistic and intellectual history. Underpinning everything from c.1750 had been a new cycle of rising prices for agricultural products. Scotland in the seventeenth century had suffered a series of economic body-blows. The first half of the century had seen famine and low prices, but from the second half of the 1640s unprecedented swathes of destruction were inflicted on burghs and rural areas by the impact of civil war, especially by the campaigns of the Marquis of Montrose, and then the whole economy was depressed by the relentless decline in farm goods between 1651 and 1688. The 1690s were harrowing due to long periods of famine. The Act of Union of 1707 may have been accepted under threat of invasion and its passage through the Scots Parliament required the usual lubricant of patronage, but it was pushed through by a Scottish political leadership quite desperate to break out of endless circles of depression and poverty, and conscious of the inability of their small state to compete in the viciously militaristic and protectionist environment of Western Christendom.

The Union initially failed to deliver its promised benefits, basically because the motor of economic expansion in the English economy faltered or at least lost impetus in the generation after 1707. By the 1740s enough promise of prosperity was coming along to save the Union, and after 1750 there was an upswing in most economic indicators, above all in population, overseas trade and the still all-important levels of prices for agricultural products. Landless agricultural labourers, especially after farm consolidation, remained very poor, but even their wages seem to have roughly doubled between 1745 and 1790, and to have gone up another 30 per cent by 1840. Though a unitary 'Industrial Revolution' is a debatable concept, there can be no doubt that by 1800 the Scottish economy had benefited since 1750 from a sharp increase in industrial activity, especially in areas like coal mining and textiles, nor that by 1832 a further industrial surge based on heavy metallurgy and eventually engineering was imminent.

Scotland had also benefited from increased agricultural output. This was originally produced by more intensive market-oriented farming exploiting growing markets within and outwith Scotland. By the late eighteenth century output was also enhanced by radical reorganisation and substantial investment. There was always a price to be paid. However, even in the Highlands a flexible response to new opportunities had by 1800 given the region comparative advantage in wool, whisky, some mineral products like slate, and organic ones like kelp. The destruction of Gaelic society probably only became irreversible in the 1840s after the convulsions produced by the great potato famine. Not all resources proved expandable under the pressure of increased demand. Lowland woodlands at least stabilised after 1775, due to positive estate policies and the availability of cheap Norwegian timber to meet increased demand. Highland pine forests, however, came under heavy pressure primarily from Highland society, with its rising demands for construction timber and wood fuel, not to mention space for types of grazing that were incompatible with natural regeneration of woodland. External forces, often blamed for destruction of Highland woods, were in fact discouraged by small tree sizes and extraction problems. By 1830 the urban revolution that turned Scotland into one of the most urbanised of northern European nations was in full swing. Though the human and environmental costs of change could be heavy, without the agricultural and industrial growth change had generated Scottish achievements would have been diminished in all fields by poverty and lack of opportunity.

One major device that increased opportunities available to a small people like the Scots was the pragmatic accommodation negotiated with England in the Act of Union. It did not allow Scots into London or the English colonies for the first time. They had been in both long before 1707, but it did make it easier for them to exploit an enlarged stage and rapidly expanding markets. It is no accident that in the last two decades before the slave trade was banned by law, twenty out of seventy-nine known masters of slavers sailing out of Liverpool were Scots, mainly from the Borders or Dumfries and Galloway. Opportunity knocked for intellectuals as well as merchants and manufacturers and a receptive, vast new reading public made the leading writers of the Scottish Enlightenment relatively affluent. David Hume had humorously declined in the 1760s to continue his best selling *History of England* 'Because I am too old, too fat, too lazy, and too rich'.

Archibald Constable (1774–1827) from Carnbee in Fife dominated British publishing at one point from Edinburgh by offering the leading Scottish intellectuals generous terms to write for him and edit his *Edinburgh Review*. His connection with the financially reckless Walter Scott proved disastrous in 1826, but his great rival, the London Scot, John Murray, followed a similar, if better managed, policy of paying his stable of writers, including the raffish George, Lord Byron, very substantial sums. Learned and literary books, published in Edinburgh and London and reprinted in Dublin and Philadelphia, were the building blocks of the Scottish Enlightenment. The commercialisation of cutting-edge intellectual work was due to cooperation between a small network of publishers and writers, to their mutual profit.

In Edinburgh between 1826 and 1838 the American John James Audubon found the skills and associates to help him sustain progress in the creation of his great book *The Birds of America*, but by 1838 the native Edinburgh literary scene was ossifying.

2: THE ENLIGHTENMENT PROBLEM

The Scottish Enlightenment is an icon of Scottish self-esteem and identity. It poses problems of definition, and its relationships with other developments of the period 1750–1832 are complex. Scotland is not the only country to lay heavy stress on its Enlightenment heritage. If the nature of the Enlightenment and its boundaries in time and space are debatable, it clearly originated within European culture, mainly in Western Europe, especially France. Its impact is most clear wherever a Western European culture was dominant, even if only in a thin layer of elite persons, as in much of Latin America, or in circles around the ruler, as in the Russia of Catherine the Great, where Scots physicians, soldiers and sailors (some of them Jacobite refugees) were very active in imperial service. Close Scottish connections with the Chesapeake and especially Virginia, connections that went well beyond the tobacco trade into education at every level from private tutors to faculty in the College of William and Mary, clearly acted as a conduit, though not the only one, for the ideas of the Scottish Enlightenment to penetrate the intellectual foundations of the new North American Union. Though there was perhaps only one British North American intellectual – Benjamin Franklin – who ranks among the great creative intellects of the period, American scholars have stressed the Enlightenment's profound influence over the Founding Fathers. It is tempting to see Scotland as in some ways the first modern nation and culture, but a small one whose destiny it was to contribute disproportionately to the first continental-scale, republican, secular, market-oriented mass society in the Western World.

Henry Commager's 1978 book *The Empire of Reason: how Europe Imagined and America Realized the Enlightenment* argued that Europeans could create most of the ideas, but only Americans could build a new society embedding them. More recently another patriotic American historian, Gertrude Himmelfarb, developed this approach in a more neutral-sounding book, *The Roads to Modernity: The British, French and American Enlightenments*, but it carries heavy ideological loadings, one of which makes it essential for her to deny the existence of a distinct Scottish Enlightenment. She is anxious to see the American Enlightenment, on which Scottish influences, especially those emanating from the Common Sense School of philosophy, were extensive as part of a broader English Enlightenment. This allows her to claim for the future United States the heritage of 'social virtues' established in England after the Glorious Revolution of 1688 and gives America a moderate, morally righteous, Enlightenment, not opposed to religion as such, where Adam Smith can be mobilised to bless American free-market capitalism. Other Enlightenments are by implication morally flawed or ineffective by comparison.

All of this should warn us of the dangers of chauvinist self-congratulation disguised as history. Some figures of the American Enlightenment were far from being ideologically moderate. Connor Cruise O'Brien, a historian from the Republic of Ireland where triumphalist republicanism has a tradition of using terror to intimidate and commit cultural genocide on rival Irish cultures, has pointed out that classical Roman republicanism was much given to talking about wading to Liberty through the blood of 'tyrants'. George III was no tyrant and neither was the unfortunate Louis XVI. Nevertheless, the future President Jefferson was for long an enthusiastic Jacobin fellow-traveller. Jefferson endorsed in private the idea that terrorism was a necessary servant of republican principles so sacred that any scale of bloodshed against domestic opponents was justified. These views he concealed later, preferring to invite Americans to join him in a successful but deeply bogus crusade against 'aristocracy' and 'monarchy' as embedded in that Great Satan, President John Adams. In the long run, the Revolution scarcely improved Franco-American relations. The French republic also used the language of the Enlightenment to ascribe universal values to its own objectives, virtually claiming to own Liberty, a bad habit to which the English, later the British, and latterly and most noisily the Americans had already become addicted. There just cannot be two Last Best Hopes of Mankind.

An iconic Scottish Enlightenment tends to encourage uncritical worship rather than realistic assessment. After all, the Whig leader C. J. Fox admitted he could never get through *The Wealth of Nations*. Yet claims for the Scottish Enlightenment can simply say that it invented the modern world, a view forming the subtitle of the work of the American historian Arthur Herman entitled, *The Scottish Enlightenment: the Scots Invention of the Modern World*. Behind this claim lies the incredible creativity of the major intellectuals of eighteenth-century Scotland and the fact that many of the issues they raised still resonate. Against this, the angry vision of many 'post-modernist' members of American English departments sees the whole Enlightenment 'project' as one of the many plots by dead white men to rape the world, depress the status of non-Caucasians with neo-scientific racist ideologies, and enslave all women in a patriarchal Hell. The unbalanced nature of these 'radical' views destroys their capacity to develop the partial insights embedded in them and tells us more about the psyches of the people advancing them, and the linguistic and conceptual gymnastics expected of them, than about a complex past world.

More serious is the inability of good historians to agree. The modern writer whose books are closest in style and spirit to the greatest intellectuals of the central era of that Enlightenment is probably Alexander Broadie, a commentator with unusual sympathy for the Scots Common Sense School of philosophy. For him the Scottish Enlightenment is a phenomenon cultivated by a small close-knit intellectual elite and it reached its peak in a few decades on either side of 1760. He would date its demise as roughly contemporary with the deaths of the philosopher Thomas Reid in 1796 and that of the geologist James Hutton in 1797. It is a point of view natural to a distinguished philosopher holding a Glasgow chair whose previous incumbents include Adam Smith. However, many other commentators would find it

too narrowly defined in time, as well as weighted towards philosophic discourse. Many important developments and books in
the history of even a narrowly defined Scottish Enlightenment
occurred in the first half of the eighteenth century, from Francis
Hutcheson's *An Inquiry into the Original of our Ideas of Beauty
and Virtue* (1725) to David Hume's *A Treatise of Human
Nature*, published anonymously in London in 1739–40. Hume's
complaint that the latter 'fell dead-born from the press' underlines the extent to which he would not acknowledge that his idea
of applying experimental techniques to moral subjects was not
as original as he claimed. His friends hailed him as the Newton
of the moral sciences but he was no more Newtonian than
his great and friendly rival Thomas Reid. The latter had been
taught by the Aberdeen University regent George Turnbull
(1698–1749), who used the experimental and deductive method
in his books on subjects ranging from classical art to moral and
Christian philosophy, and who believed that 'Liberty or a free
Constitution is absolutely necessary to uphold the Freedom,
Greatness, and Boldness of Mind'.

Then there is the problem of continuity, underlined by intellectual historians like David Allan. In a letter to his Scottish publisher in London, William Strahan, in the summer of 1770,
David Hume said, 'I believe this is the historical age and this is
the historical nation'. This was a comment on the unprecedented
success of his historical writings and also of those of his reverend
friend Principal William Robertson. Those writings were read in
translation all over Europe. Yet they were by no means the first
works by Scottish intellectuals so to be read. There is a clear continuity between the works of the Humanists and Calvinists of
Renaissance Scotland, often the same men, and the way in which
scholarship in eighteenth-century Scotland was assumed to have
a moral function. That implied a didactic duty and what we
would call a social one. We tend not to grasp the continuity
because so much of earlier Scottish achievement was expressed
in the international language of scholarship – Latin – which has
fallen into almost complete disuse. George Buchanan, who knew
John Knox, grew to hate Mary Queen of Scots, and tutored her

son James VI and I, was read all over Europe. He was hailed as
easily the best Latin poet of his time. His dazzling Latin paraphrases of the Psalms, written in the prison of the Inquisition in
Portugal, alone confirm this. He was the greatest Scottish literary figure in the neo-Latin tradition, in a land that produced
several great ones. Buchanan's paraphrases were still in use in
eighteenth-century Scotland as teaching aids. All the Moderate
intelligentsia read Latin. Principal Robertson could speak it flu-
ently and movingly when praising a colleague in his university.

Even the marked distaste that the Moderate party in the Kirk
By Law Established and many of the leading secular thinkers displayed for the bloody consequences of sectarian animosity has
a precedent in the precocious ecumenical tendencies of King
James VI. He was naively over-optimistic about reconciliation.
Moderates were realistically gloomy about what they saw as a
vein of pure evil lurking close to the heart of all organised
Christian churches, and they dreaded its reactivation through
populist appeals to intolerance. If John Knox had been in his
own quite realistic view a minor prophet, the Calvin the
Moderates read, often in Latin, was a Renaissance humanist and
civil lawyer. He wrote an Institute of the Christian religion on the
model of Roman law texts. In Scotland the legal tradition is
central to its claims to a significant Enlightenment. Lawyers were
the pervasive resident executive class in Scotland and they
achieved intellectual work of outstanding value both outside
their own field and in it. They were very much Europeans. We
must not use that adjective uncritically, as a synonym for all
things good. Their Europe was the heir of ideological total war.
There had been an Iron Curtain across Europe and very little
legal thought from the 'heretical' north of Europe had been
allowed to penetrate into the Mediterranean heartland of the
Roman Catholic Counter-Reformation. Scots law was Romano-
Dutch, one of the systems to be found in the north of Europe in
Protestant states such as the United Netherlands and North
Germany. France was an empire of law unto itself. Common
Law, an Anglo-Norman creation, survived in post-colonial
England and Ireland, where the Lordship of Ireland had been

part of a French colonial sphere in the British Isles called the Kingdom of England. From there Common Law spread to North America. South of the Alps and Pyrenees lay a different legal world. Nevertheless, Scots legal thought was most distinguished, and because of the Scots focus on the moral dimensions of man as a social being, its exponents had the breadth of interest and vision contemporaries summarised in the term 'philosophic'.

This philosophic approach to law in Scotland goes back to the *Institutions of the Law of Scotland* published by the first Viscount Stair in 1681. It was continued by a succession of institutional writers right through to David Hume (the nephew of the philosopher), who published the classic work on Scots criminal law in two volumes in 1797. He also produced a work on criminal trials under Scots law in 1800. Not every lawyer member of a legal dynasty stuck exclusively to law. A member of Stair's Dalrymple family, Sir John Dalrymple, did write on feudal property, but went on to publish important historical work in the late eighteenth century, revealing that Whig political heroes like Algernon Sydney had accepted subsidies from Louis XIV when opposing Charles II and that men like the great Duke of Marlborough had kept covert links to the exiled Jacobite court. As a representative Elder of the Kirk, Sir John had defended the playwright minister John Home against puritanical censure in the General Assembly in 1756. He also worked out how to make soap from herrings. Such men were an important part of the core of support for Enlightenment values. Another literary lawyer, Henry Home, Lord Kames, not only wrote extensively on law and literature but consciously combined benevolence with self-interest to begin the great work of clearing the bogs on his wife's estate of Blair Drummond, a task brought to fruition much later by their son and heir. This tradition of active engagement with the economic and social problems of Scottish society by eminent practising lawyers runs from Viscount Stair to Sir Walter Scott, advocate, Sheriff Depute of Selkirkshire, poet, novelist and disastrously unsuccessful businessman.

One can legitimately choose among many versions of 'The Enlightenment'. Though eighteenth-century people used the

adjective 'enlightened' in a positive sense, the concept of a phenomenon called the Enlightenment was an historical construct
after the event. Some would contend that there was no unitary
event as such but rather an overlapping series of enlightened
waves of thought in the western European world that borrowed
from one another but were ultimately shaped by national contexts. Certainly a Scottish Enlightenment, where the great majority of significant figures were either ruling elders, or in the case
of clergy, technically teaching elders with the right to administer
the sacraments in the Church of Scotland (and Calvinist
Eucharistic theology is extremely 'high'), was not like the
Enlightenment envisaged by the distinguished American historian of ideas Peter Gay. Partly by extrapolation from hugely
important French thinkers from Montesquieu to Voltaire and the
ambiguous but francophone Swiss, Rousseau, Gay described an
Enlightenment that was an international conspiracy of secular-
minded anti-clericals. There were in Scotland people like Adam
Smith and the philosopher David Hume who would have fitted
admirably into such a scenario. Indeed, both did fit comfortably
into the French scene when they went there, but they were protected at home by the greatest cultural power-broker of the day,
their friend the Moderator of the General Assembly and
Chaplain to the King, the historian William Robertson, a man
fully their equal in intellectual achievement, and infinitely better
linked to networks of institutionalised power.

The final collapse of the Jacobite option cleared the decks in
Scotland of the last arguments for Divine Right monarchy, even
if it was only the Divine Right of Indefeasible Hereditary
Succession. Jacobites had always shared in other aspects of
enlightened and 'polite' Scottish aspirations. Sir William Bruce,
the origin of the apostolic succession of classical or neo-classical
architects that peaked with Robert Adam, was an unreconstructed Jacobite after 1688, and though Hugh Trevor Roper's
typically perverse argument that the Jacobites created the
Enlightenment in Scotland (because they were 'cosmopolitan'
and, being Episcopalians or Roman Catholics, free of the dead
hand of 'Calvinism') is preposterous, there were plenty of

enlightened Jacobites. They dominated conservative fields such as Latinity, where figures like Archibald Pitcairne and Thomas Ruddiman loom large, but they also were crucial in newer fields like political economy, a fact obscured by the Whig Adam Smith's notably ungenerous silence about the achievement of the ex-Jacobite Sir James Steuart's *An Inquiry into the Principles of Political Oeconomy* of 1767. Indeed, in Steuart's field of political economy it is possible to construct a unitary Enlightenment that is non-partisan and international.

There is an argument that there was nothing unique in the case of Scotland c.1700 in the sense that other small European kingdoms such as Naples found themselves economically depressed and politically emasculated, with control lying in distant courts, in London or in the case of Naples in Madrid. Gradually, the intellectuals of both countries began to move towards the view that revitalisation could best be achieved not by feats of arms, political virtue, overt assaults on superstitious local churches or the recapture of an independence that was likely to prove illusory, but by the energetic pursuit of trade and industry. Whether it greatly matters that those who articulated this view in Scotland like David Hume or in Naples like Antonio Genovese or Ferdinando Galieni or the great Giovanni Vico, had all been influenced by the French Huguenot philosopher Pierre Bayle, may be debated. Bayle's stress on passion and self-interest as the motors of human creativity, especially in the *Dictionnaire Historique et Philosophique* he completed in 1696, was hardly original. He himself underlined, for the sake of respectability, his affinity with the pervasive Augustinian theology that stressed the inevitable sinfulness of post-Fall humanity.

The Scots connection with Huguenot culture was long-standing. It was central to the brilliant court culture of James VI before 1603, which was deeply penetrated by Huguenot theology, poetry, political theory and even music. Jean Servin set Buchanan's psalm paraphrases to wonderful polyphonic music as part of the most remarkable unsuccessful job application to a court before Bach's Brandenburg concertos. John Knox, a sounder Augustinian than Bayle, was fluent in French. The Scots elite was already doing much of what Hume wanted them to do long before Hume had written a single line. One must not confuse post-facto rationalisation with innovation.

Allowing for the fact that the phenomenon can validly be seen and described in different ways, it does seem that the concept of a western Enlightenment is a valid historical generalisation, as is the argument for a Scottish version that was both cosmopolitan and distinctive. To be avoided is the uncritical embrace of the self-hype and mutual puffery of many of its most important figures, who pretended that they had no antecedents. Unfortunately, their pose was later cemented into English-speaking literary consciousness by the Victorian historian Henry Buckle, who wrote influentially on the rise of the 'Scotch Intellect' but on the assumption that before 1707 Scotland was a primitive intellectual desert. The Scottish Enlightenment was a culmination of the long and distinguished cultural history of the nation of the Scots. It proved eminently exportable from England to India, and its Common School of Sense philosophy was still being preached, to the great comfort of conservative Americans, from the bully pulpit of the presidency of Princeton University by a Scots divine, James McCosh, in the 1870s.

3: ACHIEVEMENT, SIGNIFICANCE AND HERITAGE

Weighing the significance of intellectual currents, one has to distinguish between their importance in the ongoing history of ideas and academic discussions, and their impact on contemporary events. Ideas, especially religious ones, can create significant events when they impact on receptive societies. Scientific developments can have dramatic impacts, but the levels of scientific thought actually used in the early stages of industrialisation between 1740 and 1830 were not profound. Often ideas as such do not so much shape events as rationalise them retrospectively, though they can mould a fluid situation by defining what is thinkable by those with the power to make a difference. Thus the ideas of the Scottish Enlightenment did influence the form taken by the new republic of the United States of America, even if they partly did so by reinforcing and sharpening a commitment to English Whig ideas. *Cato's Letters*, originally contributions to *The Independent Whig* by John Trenchard and Thomas Gordon, rapidly became if anything more important than the Whig philosopher John Locke as a source for American radicals, due both to contemporary reprinting of the articles in American journals and the importation of the six London reprints in book form which appeared by 1755. Gordon was from Kirkcudbright and was taken up by Trenchard in London. He wrote a larger proportion of the *Letters* than his partner, merging physically with Trenchard's heritage by marrying his widow. The *Letters*' extreme 'country' Whiggery leaned heavily on Locke and Montesquieu but also on the writings of the Whig martyr Algernon Sidney, executed by Charles II. This reinforced the paranoia about abuse of power by any executive that lies at the root of America's precious constitutional entrenchment of checks and balances to limit executive autonomy. The fact that James Madison, fourth president of the United States, used an argument from David Hume's essay on the 'Idea of a Perfect Commonwealth' (that large size might help stabilise a republic by hindering the rise of factions) to counter the idea that republics had to be small to work at all, is an episode in the history of propaganda. Madison and his allies like John Jay and Alexander Hamilton were already committed to a large union capable of standing up to and indeed browbeating its rivals, as their writings in the *Federalist* (1787–8) show.

Nor will the argument that Scottish stadial theories of development were a decisive racist weapon against 'backward' peoples hold up. They did underpin President Thomas Jefferson's 'scientific' interest in the Virginian Indian and 'philanthropic' approach to the American Indian in general. By trying to assimilate the Indian totally to a 'higher' cultural stage, the policy eventually produced a rationale for his forcible removal across the Mississippi, where time and segregation would prepare him to vanish into total integration. Yet if Jefferson had not supplied 'enlightened' platitudes, some other vocabulary would have been dredged up to justify land seizures and the removal of Indians. Even Virginia's last governor, the Scottish Lord Dunmore, was popular when waging war on Indians. Grabbing a continent was always central to the American vision. Most Americans had never heard of stadial theory, but as Walter MacDougall points out in *Freedom Just around the Corner*, a high proportion of them were hustlers.

One must not ascribe to eighteenth-century Scots the racism of the late nineteenth century. They accepted without comment the large number of children of mixed race sent back to be educated in Scotland after the death of their Scottish fathers in India. In the case of George Bogle, pioneer of British contact with Tibet, his three daughters by a Tibetan lady came back to be educated after his premature death and married into the Ayrshire gentry. Lord Liverpool, leader of a government that ran the United Kingdom for nearly fifteen years after 1812, was himself part-Indian. The intellectuals of the Europe of the Enlightenment did tend to be unsympathetic towards Islam. They identified it with fanaticism (which is why when Voltaire wanted to attack a Pope he did so under the guise of writing about Mohammed). Yet in the world of the East India Company there was much in common in lifestyle between the Muslim gentry that the Company was gradually ousting from power and its own Scots servants, often lairds' sons.

A Scot working in a diplomatic capacity for the Company, which meant he had to have some Persian, could form an intimate and stable relationship with a noble Indian lady whose father had become a colonial civil servant when he left Persia to help run Mysore, a new South Indian regional empire founded by a Muslim adventurer. Scots were participating, consciously and with few inhibitions, in the long-standing globalisation of European interests through maritime expansion. James Gibb, the Aberdonian architect, trained in Rome under the papal architect Carlo Fontana, left architectural achievements from the church of St Martin-in-the-Fields in London to the revamping of West St Nicholas Kirk in Aberdeen. He also in the 1750s translated and published a history of early Portuguese overseas expansion.

As with the Portuguese, there was a deal of roguery in the Scottish contribution to European expansion. Americans may have had unprecedented opportunities for hustling, but even they produced few scams as outrageous as that of General 'His Highness' Sir Gregor MacGregor (the rank and title were foreign), who after fighting in the Peninsular War and the wars of liberation in South America, turned up in London in 1822 to exploit a stock market bubble and sentimental affection for the persecuted Clan Gregor that had played such a prominent role in George IV's jaunt to Scotland. He invented a non-existent country, Poyais, situated appropriately on the Mosquito Coast in Central America, appointed himself its 'Cazique', and then conned people in France as well as the United Kingdom into giving him loans and buying shares in his fraudulent enterprise. In 1823 a boatload of Scottish emigrants even sailed from Leith to 'St Joseph', the non-existent capital of non-existent Poyais.

Nevertheless, without the stimulus of underlying economic growth, plus the global experience gathered through active participation in an incoherent sprawl of interests under the British Crown, and their astute use of the opportunities offered by the international metropolis that was London (not the least of which was the Scottish mafia of friendly publishers like William Strachan or Strahan, and later John Murray), the Scottish intellectual achievement in the 'high' Enlightenment after 1750 would have been poorer. It left a heritage in the sciences, what we would call the social sciences, literature and the arts which is stunning in volume and calibre. Political stability within an elitist framework of regional power was essential. There was little self-conscious cultivation of 'the democratic intellect' in Scotland, though noble patronage could secure advancement for those of relatively humble origins, and social mobility was high especially for the expanding professional and mercantile classes. Scottish university education cost perhaps a tenth of its English equivalent but there were only about a thousand students in Scots universities c.1700, and perhaps only a couple of thousand by the end of the century. On the other hand, Scots were exceptionally adept at accessing the patronage of the Union state. By the 1790s an astonishing 40 per cent of full regimental colonels in the British army were Scots.

Scottish intellectuals were not attracted by dogmatic republicanism. Hume, Smith and their much more radical friend John Millar, author of the 1771 *Origin of the Distinction of Ranks*, and of *An Historical View of the English Government* (1787), all assumed that economic and social development would generate developments turning civilised monarchies necessarily into governments of law guaranteeing property rights from arbitrary violation as effectively as any republic, if not better. Order and moderation were central to Scottish Enlightenment thought, even in the field of geology, where James Hutton and his contemporaries identified 'catastrophist' theories of the evolution of the Earth with religious fanaticism. Hutton and his heir Sir Charles Lyell, who summed up the contribution of the Scottish Enlightenment to the field in his *Principles of Geology* (1830–33), founded modern geology by insisting that geological forces were always the same observable everyday ones. Ironically, they also made it difficult for their successors to accept that there have been apocalyptic catastrophes, like the extinction of the dinosaurs, or the much more extensive Permian extinction of nearly all life on Earth approximately 250 million years ago. Classicism and neo-Classicism in architecture encapsulated the calm, cosmopolitan, disciplined taste of contemporary Scots elite culture.

France remained the arbiter of style and intellectual chic. Legal relationships with the Netherlands continued to flourish until the French conquest of the Dutch Republic in 1795, and Italy gave Enlightenment Scotland much, including its predominantly Italian classical music tradition. Scots touring Italy could be serious students of the great Neapolitan musician Domenico Scarlatti (1685–1757). Sir John Clerk of Penicuik, best known as an early agricultural improver, had in 1697–8 taken violin and composition lessons from 'il divino' Archangelo Corelli in Rome and showed real promise as a composer. In Scotland there was always a dialogue between elite and 'popular' culture, as Lady Nairne's songs show. The elite still usually spoke Lowland Scots rather than Standard English. The lack of documentation for 'folk' music before 1780 probably reflects an assumption that everyone was familiar with it.

Nevertheless, this cultural balance was time-limited. There had probably been at least 100,000 religious Dissenters in Scotland as early as 1766. By 1832 they were formidable in most Scottish cities. The French Revolutionary and Napoleonic wars destroyed the easy international intercourse of their enlightened betters. Lord Elgin, notoriously, was detained by Napoleon in Paris between 1803 and 1806, with disastrous personal and financial consequences for him, despite an ambassadorial status that would have guaranteed immunity at any previous time. Aristocratic Continental elites after 1815 were increasingly driven by social paranoia into the arms of the reactionary politics and ultramontane Roman Catholicism they had tacitly rejected for much of the eighteenth century. Freemasonry, invented in Scotland and one of the major vehicles of Enlightenment values, became suspect as a source of revolutionary ideas to the Catholic monarchs who had protected it from papal hostility. A broadening franchise in Scotland meant inevitably a massive reinforcement of sectarianism and demagogic populist politics.

Enlightened thought had always had its limits in Scotland. There were never female Freemasons, though in the Netherlands and France in the eighteenth century elite women had been admitted to many lodges. Romanticism further accentuated the stress on a maudlin vision of soft, companionate 'feminine virtue' that an Edinburgh Whig political hostess and writer like Elizabeth Hamilton, a friend of Professor Dugald Stewart, could see was locking upper-class women into a domestic prison. The *Edinburgh Review* could accept women novelists, but assumed they could never match the grandeur and force of the 'best' male authors. Women of the lower orders were of course always working to make ends meet, many of them underground in coal mines, some breastfeeding babies in the intervals of heaving coal.

Scotland ever after remained in some sense an enlightened country where most intellectuals revered the Scottish Enlightenment's central values of Reason, Tolerance, Moderation and Social Empathy with other humans. However breached in the observance, these were the greatest gifts of an unprecedented efflorescence to a nation whose heritage it enriched in many ways. Its shortcomings could always be criticised using its own rational principles. Its heritage is so potent that it has been abused especially by free-market fundamentalists whose misappropriation of the name of Adam Smith, a Professor of Moral Philosophy for whom economic activity had to operate in a framework of moral values and justice between human beings, was outrageous. Walter Scott died fearing for the survival of Scottish identity. Yet a distinctive regional Enlightenment under the ascendancy of Islay and the Melvilles had left a confirmed sense of Scottish national identity which was socially inclusive, 'British' (however ill-defined that term) and enduring.

Its leading intellectuals were antipathetic to the tendencies to cultural and physical genocide so close to the heart of the new, exclusive nationalisms doomed to repeat the tragedies of the old religious wars, and sometimes rooted in them. Adam Smith reviewed Samuel Johnson's *Dictionary of the English Language* in 1755 saying what a great achievement it was and demonstrating how much better he himself might have done it had he been so inclined. Noah Webster's hubris was different. His 1828 *American Dictionary* was aimed at driving the (admittedly anti-American) Johnson from the market and inventing a distinct form of English, but he could foresee an overbearing imperial republic of 300 million Americans within 200 years (it came in 180). Smith, like Hume, who saw in colonial British America the future of the English language, belonged to a small people who could engage in great enterprises, like the invention of Standard English and its literary canon, only in cooperation with others.

In 1729 the early Scottish Enlightenment had been enriched when the Irishman Francis Hutcheson, an Ulster Presbyterian, was called to Glasgow University's chair of Moral Philosophy after a successful teaching career in Dublin. In 1832, in the twilight of the Scottish Enlightenment, another Ulsterman, William Thomson, still a young boy, came from his native Belfast to Glasgow where his father had taken a chair of mathematics. As Lord Kelvin, William was to be a towering figure in the scientific-industrial complex of late-Victorian Scotland, but that was a very different world erected after the fragile social, political and intellectual balances underpinning the age of Enlightenment were swamped by reform, emigration, immigration and the rise of manufacturing industry, fastest of all in Glasgow. William Thomson entered the wings in the year that conservative Dundas man, Sir Walter Scott, who always distrusted 'enthusiasm', left the stage. By 1825 a charismatic Scots clergyman, Edward Irving, was preaching the imminence of the Second Coming from the pulpit of the Caledonian Church in London. Another successful preacher of the signs of the end of the world, John Cumming, was to see David Hume as an Arch Frog creeping from the mouth of the dragon in the Book of Revelation to spawn a progeny of Scripture-subverting geologists. To every thing there is a season and a time to every purpose under the heaven; 1832 was a good year for Walter Scott to die.

Selected Further Reading

1: GENERAL SURVEYS

David Allan, *Scotland in the Eighteenth Century* (London, 2002).

T. M. Devine, *The Scottish Nation 1700–2000* (London, 1999).

T. M. Devine and J. R. Young (eds), *Eighteenth Century Scotland: New Perspectives* (East Linton, 1999).

R. A. Houston and W. W. Knox (eds), *The New Penguin History of Scotland* (London, 2001).

Michael Lynch, *Scotland: A New History* (London, 1991).

N. T. Phillipson and Rosalind Mitchison (eds), *Scotland in the Age of Improvement* (Edinburgh, 1970).

T. C. Smout, *A History of the Scottish People 1560–1830* (London, 1969).

2: SOCIAL HISTORY

Andrew Blaikie, *Illegitimacy, Sex and Society, Northeast Scotland, 1750–1900* (Oxford, 1993).

T. M. Devine and Rosalind Mitchison (eds), *People and Society in Scotland Volume I 1760–1830* (Edinburgh, 1988).

Michael Flinn, *Scottish Population History* (Cambridge, 1977).

Hamish Fraser, *Conflict and Class: Scottish Workers, 1700–1838* (Edinburgh, 1988).

A. J. Gibson and T. C. Smout, *Prices, Food and Wages in Scotland 1550–1780* (Cambridge, 1995).

R. A. Houston, *Social Change in the Age of Enlightenment: Edinburgh 1660–1760* (Oxford, 1994).

R. A. Houston, *Scottish Literacy and the Scottish Identity* (Cambridge, 1985).

R. A. Houston, *Madness and Society in Eighteenth-Century Scotland* (Oxford, 2000).

Anne-Marie Kilday, *Women and Violent Crime in Enlightenment Scotland* (Woodbridge, 2007).

Leah Leneman, *Alienated Affections: The Scottish Experience of Divorce and Separation, 1684–1830* (Edinburgh, 1998).

Rosalind Mitchison, *The Old Poor Law in Scotland* (Edinburgh, 2000).

Rosalind Mitchison and Leah Leneman, *Sexuality and Social Control: Scotland 1660–1780* (Oxford, 1989).

Rosalind Mitchison and Leah Leneman, *Girls in Trouble: Sexuality and Social Control in Rural Scotland, 1660–1780* (Edinburgh, 1998).

Rosalind Mitchison and Leah Leneman, *Sin in the City: Sexuality and Social Control in Urban Scotland, 1660–1780* (Edinburgh, 1998).

Elizabeth Sanderson, *Women and Work in Eighteenth Century Edinburgh* (London, 1996).

Ian D. Whyte, *Scotland before the Industrial Revolution* (London, 1995).

Christopher A. Whatley, *Scottish Society 1707–1830* (Manchester, 2000).

3: INDUSTRIAL AND COMMERCIAL HISTORY

R. H. Campbell, *Scotland since 1707* (Oxford, 1965).

R. H. Campbell, *The Rise and Fall of Scottish Industry, 1707–1939* (Edinburgh, 1980).

T. M. Devine, *The Tobacco Lords* (Edinburgh, 1969).

Alastair J. Durie, *The Scottish Linen Industry in the Eighteenth Century* (Edinburgh, 1979)

M. W. Flinn, *The History of the British Coal Industry Volume II, 1700–1830: The Industrial Revolution* (Oxford, 1984).

Eric J. Graham, *A Maritime History of Scotland 1650–1790* (Edinburgh, 2002).

Henry Hamilton, *An Economic History of Scotland in the Eighteenth Century* (Oxford, 1963).

Henry Hamilton, *The Industrial Revolution in Scotland* (Oxford, 1932, reprint 1996).

A. J. Slaven, *The Development of the West of Scotland 1750–1960* (London, 1975).

A. G. Thomson, *The Paper Industry in Scotland, 1590–1861* (Edinburgh, 1974).

Christopher A. Whatley, *The Scottish Salt Industry, 1570–1850* (Aberdeen, 1987).

Christopher A. Whatley, *The Industrial Revolution in Scotland* (Cambridge, 1997).

4: FARMING, FORESTRY AND FISHING

T. M. Devine, *The Transformation of Rural Scotland: Social Change and the Agrarian Economy, 1660–1815* (Edinburgh, 1994).

T. M. Devine, *Clanship to Crofters' War* (Manchester, 1994).

R. A. Dodgshon, *From Chiefs to Landlords: Social and Economic Change in the Western Highlands and Islands, c.1493–1820* (Edinburgh, 1998).

M. Gray, *The Highland Economy 1750–1850* (Edinburgh, 1957).

M. Gray, *Fishing Industries of Scotland, 1790–1914* (Oxford, 1978).

Allan I. Macinnes, *Clanship, Commerce and the House of Stuart, 1603–1788* (Edinburgh, 1996).

Rosalind Mitchison, *Agricultural Sir John: The Life of Sir John Sinclair of Ulbster 1754–1835* (London, 1962).

E. A. Richards, *A History of the Highland Clearances: Agrarian Transformation and the Evictions, 1746–1886* (London, 1982).

T. C. Smout, Alan R. MacDonald and Fiona Watson (eds), *A History of the Native Woodlands of Scotland 1500–1920* (Edinburgh, 2005).

5: BANKING

S. D. Checkland, *Scottish Banking: A History, 1695–1973* (Glasgow, 1975).

C. W. Munn, *The Scottish Provincial Banking Companies, 1727–1864* (Edinburgh, 1981).

Richard Saville, *Bank of Scotland A History, 1695–1995* (Edinburgh, 1996).

6: POLITICS

T. M. Devine, *Conflict and Stability in Scottish Society 1700–1850* (Edinburgh, 1990).

Michael Fry, *The Dundas Despotism* (Edinburgh, 1992).

Bob Harris (ed.), *Scotland in the Age of the French Revolution* (Edinburgh, 2005).

Bob Harris, *The Scottish People and the French Revolution* (London, 2008).

Kenneth Logue, *Popular Disturbances in Scotland, 1780–1815* (Edinburgh, 1979).

George McGilvary, *East India Patronage and the British State* (London, 2008).

Alexander Murdoch, *The People Above: Politics and Administration in Mid Eighteenth-Century Scotland* (Edinburgh, 1980).

John Shaw, *The Management of Scottish Society, 1707–1764* (Edinburgh, 1983).

John Shaw, *The Political History of Eighteenth-Century Scotland* (London, 1999).

Ronald Sunter, *Patronage and Politics in Scotland 1707–1832* (Edinburgh, 1986).

7: EMPIRE AND EMIGRATION

Ian Adams and Meredyth Somerville, *Scottish Emigration to North America 1603–1803* (Edinburgh, 1993).

William R. Brock, *Scotus Americanus* (Edinburgh, 1982).

J. M. Bumsted, *The People's Clearance 1770–1815* (Edinburgh, 1982).

T. M. Devine, *Scotland's Empire 1600–1815* (London, 2003).

Gordon Donaldson, *The Scots Overseas* (London, 1966).

Michael Fry, *The Scottish Empire* (Edinburgh, 2001).

Douglas J. Hamilton, *Scotland, the Caribbean and the Atlantic World 1750–1820* (Manchester, 2005).

Alan L. Karras, *Sojourners in the Sun: Scottish Migrants in Jamaica and in the Chesapeake, 1740–1800* (Ithaca and London, 1992).

Ned C. Landsman, *Scotland and Its First American Colony 1683–1765* (Princeton, 1985).

Ned C. Landsman, *Nation and Province in the First British Empire: Scotland in the Americas, 1600–1800* (Princeton, 1985).

Susan Leiper, *Precious Cargo: Scots and the China Trade* (Edinburgh, 1997).

Anthony W. Parker, *Scottish Highlanders in Colonial Georgia* (Athens, GA, 1997).

David Sinclair, *Sir Gregor MacGregor and The Land that Never Was* (London, 2003).

Iain Whyte, *Scotland and the Abolition of Black Slavery, 1756–1838* (Edinburgh, 2006).

8: RELIGION

Callum Brown, *Religion and Society in Scotland since 1707* (Edinburgh, 1997).
L. Drummond and James Bulloch, *The Scottish Church, 1688–1843: The Age of the Moderatues* (Edinburgh, 1973).
Robert Kent Donovan, *No Popery and Radicalism, Opposition to Roman Catholic Relief in Scotland, 1778–1782* (New York, 1987).
David Hempton, *Religion and Political Culture in Britain and Ireland* (Cambridge, 1996).
John R. McIntosh, *Church and Theology in Enlightenment Scotland: The Popular Party, 1740–1800* (Edinburgh, 1998).
Leigh Eric Schmidt, *Holy Fairs: Scottish Communions and American Revivals in the Early Modern Period* (Princeton, 1989).

9: ART, MUSIC, ARCHITECTURE, TOWNS AND CITIES

Ian Adams, *The Making of Urban Scotland* (London, 1978).
Julius Bryant, *Robert Adam Architect of Genius* (London, 1992).
Thomas Crawford, *Society and the Lyric: A Study in the Song-Culture of Eighteenth-Century Scotland* (Edinburgh, 1979).
Kitty Cruft and Andrew Fraser (eds), *James Craig 1744–1795* (Edinburgh, 1995).
E. Patricia Denison, David Ditchburn and Michael Lynch (eds), *Aberdeen Before 1800* (Edinburgh, 2002).
T. M. Devine and Gordon Jackson (eds), *Glasgow Volume I: Beginnings to 1830* (Manchester, 1995).
John Fleming, *Robert Adam and His Circle in Edinburgh and Rome* (London, 1962).
James Holloway, *Patrons and Painters: Art in Scotland 1650–1760* (Edinburgh, 1989).
David and Francina Irwin, *Scottish Painters at Home and Abroad 1700–1900* (London, 1975).
David Johnson, *Music and Society in Scotland in the Eighteenth Century* (London, 1972).
Ian G. Lindsay (revised by David Walker), *Georgian Edinburgh* (Edinburgh, 1973).
Duncan Macmillan, *Painting in Scotland: The Golden Age* (Oxford, 1986).
Thomas A. Markus (ed.), *Order and Space in Society* (Edinburgh, 1982).

John Purser, *Scotland's Music* (Edinburgh, 1992).

Margaret H. B. Sanderson, *Robert Adam and Scotland* (Edinburgh, 1992).

William Sinclair, *Lord Elgin and the Marbles* (London, 1967).

A. A. Tait, *The Landscape Garden in Scotland* (Edinburgh, 1980).

C. A. Whatley, A. M. Smith and D. B. Swinfen, *The Life and Times of Dundee* (Edinburgh, 1993).

A. J. Youngson, *The Making of Classical Edinburgh* (Edinburgh, 1966).

10: EDUCATION AND ENLIGHTENMENT

David Allan, *Virtue, Learning and the Scottish Enlightenment* (Edinburgh, 1993).

Robert Anderson, *Education and the Scottish People 1750–1918* (Oxford, 1995).

Stephen Baxter, *Revolutions in the Earth* (London, 2003).

Christopher J. Berry, *Social Theory of the Scottish Enlightenment* (Edinburgh, 1997).

Alexander Broadie, *The Scottish Enlightenment* (Edinburgh, 2001).

Alexander Broadie (ed.), *The Cambridge Companion to the Scottish Enlightenment* (Cambridge, 2003).

Stewart J. Brown (ed.), *William Robertson and the Expansion of Empire* (Cambridge, 1997).

James Buchan, *Capital of the Mind* (London, 2003).

R. H. Campbell and A. S. Skinner, *Adam Smith* (London, 1982).

Jennifer J. Carter and Joan H. Pittock (eds), *Aberdeen and the Enlightenment* (Aberdeen, 1987).

Robert Crawford, *The Scottish Invention of English Literature* (Cambridge, 1991).

Roger L. Emerson, *Academic Patronage in the Scottish Enlightenment* (Edinburgh, 2008).

Arthur Herman, *The Scottish Enlightenment* (London, 2001).

Andrew Hook, *Scotland and America: A Study of Cultural Relations 1750–1835* (Glasgow, 1975).

Andrew Hook (ed.), *The History of Scottish Literature Volume 2 1660–1800* (Aberdeen, 1987).

Andrew Hook and Richard B. Sher (eds), *The Glasgow Enlightenment* (Edinburgh, 1995).

Colin Kidd, *Subverting Scotland's Past* (Cambridge, 1993).

Nicholas Philipson, *Hume* (London, 1989).

Jack Repcheck, *The Man Who Found Time: James Hutton and the Discovery of the Earth's Antiquity* (London, 2003).

John Robertson, *The Scottish Enlightenment and the Militia Issue* (Edinburgh, 1985).

John Robertson, *The Case for the Enlightenment: Scotland and Naples, 1680–1760* (Cambridge, 2005).

R. B. Sher, *Church and University in the Scottish Enlightenment* (Edinburgh, 1985).

R. B. Sher, *The Enlightenment and the Book* (Chicago, 2006).

Fiona Stafford, *The Sublime Savage: James Macpherson and the Poems of Ossian* (Edinburgh, 1988).

Donald Winch, *Adam Smith's Politics* (Cambridge, 1978).

Charles W. J. Withers and Paul Wood (eds), *Science and Medicine in the Scottish Enlightenment* (Edinburgh, 2002).

Appendix: Chronological Table

1746 Battle of Culloden.

1747 The Abolition of Heritable Jurisdictions (Scotland) Act (20 Geo. II. Cap. 43).

1749 Prestonpans Sulphuric Acid Works established by John Roebuck and Samuel Garbett.

1755 Dr Alexander Webster's private census 'Account of the Number of People in Scotland, 1755'.

1756–63 The Seven Years War or 'the Great War for Empire'.

1759 Carron Ironworks founded near Falkirk by Roebuck, Garbett, and William Cadell. Robert Burns born near Ayr.

1760 Accession of George III.

1761 Death of Archibald Campbell, first Earl of Islay and third Duke of Argyll, first great political manager of Scotland.

1761–3 Ministerial career of John Stuart, third Earl of Bute and favourite of George III.

1766 James Craig wins the competition for the plan for the New Town of Edinburgh.

1767 Craig lays, in Rose Court, the foundation stone of the first house in the New Town.

1769 James Watt's first patent for an improved steam engine.

1771 Birth of Walter Scott in Edinburgh.

1772 Failure of the Ayr Bank.

1774 Major-General Simon Fraser granted the estates forfeited by his Jacobite father, Lord Lovat.

1776 Publication of Adam Smith's *An Inquiry into the Nature and Causes of the Wealth of Nations*.

1776–83 The War of the American Revolution.

1784 General Election confirms the administration of William Pitt the Younger and the importance of his principal Scottish ally, Henry Dundas, later first Viscount Melville. Remaining Forfeited Annexed Estates returned to the representatives

	of the forfeited families. Agitation for burgh reform in Scotland.
1788	Death of Charles Edward Stuart ('Bonnie Prince Charlie') in Rome.
1789	Outbreak of the French Revolution.
1790	Introduction of water-powered spinning machinery into Scotland.
1791	Henry Dundas becomes Home Secretary.
1792	Episcopalians' religious disabilities removed. 'General Convention of the Friends of the People in Scotland' meets in Edinburgh in December.
1793	France declares war on Britain in February. Third General Convention of the Scottish Friends of the People held in Edinburgh in October. In December it is forcibly dispersed by the authorities and its leading figures tried and sentenced to transportation.
1796	Death of Robert Burns.
1797	Extensive rioting in Scotland against the Militia Act. Professor Robison of Edinburgh University publishes his *Proofs of a Conspiracy against all the Religions and Governments in Europe*.
1800	Watt's basic patent rights over his improved steam engine lapse.
1801	William Pitt resigns as first minister of the Crown.
1802	Peace of Amiens with Napoleon's France. New opposition periodical, the *Edinburgh Review*, commences publication.
1803	Renewal of war with France.
1804	Pitt returns to office with Viscount Melville as First Lord of the Admiralty.
1805	Melville impeached and compelled to resign.
1806–7	So-called 'Ministry of all the Talents' headed by C. J. Fox and the Duke of Portland.
1809	Tory *Quarterly Review* commences publication.
1812	Great weavers' strike in Glasgow and the west of Scotland.
1813	'Tron Riot' in Edinburgh.
1814	Walter Scott publishes his novel *Waverley* anonymously.
1814–15	Defeat of Napoleon and European peace settlement. Radical Hampden Clubs set up in Scotland.
1816	Post-war business depression becomes severe.
1817	Series of political trials in Edinburgh and revival of agitation

for burghal reform in Scotland. *The Scotsman,* a radical paper, established. *Blackwood's Magazine* appears as a Tory reply to *The Scotsman.*

1820   So-called 'Radical War' in the west of Scotland.

1822   King George IV's state visit to Edinburgh, stage-managed by Sir Walter Scott.

1824   Repeal of the Combination Acts through the agitation of Joseph Hume and Francis Place removes legal ban on trade union activity.

1825   Spectacular collapse of business boom decimates Scottish industry.

1826   Sir Walter Scott and his principal associates declared bankrupt.

1827   The second Viscount Melville resigns office.

1828   'Hot blast' iron-smelting process invented by James Beaumont Neilson.

1829   Catholic emancipation.

1830   Fall of Wellington's Tory ministry. Whigs take office.

1832   Passing of the Reform Act (Scotland) largely shaped by Jeffrey, Cockburn and Kennedy. Death of Sir Walter Scott.

1833   Burgh Reform Acts restructure Scottish burgh government.

Index